Eighty-Five Halloweens

BURT HARRIS

Editing, formatting and cover design by Great Lines & Designs, Gr8Lines@comcast.net.

"Eighty-Five Halloweens: Tales from a Lifetime of Tricks and Treats," by Burt Harris. ISBN 978-1-60264-638-4.

Published 2010 by Virtualbookworm.com Publishing Inc., P.O. Box 9949, College Station, TX 77842, US. ©2010, Burt Harris. All rights reserved. No part of this publication may be reproduced, stored in a retrieval system, or transmitted in any form or by any means, electronic, mechanical, recording or otherwise, without the prior written permission of Burt Harris.

Manufactured in the United States of America.

Acknowledgements

Without the dedication and expertise of my editor
I would not have started, and certainly
would not have completed, this book.
Her skill in editing, organizing, and formatting
was as responsible as my own efforts for any
success this book may enjoy. Thank you, RK.

Pamela, my wife and my gift—thank you for your
encouragement, patience, and good humor during the
writing of this book. Your assistance was invaluable.
You fill my days with joy!

George, when you became my muse, I gained the
inspiration to begin this book. Thank you, Wizard.

Contents

My shrink, Dr. Geisenberg, died recently. I found out through a note from his wife. I don't know how he died. His wife didn't say. Personally, I think he exploded.

For more years than I care to count, Dr. G and I sat across from one another. I mainly talked; he mainly listened. He was a terrific listener. The more Dr. Geisenberg listened, the fatter he got. It seemed as though all my words were being stored in his body. He listened so well that finally, I ran out of things to say. We had to stop my therapy. I needed time to go out into the world and find more problems so he could listen to them. It became my mission in life to bring problems to therapy so my therapist could listen and prosper. If I didn't have a problem, I would create one. I became an expert at this.

I'm certain he finally got so full of my words that he exploded. What I want to know is, what happened to all those words? When Dr. G exploded, did they all scatter out like papers thrown from an airplane? Are they out there somewhere floating around? Should I gather them up and feed them to another therapist? I sure as hell don't want them back for myself.

If he had talked more, some of the words would have escaped and he probably would have been saved. The newer therapists know this. They talk a lot. They are not willing to sacrifice themselves as my doctor did. The new therapists throw so many words back at you that sometimes you wonder if they were all yours in the beginning. The new therapists also have pills to dissolve words when the pressure becomes too much to bear.

I like to remember the old days, when I would sling those words at Dr. G and he would absorb them like a sponge. He would sit there in that big chair nodding and soaking in waves of verbiage, growing larger and larger. Looking back, I should have realized it had to happen to one of us. If I hadn't unloaded to Dr. Geisenberg, it could have been me who exploded.

I like my old doc's way.

Better *he* should explode than me.

The Making of a SUEDE

After my shrink died, I decided to recapture some of my words and write a book. It seemed a better idea than taking pills. After a bit of thought, I decided writing a book was not a good idea. That made about the tenth time I had flip-flopped. When I realized this, a cold spasm of fear ran through my belly. Had I become what the politicians and media pundits decry in derisive tones—A FLIP-FLOPPER?

I think I may be getting really good at flip-flopping. As I age, I see so many nuances and conflicting influences that I am considering becoming a *professional* flip-flopper. When I left the Army, I decided I would never work for the government again. Now, in the light of my increasing expertise, I am considering flipping that decision and applying for an executive position in our government.

Really clever flip-floppers break decisions down into categories. That way they can expand one decision into two or three or fifteen. With this technique, it is possible to make not only the original decision more complicated, but also to make the flop or the flip (whichever) more intricate. A practiced expert, using this technique, can break the original decision down to so many sub-decisions that the original flip is lost in the flopping—therefore, he can never be held responsible. That qualifies him for a very high position in the corporate world, or a permanent position in our federal government.

People who have limited expertise in this multiple flip-flop/flop-flip operation qualify only for the lower echelons of governmental or corporate positions. Successful lower echelon decision people practice flipping and flopping until they become proficient at losing the point.

When they reach this exalted plane, they are ready for graduation. Their cumulative history is reviewed. If their record is found to be lacking all traces of responsibility, the candidate may be ready to join the truly elite group of Super Upper Echelon Decision Experts—SUEDEs.

SUEDEs occupy the top level of governmental and corporate command. Political candidates, CEOs, and our top economic advisors fall into this category. Bankers and insurance executives are the truly elite. Their expertise is easily measured by examining their pay.

After breaking down my own decisions into their various components and flipping the flop several times, I have tentatively decided to try to attain the exalted position of SUEDE.

I may have inadvertently already reached my goal, since I have managed to lose the whole point of this discourse and therefore can never be held responsible.

I think I may now be qualified to write my book.

I'll flip a coin and see how it flops.

The Gauntlet

My wife, Pamela, and I visited a downtown Carmel, California bookstore where I asked for a book for writers. The clerk said, "Do you want to know where you can sell your work?" I beamed. That brilliant clerk knew a writer when she saw one. In some other part of the country, they might have asked if I wanted a book telling me how to write, or a book of famous authors or quotations, or maybe a dictionary? In Carmel they assumed—correctly—that an accomplished writer wanted to market his brilliantly written work. Or perhaps it was not my location, but my bearing that bespoke my talent. Regardless, that clerk had class.

Carmel is a kind of haven for writers. They come here from all over the world. Discussing a book or the writing of a book over lunch or breakfast is usual. It is customary to hear conversations in French or Italian or even Latin as you pass people on the street. That's the atmosphere of the town.

Pamela is a writer in her own right. She can turn a phrase with the best of them. If I told her once, I told her a thousand times: in Carmel you have to be careful. A good line is worth a fortune to an author. In Carmel you are surrounded by writers. Keep your great lines to yourself and never—but never—utter them out loud.

So, we were in this bookstore and I said to Pamela, "I think I'll write a book of memoirs." My wife is an impassioned competitor as well as a loyal partner. I couldn't say I was going to embark on a literary project when Pamela was around unless I was ready to defend my writing skills. She instantly interpreted my remark as a challenge.

She fixed me with one piercing eye—the eye that always focuses on a food spot on my shirt or an insect on the wall, and said, "Do I hear the clank of a gauntlet hitting the floor?"

What a great line! A talented writer could write an entire book around a line like that. Ten people came to attention at once, opened their notebooks, and scribbled frantically. I don't ever remember being so angry.

I told Pamela. I said, "You don't go yelling a great line like that all over town! You use it yourself or you give it to your husband. There just isn't any excuse for that kind of behavior."

I told her plenty. I said, "How do you think William would have felt if Mrs. Shakespeare had run around yelling 'Out, damned spot!' or 'To be or not to be' all over Carmel? I can tell you right now, Bill would be plenty mad, just like I am."

Right after that Pamela apologized and I started writing "Eighty-Five Halloweens." I figured Pamela could clank her own gauntlet.

I told her. I said, "Frankly, my dear, I don't give a damn."

It Works in Practice,
But it Will Never Work in Theory

Writing a book was a new adventure for me, and I decided it would be a good idea if I contacted Fred Query, a local publisher friend of a friend, for a bit of advice. The dialogue over lunch unearthed an amazing amount of helpful information. The insider tips really started to flow after Fred's third cocktail.

I learned that for a piece of writing to be legitimately labeled a "book," it must have a reasonable number of pages. You can't ask someone to pay $24.95 for a book that consists of only two pages. Fred pointed out that we're all used to being cheated, but readers generally draw the line somewhat short of a two-page book—unless it's cleverly disguised.

Fred said, "Take for instance the How-To books. They all have one thing in common: they are all two-page books. Somewhere, tucked in amongst the filler, usually in the last chapter, are the only two pages that mean anything. After you wade through the trials and mistakes of the author's life, slog through his unhappy marriage and his business failures, delve into the problems with his crazy brother and his silly in-laws, then—and only then—will he reveal how to do whatever it is you bought the book to find out how to do. This never takes more than two pages. Often one is enough."

We were finishing our fifth cocktail when Fred said, "I missed the big one this year. The author contacted our office first with his idea for a book. My reader didn't catch the true potential of the manuscript."

ME: Really? Tell me about it.

FRED: The author had bought some land to grow earthworms and when he dug his water well, he struck oil and became a millionaire. It was an obvious slam-dunk for a How-To book—all it needed was a catchy title.

ME: Yeah, how about something like, "How to Oil Your Way to the Top"?

FRED (WITH A BITTER GRIMACE): The publisher called it "How to Worm Your Way to a Million Dollars in Real Estate." The book hit the Times Best Seller list last week.

ME: What a shame. Let's have another drink.

Fred: Good thinking.

ME: How are 350-pagers selling this year?

FRED: The 300-pager is our big seller. If you go above 325, we have to raise the price a couple bucks.

ME: Okay, I'll put my best two pages at about 275 and 276. That way they won't get to the real meat of the thing until it's too late to return the book.

FRED: Good thinking.

ME: I'll pick up the lunch check.

FRED: Good thinking.

Origins

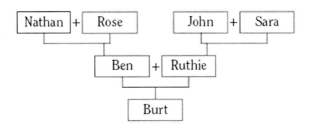

If I were a rich man

The year is 1890, and that could have been Nachman, my paternal grandfather, singing while his donkey took a dump in the middle of a dusty country road in Eastern Europe.

A Rose by any other name

My grandfather, Nachman, was an itinerant seller of pots and pans. One miserably hot July day, my grandfather was guiding his donkey cart on a shortcut from town to town. As he traveled along the lonely backwoods road, he imagined how he would make his fortune when he migrated to the United States. Through a break in the thick brush lining the bank of a stream, he glimpsed a beautiful young girl bathing in the river. Nachman was twenty-five years old. The water nymph was fifteen, in the flower of young womanhood. Nachman did what any fellow orthodox Jew would have done. He thanked God for granting him this wonderful opportunity.

My grandfather stopped his donkey cart and sat on some rocks behind a large tree to enjoy his heaven-sent gift. He quietly unwrapped his salami sandwich, chewed on his garlic clove, and soaked up the irresistible scenario. Love blossomed for him that day during lunch. He yearned for the beautiful naked Raisa to be by his side every day of his life.

As was the custom in that time and locale, Nachman negotiated with Raisa's father to marry his daughter. A monetary deal was struck: when Nachman made his fortune in the United States, he would pay Raisa's family the negotiated amount and send for her to join him in the United States. Nachman gave Raisa's mother a (non-refundable) five-gallon iron cauldron as a down payment and made his plans to go to the U.S.

At Ellis Island the officials mispronounced and recorded Nachman's first name as Nathan. For efficiency, they also dropped a couple of syllables from his last name. Nachman became a certified American by the name of Nathan Harris. From New York City, he begged, borrowed and BS-ed his way to St. Louis, Missouri, took up residence with some relatives, and resumed selling pots and pans door-to-door.

He prospered, saved his money, and moved to his own apartment. He then sent for his Raisa. On Ellis Island, Raisa was transformed into Rose. She lost none of her beauty in the process. In short order, Nathan and Rose produced Ben, their first truly American product.

Four more kids later, Nathan was the proud owner of a successful general store. He may have been a certified American, but he still believed in the Old World absolute of the patriarchal family. He ruled his wife and five children with an iron hand.

Nathan's oldest boy, Ben, rankled under his father's firm command. He and Nathan were combatants from the start. Partway through high school, Ben had had enough. He left home to fend for himself. He looked old for his age and spent the next ten years running special sales events for retailers. He had a knack for promoting and was quite successful at his job.

Romance in rag-top time

Like his father, Ben Harris had an eye for beauty—and Ruthie Goodman was a beauty. Her oval face was framed by a glorious crown of black hair, and her skin glowed with a flawless beauty.

Her features were lovely with a suggestion of sultriness and behind her dark eyes and soft smile you could sometimes see a fire burning. Ben spotted her on the school grounds a few months before she was to graduate from high school. His predatory instincts went into full gear. He swept the young innocent off her feet with his charm and sophistication.

Ruth declared immediate and undying love for Ben as she snuggled into the fragrant soft leather of his brand-new 12-cylinder Packard convertible. She told her parents if they didn't let her marry Ben she would elope in his convertible—with or without Ben.

I did it my way

John Goodman, Ruthie's father, had a certain respect for his daughter's suitor. The two men had a lot in common. Like Ben, John was successful in spite of his limited formal education. Both men's fathers had migrated from Europe and retained many of the Old World's patriarchal traditions. John's father had used his belt to beat John into submission once too often. At age fifteen, John wrestled his father's favorite weapon away and threw the belt in the fire. His father announced, "If John is big enough to do that, he's big enough to fend for himself." John was ordered out of his father's house. They never spoke to each other again.

John Goodman became proficient as a pattern cutter and sewing machine operator in a St. Louis sweatshop. When he gained enough experience, he started his own apron factory and employed five women as sewing machine operators. He married Sara, his childhood sweetheart.

Little Ruthie was the pride and joy of John and Sarah Goodman's life. She was as spoiled and headstrong as an only child can sometimes be. Her parents knew that if Ruthie said she would run away, she would keep that promise regardless of their concerns.

A GoodMan knows when to hold 'em and when to fold 'em

Ever the pragmatist, John knew when to stop fighting and start negotiating. He proposed a deal: the Goodmans and Ben would pool their carefully saved money and open a retail store together. To save money, the new extended family would live together in one big house. Ben would have his child bride. The Goodmans would still have their daughter. Ruthie would have her convertible. Everyone would live happily ever after.

Money, as usual, influenced the balance of power. Ben had contributed the most, so he became the leader. Mercurial, talented, inventive, and fiercely competitive, Ben was willing to break the rules and take chances. John was quiet, funny, lovable, and always the noble gentleman. Ben was the motor that powered the boat; John was the rudder that held the steady course. Ruth was beautiful, flirtatious, and a natural saleslady. Sara could also sell, and she spent her life selling everyone on the idea that no matter what happened, it would turn out for the best. They were all very hard workers dedicated to a common cause. It looked like a winning combination.

Boil and bubble, toil and trouble

Ben found a general store for sale and just the right big house for the two families in Bullneck, a small Illinois town a few hours from St. Louis. The family figured that with such a winning team, in a few years they would all have enough money to return to the St. Louis they loved and resume their lives. But notwithstanding their hard work and collective dream, "a few years" turned into a dozen, and a dozen more. The family never really got to "resume their lives." They lived for a future that would never be.

On Halloween, a year after Ben and Ruthie were married, the doctor clamped a pair of forceps over my head and I was dragged, protesting loudly, out of Ruthie's womb and into this world of damaged men and strong but gentle women.

The Apple Tree

Wild apple trees can grow more than fifty feet tall if they aren't topped. We had a tree like that, wild and lonesome, growing in our back yard in Bullneck, Illinois. We called its fruit June Apples, and I have never tasted anything so delicious before or since. From my six-year-old perspective, I felt our apple tree towered over all trees that had ever been—or ever would be.

Each summer, when the oppressive Midwest heat made your heartbeat pound in the back of your eyes, I would sit in that untamed old tree and pick the wild apples. I can still feel the sun-hot juice squirt to the back of my mouth and run down my chin. I would eat until my stomach ached and I could hold no more.

There was only one person who liked those apples as much as I did: my grandfather, John. Gramps would take out his pocketknife and cut a big slice of his apple while I chomped a big bite out of mine. We would talk about the world and why the sky had clouds and what made the grass green. We talked about what made home-grown tomatoes taste so good. I guess my Gramps and I talked about almost everything.

Everybody called him "Mr. Goodman, that marvelous man." Just as that apple tree towered over all other trees, he towered over all other men. He walked with his shoulders back and his white-haired head held high. He commanded respect wherever he went. I was lucky he was my grandfather, and I knew how lucky I was.

One lazy day, I was climbing my apple tree and spotted the perfect apple. Fat and round, vibrant green in color with a tantalizing splash of red, it hung from a branch higher than I had ever gone. But that apple called to me—I had to have it. I reached my perfect apple that day in July, but when I got there and looked down, the ground seemed far away. I got scared and couldn't move. I clung to the tree branch and yelled for help.

It was Sunday, and nearly everyone was home. My mother and father heard my cries and came running into the yard. We didn't have a ladder high enough to reach me, and my perch was too thin to support more than a scrawny six-year-old. Tears were streaming down my face. I couldn't unclasp my death grip.

My mother called the fire department. My father tried to take control. He rallied his authoritative grasp of language and deep understanding of human nature and commanded me to "Climb down from that tree this very minute!"

The volunteer fire department showed up and ran around like circus cops, making all kinds of noise. Bullneck was a very small town. There wasn't a house or a business more than two stories tall. Even the firemen's ladders couldn't reach me. The firemen spread a net and Moishe Grimsley, the volunteer fire chief, asked me to jump. But I was immobilized in that apple tree. I couldn't budge.

Sunday services were just ending at the Baptist Church across the street. Preacher Elijah "Spud" Hall saw the commotion and came over to pray me down. He had the entire congregation in tow. The sheriff promised he would let me shoot his gun if I came down to get it. Half the town was in our back yard. But nothing could move me.

Gramps had been taking his usual Sunday stroll that morning. He came home for lunch and strode through the gathered crowd to the back yard. He looked up at the white-faced little kid clutching a skinny branch and shivering with terror. With a gesture, Gramps silenced the yelling and cajoling and praying. He told everybody it would be best if they all left.

Reluctantly, the helpful horde cleared the scene. Gramps looked up at me and said, "Jump, I'll catch you." I looked down and saw my grandfather standing down there, so far away, smiling, arms outstretched. I knew if he said he would catch me, he would.

I jumped.

Mr. Goodman, that marvelous man, caught me and broke his arm doing it. I cried because I had hurt him, and he told me to forget it because it didn't hurt at all.

Gramps wore a cast for weeks, and I brought him apples every day, freshly picked from the tree. We ate our apples together, and we talked about the world, and why there were clouds in the sky, and why home-grown tomatoes tasted so good.

Stalking

When I was in third grade I decided to rid the world of flies. I put sugar out on the back porch, and when the flies landed I slapped them with my fly swatter. But one day our teacher explained that a single fly would lay thousands of eggs in a lifetime. She said it was impossible to control flies by killing a few at a time with a fly swatter.

Thus ended a favorite pastime of mine. It just didn't make sense anymore.

I decided to go back to lassoing the cat. I had almost given up trying to lasso the cat. In those Western movies I loved so much, Tom Mix had no trouble lassoing anything that moved. A cat should be easy for Two-Gun Slim Goldberg. Back in those days, Two-Gun Slim Goldberg was my cowboy name. I knew I would be the first Jewish president when I grew up. I decided to be the first Jewish cowboy in preparation.

I had been trying to lasso our cat, Penny, for about a month. She was always too fast. Once I almost nabbed the little bugger. The noose landed on her head, but she backed off in the wrong direction and it didn't hold. But Two-Gun Slim was determined.

The day was bright with promise. The morning dew still hung on the blades of grass. The big cat's yellow eyes gleamed as she stalked a bird feeding on seeds not five yards away. As the bird would feed, Penny would move two steps closer to her prey and then hunker down and become a stone. The bird would bend to feed. The stone would move an inch closer.

In true Indian fashion, Slim watched cat and bird in silent admiration. You must understand: Two-Gun Slim Goldberg was a Jewish cowboy who was part Indian. There weren't too many of those on the Illinois plains. Being Indian, Slim could appreciate a good stalk; being Jewish, he could sympathize with the bird. But Slim had his own script for the day. He had to lasso and brand that cat.

Slim tightened the belt that held his two pearl-handled six-guns and lumbered down to the barn for his rope. Penny's day had come. It was branding time at the Goldberg Corral.

Slim had learned something while watching the cat. He would do his own stalking. While Penny was intent on bird creeping, Slim became intent on cat creeping. He approached the cat from her blind side and then froze. One step, then stone. Two steps, then stone. As Penny came closer to the bird, Slim was sneaking up on Penny. Bird, cat, and Slim were a trio in the ballet of the hunt.

Two-Gun Slim Goldberg readied his lasso. With a quick and practiced swing he threw the noose over Penny's head. The cat was caught! She jumped, struggled, and began to scream. Bent on escape, Penny made a frantic beeline away from her tormentor, only to be jerked into an airborne somersault when the rope suddenly ran out.

Penny ran and somersaulted and screeched like a banshee. Indian Slim was petrified with fear. Jewish Slim was sure he was killing his mom's cat. Two-Gun Slim Goldberg didn't know what the hell to do. He had noosed a cat, and he couldn't let go.

With a mighty lunge, Penny finally jerked the rope out of Slim's hand and the frenzied animal disappeared into the neighbor's yard, dragging the length of rope behind her behind. Slim was convinced that Penny had run away to die alone in horrible pain. He started to cry and ran into the house blubbering, "I killed the cat—I killed Penny!" Two-Gun Slim Goldberg, the first Jewish cowboy, was consumed with grief at his first "kill" and frightened out of his chaps for the reckoning to be faced when his father came home after work.

Two-Gun called on his God for mercy. He even promised to eat his green beans if only God would bring Penny back to life. Two-

Gun prayed all morning and spent the rest of the day staring at the place where the cat had disappeared, hoping for the miracle he suspected would never happen. He was afraid to look around the yard for fear he would come across Penny's dead, strangled body. His eyes filled with tears as he pictured her tortured carcass.

Then the miracle happened: Penny appeared! She was playing with a rubber ball. The rope was gone. It was as if nothing had ever happened. Two-Gun Slim breathed a sigh of relief and asked God if he really had to eat his green beans. God told him that since he had promised, it would be a good idea for him to honor his pledge. Two-Gun Slim Goldberg grunted an Indian grunt and sighed a Jewish sigh.

The following day when Slim went back to school, a substitute teacher was on duty. She opened the lesson plan and repeated the previous week's lesson on reproduction. She explained that every fly would produce thousands of eggs during its lifetime. Taking this fact into account, the new teacher explained, every fly you killed was like killing thousands of unborn flies.

Two-Gun Slim Goldberg went home and strapped on his pearl-handled sixguns. He went to the kitchen for a load of sugar and a fly swatter.

Life made sense again.

The Goblins Will Get You
if You Don't Watch Out

They got out. I knew they would, those miserable monsters.

As long as I could keep that closet door closed, nothing bad could happen.

Our big old gnarly apple tree was just outside my bedroom window. The wind would howl and that tree would shake. Lightning would brighten the sky and throw fearsome shadows of grasping hands against the wall. The branches of that tree would knock against the window with furious rage at being outside in the storm. But I was safe, because the window was securely locked and my closet door was closed.

I don't know why, but all the demons in the world were locked up in my bedroom closet.

Everyone knows that demons only come out at night. So it was okay to leave the closet door open during the day. It was okay to hang clothes in the closet. It was okay to clean it or to store toys there. Just make sure you did all those things during the day! Because you didn't dare open that closet after sundown. Those demons would come right out and nobody knew what they might do.

That was me at six and eight years old. Maybe even ten. My mother said she wasn't allowed to open that closet door after dark until I got back from the Army, but I don't believe that.

I know it's not true, because after I got back from the Army I used to leave that door open at night, right up until the time I went to bed. I would close it then, of course. There's no sense taking chances when you are asleep and can't defend yourself.

It's strange how something like that gets started. It was sort of a family joke—but it wasn't funny to me. When I was six I had seen the demons, one moonless night when the wind howled and the rain pounded and the tree was clamoring to come in out of the storm. When I saw those monsters I howled louder than the wind. I scared the hell out of them, and they shot back to the safety of their closet. Before they regrouped, I was able to slam the closet door closed. I thought I had trapped them for sure.

It seemed to me that although the family thought it was funny, they didn't open that door at night, either. And they sure stayed away from that closet when a Midwest storm was raging and the lights were out and the house moaned in misery from the pounding outside.

It was kind of a miracle to have all those bad things imprisoned in my closet. In a sense, it was comforting to know where they all were. I could keep that big door closed and believe I was safe.

Big Steve vs. Buck Jones

Everyone knew it was just a question of time until Big Steve Monahan decided to cream the little kid. It had been a while since Big Steve had moved to Bullneck. He'd had time to size me up and had decided it was time to take action.

He picked the middle of a ball game, just after I had dropped a pop fly to the infield. He was captain of the team. He was always captain of the team. He strolled over to me, curled his lip into a sneer, spit in the dirt, and said, "Want to join the girl's team, Shorty?"

No self-respecting eight-year-old could take an insult like that. Big Steve was lucky my name wasn't Shorty! I summoned my dignity and walked off the field.

Even at eight, I knew this was just the beginning of my problem. If I wanted to hold my head up in that neighborhood, there would have to be a face-off. I was scared. Big Steve was about twice my size. He was ten times as mean.

Like many kids of my generation, I loved the Western movies of the 1930s. Tom Mix, Hopalong Cassidy, Bob Steele, Buck Jones. They were my heroes and my gods. No time was better than all day Saturday, when I got to watch the latest cowboy movie. I would see it over and over, until finally after the last show the theater would clear and the manager would throw me out.

Buck Jones was my favorite. There always came a time when the bad guys just pushed Buck too far. You'd see a close-up of his craggy face. His eyes narrowed to dangerous slits. He set his jaw and bunched the muscles in his cheeks. His hands fell to his holsters, his knees bent, and his shoulders curled in a half crouch. It was Buck's action stance, and the bad guys knew it. They cowered with fear and Buck would wipe them out.

In my eight-year-old brain, it made sense that if every Saturday afternoon Buck Jones could terrorize ten or twenty bad guys, I should be able to do it on a single day with a single bad guy: Big Steve.

I knew I would need to practice. I set myself up in front of the full-length mirror in my mother's dressing room and began rehearsals. My eyes became slits, my nostrils flared; I flexed the muscles in my cheeks until my jaw ached. I added a few touches of my own. I let spit foam in the corners of my mouth, and I perfected the sound of labored heavy breathing.

My little brother wandered in on one of my practice sessions and went screaming for my mother, yelling that I was having a fit. I knew then that I was ready to make my move on Big Steve.

It was late on a quiet summer day when I sauntered toward Big Steve's house. I had on my heavy belt. A dirty bandana hung loose around my neck. My feet were sweating in my fur-lined snow boots. My father's best black felt hat, creased cowboy style, hung down around my ears. The sun was setting at my back when I called out Big Steve.

The bad guy came out of his house and stood looking at me with his little pig eyes. He didn't say a word—he just stared.

My eyes narrowed to dangerous slits, my nostrils flared, my cheek muscles bunched, and foam appeared at the corners of my mouth. I crouched like a gorilla and started breathing like a bull. In a low wheeze, I snarled, "Okay, Big Steve, you wanna fight—now's the time."

Steve said, "Don't bother me, Shorty." He turned around and went back into the house. After I quit shaking, I realized that I had won! Me and ole Buck had beaten the bad guy.

Big Steve never called me Shorty again.

The Show Stopper

My friend Frank had this ratty dog who knew only one trick. The dog was a big shaggy thing who stuck by Frank as though they were glued together.

They had adopted each other by accident, as kids and dogs will do. One day when they were playing around, Frank pointed his cap pistol at the dog and fired off a round.

The dog stopped dead in his tracks, his legs stiffened, and he fell over as if he'd been struck dead. He lay there, barely breathing, until Frank said "Okay, Old Shaggy." Then Shaggy got up and took a bow.

That was his only trick, and it was a showstopper.

Frank would run around, this big bag of rags chasing after him with wild eyes and tongue hanging out. And suddenly, without any warning, Frank would pull out his cap pistol and fire at the dog. The dog would go into his act, Frank would say, "Okay, Old Shaggy," and anybody who happened to be around would crack up laughing.

One day when Frank and the dog were making castles out of old boxes behind the local food market, Frank pulled out his cap pistol and fired. Mr. Shaunessy, the manager of the market, saw the act and thought it was about the funniest thing he had ever witnessed.

Shaunessy was also the organizer of our local annual dog show, and he figured an act like this would be great entertainment at the next show. He made a deal with Frank. Shaunessy offered to save all the market's old boxes and designate the back of the market as Frank's permanent territory. All Frank had to do was loan Old Shaggy to Shaunessy for a few hours during the next dog show. No kid in his right mind could resist an offer like that!

Shaunessy couldn't wait to enter the dog's name in the next dog show obedience trial.

To understand the rest of this story, you have to understand dog owners. Especially dog owners who frequent dog shows. These owners are positive that their dogs are capable of thinking and reasoning. These owners don't own "dogs." They own *people* who are *shaped* like dogs.

You can insult a regular person. You can maim a regular person. You can knife them, club them, shoot them. . . show dog owners wouldn't even turn around to look at you.

But if you are at a dog show, you'd better not think of hitting or even yelling at a dog. It doesn't make any difference whether it is your own dog or someone else's. The results would be the same. A show dog owner would rise like an avenging angel and smite you.

Shaunessy knew this, and that made his plan doubly funny.

The big day came. The dog owners, handlers, and groomers were going through their paces. Old Shaggy had been bathed and clipped and prettied until he didn't even look like himself. Frank refused to attend the show because his dog didn't smell right anymore.

You could tell Old Shaggy wasn't very happy, either. He wanted his old smell back. He missed his tangled mass of hair. He missed Frank. He hated Shaunessy for destroying his shaggy, smelly identity.

The day dragged on and finally, it was Old Shaggy's turn at the trial hurdles. He knocked over the first hurdle, as Shaunessy knew he would. Shaunessy yelled an obscenity. The onlookers gave a gasp.

When Old Shaggy knocked over the second hurdle, Shaunessy pulled out a pistol loaded with blanks and fired at Old Shaggy.

Shaggy stopped cold in his tracks, his legs stiffened, and he fell over as if he'd been shot dead. A silence enveloped the crowd.

And then, as if they were one body, they gave out with a blood-thirsty yell and charged toward Shaunessy.

Shaunessy smiled at his cleverness and said, "Okay, Old Shaggy."

Old Shaggy never moved a muscle. Shaunessy said, "Okay, Old Shaggy!" and pushed Old Shaggy with the toe of his boot. The dog didn't even breathe. Shaunessy took one look at the approaching crowd and started to run for his life.

The screaming crowd and Shaunessy disappeared in a wild chase out of the show ring.

Old Shaggy got up, shook himself, and trotted off to find Frank.

Honesty Is the Best Policy?

It had a bent neck and was U.S. Army khaki-colored. It had an adjustable lens and a hook for carrying it on your belt. It was waterproof and unbreakable and had three settings for controlling the light. It was lightweight for easy carrying, but heavy enough to be used as a weapon in case you were attacked by a jungle animal.

It was the Official Boy Scout Flashlight.

When I was ten years old, the Fleischmann Bubble Gum Company held a contest to give these babies away. Printed on the wrapper of each piece of bubble gum was a random series of letters. To win the contest, you had to accumulate enough of these letters to spell the words "FLEISCHMANN BUBBLE GUM."

It was easy enough to accumulate letters. I was a voracious bubblegummer and had a stack of wrappers. The problem was in acquiring the correct combination of letters. No matter how many bubble gum wrappers I saved, I could never find an "H" or a "G."

Two weeks was about the limit to my patience. After that, I figured if I couldn't *find* the letters, I would *make* them.

I got out my glue and my scissors. My ingenuity was as unlimited as my supply of letters. I took fragments from spare letters, glued them together, and completed the letters I needed. I completed "FLEISCHMANN BUBBLE GUM" in short order.

I stuck the whole glue-laden mess into an envelope and sent it off to the Fleischmann Bubble Gum Company. It must have been received by a blind clerk completely devoid of human intelligence.

Ten days later, my flashlight arrived.

It was then I made my mistake. I showed my parents the handsome addition to my belt and bragged to them of how cleverly I had acquired my ill-gotten prize.

They were appalled. Their son was a cheat! I was instructed to sit down and write a letter to the Fleischmann Bubble Gum Company. I was to explain my criminal action and ask for instructions for returning the loot. It took much longer to write the letter than it had taken to commit my heinous crime.

My precious flashlight—earned by the sweat of my glue-laden hands and the inventiveness of my devious ten-year-old mind—was placed in the custody of my mother, pending a reply from Fleischmann.

Very shortly, an official-looking letter arrived. It was a long letter extolling the virtues of Fleischmann Bubble Gum, signed by the company's president. He said he had become the president of his firm through his honesty and hard work. He expected me to do the same.

As a reward for my honesty in confessing my crime, the Board of Directors of Fleischmann Bubble Gum Company had decided to allow me to keep the Official Boy Scout Flashlight.

In bold capital letters, just above the president's signature, was the admonition:

"HONESTY IS THE BEST POLICY."

To me, it was a lovely letter. I couldn't wait to get my hands back on my flashlight.

But even at my tender age, something didn't ring right. The slogan stuck in my mind: Honesty Is the Best Policy. It seemed to me that I would never have gotten the prize if I hadn't cheated in the first place.

The World According to Old Charlie

Everyone in Bullneck loved Old Charlie. He had been born and raised in our little town and was one of Bullneck's oldest citizens. When France declared War on Germany in 1914, Charlie joined the French Army to fight the "War to End All Wars." He was wounded in the Battle of the Ardennes and returned home a local hero.

The grateful French government awarded him a small pension. He led a modest life and became the honorary historian of Bullneck.

When the weather was good, we would find Charlie sitting outside on the library bench, reading. When the weather was bad, Charlie would camp inside the library huddled over a pile of papers, his nose buried in some periodical or book.

Charlie always smiled. He never had a bad word for anyone. I think he may have been the happiest person I ever knew.

Charlie didn't look like much with his rumpled clothes and little rimless glasses. He always seemed to be ruminating over what he was going to say next as he squinted out of his shining blue eyes. He slumped in his chair with a permanent slouch, and he walked with a sort of shuffle. But Charlie could unravel a yarn with more humor and style than any storyteller I ever knew.

Charlie would lean back, get a faraway look in his eyes, and take his listeners on a journey to lands that never existed and characters who were bigger than life. True, partly true, or pure fiction, Charlie didn't care and neither did his spellbound audience. His rapt listeners always felt they had learned something. We thought we were a little bit more worldly because we had gone on Charlie's latest flight of fantasy. I think it might have been one of Charlie's stories that first made me realize life wasn't as simple as it seemed on the surface.

In school we had been studying ancient history and the stories of the old Roman and Greek gods and goddesses. I was returning a book to the library, and Charlie was sitting on his usual perch in front of the building. I stopped to talk to him. Somehow Pandora's name got into the conversation. I told Charlie in no uncertain terms what I thought about that miserable female who had brought mankind all our troubles.

Charlie leaned back and sighed. He fixed me with one of his thoughtful looks and said, "I've done a lot of thinkin' and readin' about Pandora. If you know the true story, I think she got a bad rap."

Charlie slouched a little lower on his bench, and I knew this was going to be a long one.

He said, "The ancient Romans and Greeks had lots of goddesses and gods. In the beginning, the gods had most of the power, while the female goddesses did all the work. They had to manage the palaces and do all the cooking. In addition, they answered most of the earthly prayers while the male gods were out playing tricks, manipulating battles, and cavorting with the mortal womenfolk.

"As they began to wise up, the goddesses started the women's lib movement. Once the ladies got involved with the parades and the meetings, they were too busy to bother with the problems of mankind, and that included answering prayers. With the gods busy having fun and the goddesses busy enjoying their liberation, nobody up there was listening to the people on Earth. The Romans and Greeks finally gave up praying.

"That's the *real* reason the ancient religions aren't practiced anymore."

Charlie paused and said, "I just thought you might be interested in a little background history. Now back to Pandora. It is true that Pandora—a woman—opened the box of plagues and released all those terrible troubles on the world. However, it was Zeus, the king of the gods—a male, mind you—who loaded all the world's troubles into that box in the first place. It was Zeus who told Pandora that the box contained a mink robe, an 18 karat diamond-studded watch, and a double strand of nine millimeter pearls. Then, just before he left the room, he gave her the container and sunk the real hook. He forbade her to open the box. Remember this, kiddo: you just don't *forbid* women to do anything. Zeus should have known this.

"Pandora opened the box before Zeus had even passed through the door. All the troubles of the world flew out, and then the box was empty. She was mad as hell. Pandora searched the box for a hidden goodie. There wasn't even a gift certificate from Macy's inside. That's the kind of god Zeus was. I think it's time we stopped blaming Pandora and women for all our problems. That lowlife Zeus should shoulder the blame."

That was about as worked up as I ever saw Charlie get about anything.

I thought about Charlie's story. I didn't know Zeus had "set up" Pandora like that. It made me wonder how many other inaccurate stories I had believed. The facts had changed my mind about Pandora. If I knew more of the facts about other things, maybe I would change my mind about them, too.

I looked at Charlie and asked, "Is that a true story?"

Charlie looked back at me and said, "I don't know. Is the one you read in school true?"

Charlie always left you thinking.

Wherever he went, Charlie carried an old beat-up book. It was covered in what Charlie claimed was genuine buffalo skin. Exotic Indian markings covered the outside. Beads glistened all around the edges. Charlie was always scribbling in that strange-looking book.

Charlie guarded that book as though it were the ticket to heaven, but as eager as he was to share a story, the book was something he never mentioned. He never showed the contents to anybody. He treated it like some kind of sacred thing that had to be protected from harm at all cost.

Kids being kids, my friend Bill and I decided to get a look in that book whether Charlie liked it or not.

Late one night, when he was sound asleep, the two of us crept into Charlie's shack and stole his beloved book.

We couldn't wait to get to the nearest light and see what Charlie had been writing all those years.

Bill opened the book, and we saw that the pages were all blank! In spite of all the scribbling, that precious book of Charlie's was a complete zero. All this time, Charlie had been faking.

At first, we laughed. We couldn't wait to spread the news about Old Charlie's famous book. Then we did something I'm proud of to this very day. We got to thinking about all the times Charlie had helped us when we needed him, and all the hours he had spent telling us his stories.

I guess right then we sort of grew up a notch. We replaced Charlie's book where we had found it, and never told anyone what we had done.

It wasn't until many years later that I learned the power of that special book.

The Nail That Sticks Up
Will Get Hammered

1933 had hardly begun when my family came home early from work. They had closed the store for a week because there was no money to pay the employees. My father had a look on his face that promised trouble. He announced, in funereal tones, that the bank had defaulted and closed its doors. We had lost all our money and we were on the road to the poorhouse.

I said, "I have some money in the bank. We can use that." My father looked at me and said, "That's gone, too."

My young mind couldn't quite grasp why that nice Mr. Roberts, the bank teller, would take away my hard-earned savings. Mr. Roberts and I had lovingly opened my little steel barrel bank once or twice every year since I was old enough to see over his counter. The coins would spill out on the counter, and Mr. Roberts and I would sort and count them together. Then he would enter the amount into my cherished blue bankbook and congratulate me on the "staggering" amount I had saved.

My dad's announcement made me wonder if Mr. Roberts had taken away my carefully saved collection of marbles as well as my savings. I ran to the closet where I kept my stash. All the marbles were still there. I was glad I hadn't entrusted them to the local bank teller. They probably would have been gone, just like the money in my savings account.

The Great Depression had thrown its pall over the nation. A railroad ran through Bullneck and the "hobos" would jump off the train as it slowed down on its way through town. Ragged beggars, down on whatever luck they had enjoyed in past years, knocked on our back door for work or a handout. If my mother was at home, she always made time to brighten the day of these unfortunate men. She fixed them sandwiches, coffee, and pie, all carefully arranged on a wooden tray. They sat on the back porch and quietly ate this bounty, sometimes telling me stories of their transient lives as if they were great adventures.

But I wasn't fooled. Our whole family knew that "There but for the grace of God go we."

Everyone worked in our family: six days a week, ten hours a day, and fourteen hours on Saturday when the farmers came to town for their weekly shopping. By the late 1920s my family had opened seven clothing stores in various small towns in Southern Illinois. We were well on our way to realizing my father's vision of a chain of department stores.

But after the banks were shuttered, we lost all except one of the stores. Our main customers, the area's farmers, were now living hand-to-mouth—eating what they could grow and trading their produce for other essentials. There wasn't much in the kitty for new clothes.

Ben and John were devastated. Our normal dinner conversation was dominated by my father's doleful descriptions of his struggle to save us from our inescapable destiny to be sent to the poorhouse. To me, the threat of the poorhouse was real and imminent. In this place of utter despair, even the bread in my imagined dinners of bread and water would be green with mold. My father's harping about the poorhouse gave me recurring nightmares that would haunt me forever. I started to believe that no amount of money would be enough to protect me from this ever-present threat.

When Ben tired of sending us to the poorhouse, his tirades usually would turn to current events. He was an expert on every subject, and his views were chiseled in stone. Those who disagreed would feel the pain of prolonged ridicule and derision—not only for their views of the current subject, but also for their sins since the time of Genesis.

For the sake of their digestion, most members of the family

refrained from comment during Ben's ravings, hoping he would finally run out of steam. Once in a while, Gramps would make a joke to relieve the tension. Otherwise, I was the only one foolish enough to ever comment or laugh.

I was precocious. From the age of about six, I never kept my mouth shut. I was fearless, contrary, and—looking back—more than a bit stupid. I knew exactly how to get my father's blood to boil. I took Ben's old-country need for patriarchal control and obedience as a continual challenge. His dinner rages against me were a regular family event.

I would like to think that Ben was a product of his time. Ben's father, Nathan, had set the example: rule your family with an iron hand, cherish your womenfolk, and worship the power of money.

The Depression robbed my father of his life's mainstay—his control. Unable to protect his business from the crushing effects of the economy, he felt emasculated, out of control, and continuously on the verge of rage. Ben's rage infected both me and my brother, Earl, with permanent feelings of inadequacy and a lasting fear of being poor and powerless.

"Boiled-Over" Sunday happened after one of our neighborhood football games had ended. In the last minutes of the game, I had been alone in the end zone when Big Steve threw me a desperation pass. I juggled the ball, and miracle of miracles, finally captured it for a last-minute touchdown. My team lost the game, but that didn't diminish my elation. Even Big Steve momentarily treated me with more respect. It was a couple of hours after that, while I was still swollen with pride, that "Boiled-Over" Sunday occurred.

As a rule, we had dinner early on Sundays. We always had chicken soup garnished with my mother's fourteen-pound cannonball dumplings.

No one in our family liked to eat the boiled chicken used to make the soup. In the long-cherished custom of Jewish cooking, dishes were cooked until all the ingredients joined to become an unidentifiable stew. The mystery meat in this mixture—beef, lamb, or whatever—we called "flesh."

My mother was always praised for her cooking skill, but what she cooked often remained unnamed because no one really knew what it was supposed to be. Of course, if a wing managed to remain intact, we knew cows didn't fly and it had been a long time since a lamb had fallen from the sky. We knew the meal must have started out as chicken, or maybe turkey. If we cracked a tooth on a buckshot, we knew that our neighbor had been quail hunting. Between chews we were able to identify enough "flesh" to safely murmur, "Good. Bird?"

As a rule, the relentlessly boiled chicken from the soup was given to the dog. Ruthie's cannonball chicken soup would be followed instead by juicy fried chicken and mashed potatoes.

Feeling invincible on this Sunday, I decided I would claim the boiled chicken that no one else wanted. As I was helping her clear the soup bowls, I asked my mother to give me the soupy remnants of chicken for my main course.

A heaping platter of fragrant and steaming fried chicken was placed at its usual place in front of my father. As Ben was selecting the choice fried morsels, my mother brought in my plate of stringy boiled chicken.

Ben took one look at the plate of boiled chicken in front of his elder son—the one member of his family who was his special pain in the ass. His face turned the bright red that could have signaled a stroke, but in this case merely signaled the onset of one of his monumental fits.

My father threw my plate of boiled chicken across the table and raged, "Why in hell does that kid get boiled chicken when all the rest of us have to eat it fried?"

My chicken was sent back to the kitchen. Later, it was fed to the dog.

The Magic Perfume

How fun it is to read about places exotic: Shanghai, Tokyo, Moscow, and especially Paris. I have been to Paris twice, maybe three times. My memory is not my greatest asset. One thing I do remember is how my grandmother, Sarah, loved "Evening in Paris" perfume.

As a kid, I couldn't understand why Sarah loved that perfume so much. To me it smelled terrible. And it wasn't cheap, either. I used to make jokes about the blue box with all the phony-looking stars and the stinky perfume. But every Christmas I gave my grandmother the smallest bottle of Evening in Paris I could find. That was all I could afford, and I wanted to please her.

Sarah was well into her fifties when the family started worrying about the way she was acting. She had always been a bit scattered, but she started forgetting all kinds of things, and was given to crying spells. The family called a conference and badgered her into seeing the doctor.

A couple of days and more than a couple of dollars later, old Doc Kindly diagnosed her with a nervous breakdown and handed her a bottle of pills. Back then, "nervous breakdown" was the medical term for "beats me."

Today the terminology has become more sophisticated. "Stress" or "anxiety syndrome" are favorite diagnoses. If that doesn't satisfy the patient, "auto-immune disease" is another good, indefinable term. Regardless of the diagnosis, an expensive bottle of pills is always prescribed.

But now is now and then was then, and our family accepted the diagnosis of a nervous breakdown. Sarah's disease generated another family conference. Even Gramps was at his wit's end. My dad ended the debate in his typically compassionate way: "Nervous, schmervous, what the hell is a nervous breakdown? Let's ship the old lady off to her cousins in California. Let them put up with her."

So that's what we did.

My grandmother blossomed in her new environment. For the six months of her "California Cure," she sent glowing reports of all the sights and activities. She wrote about the restaurants with buildings shaped like hot dogs or derbys. She enthused about the blue ocean, the red sunsets, and the beaches that stretched forever.

She wrote to us about the odd-looking bushy trees that grew in the fields beside the country roads. Trees that sprouted oranges like Christmas tree ornaments. And the farmers would let you pick a small basket for free, right off the trees! When she returned home, she announced that traveling was what she wanted to do for the rest of her life. She started making lists of all the places in the world she wanted to see.

But in the '30s, there was no money to "waste" on travel. Sarah did the only thing she could do. She read travel books and sent for brochures. No place was too far away or too exotic for her imagination—but Paris was her dream destination.

Sarah and I used to sit for hours and pour over her collection of brochures. We "traveled" all over the world. It was nothing to have breakfast in Rome, fly to Tokyo for lunch, and end up in an exclusive hotel in London for dinner. No matter where the trip started or where it ended, we always managed to visit Paris. And though I was too young, the debonair French waiter would wink at us and bring two glasses of vintage red wine. We would smile and thank the waiter (in French, of course). Together, we would savor our imaginary drinks as we watched the imaginary Parisians stroll down the imaginary Champs-Élysées.

My grandmother cherished two things above all in her simple life: her family, and her dreams of exotic places.

One day I was waiting for Sarah to take me to see "Top Hat" at the movies. The mirror on her bedroom door reflected her ageless image as she applied her lipstick. Then she carefully removed her Evening in Paris perfume from her bureau drawer. I saw the blue cardboard box with the stars, and I noticed how protectively my grandmother handled her treasure.

She tenderly held the box and looked at the stars and opened the lid. Sarah withdrew the bottle and for a few moments, lovingly cradled the precious elixir. She removed the applicator and fragrance filled the air. I looked at Sarah's eyes, and I knew she was in Paris. It was as plain to me as if the French waiter had just delivered our wine.

You Can't Steal Second Base
With Your Foot on First

When I was in elementary school, the neighborhood kids played baseball in an old field where cattle grazed part-time. There were just enough cow deposits left around to make playing in the outfield a distinct challenge.

There were no leagues or coaches or uniforms, but we played to win, even though our opponent on Monday was probably our teammate on Tuesday. As I remember it, the outcome of any game always depended on me.

Why did the pop fly that would end the game and make us the winner always fall to my side of the outfield? Why was my turn at bat always when the bases were loaded and there were two outs?

And why was my nemesis, Big Steve, always the captain?

It was the slow stuff that did me in. A high pop fly coming right at me in center field, the kind of thing where you didn't even have to move to catch it. The sun at your back and the ball lazily floating right to where you have been standing for the past hour and a half. Mary Webster yelling for you to make the last easy out, your team already swaggering off the field in victory. . .

That ball would go right through my hands and plunk down to the ground. I wanted to follow that dropped ball and hide in one of those deposits that dotted the field.

I never had any trouble catching a line drive. Any baseball that came at me in a flat speedy trajectory was meat for my trusty glove. As if it had eyes, it would smack into the pocket with a satisfying thump.

The problem came when I had too much time to think. A pop fly would soar slowly toward my glove, and I would watch the seams turn and start to think. What if I missed it? Would Mary Webster quit coming to the games? Would I have to quit school in shame?

Sometimes I had time to think ahead seventy years and envision myself and "Captain" Big Steve in rocking chairs at the old folks' home. I could hear him saying in a croaky old wheeze, "Remember how you missed that pop fly back in nineteen-and-thirty-one? Cost us the game? Yessir," he would croak, false teeth clicking in his skeleton-like head, rocking fiercely back and forth as the chair squeaked rhythmically, "You sure did cost us that game."

That's when the pop fly would hit the cow plop.

It was the same with batting. Give me a fast pitcher and a fast ball, and I could zap that sucker right out of the old ballpark. It was the slow, fidgety pitchers that got to me. You know the ones.

The pitcher would wet his fingers, take a look around the bases, adjust his hat, and look down at the catcher. I would be crouched in my batter's stance—steely-eyed and ready. The pitcher would straighten up and shrug off the catcher's sign. That would start my thinking. What if I struck out? What if I got hit by the pitch? What if I let down my whole team (again)?

Then the pitcher would start his routine again. He would re-adjust his vital body parts, touch his hat, look around at all the bases, wet his fingers again, and look down at the catcher. He would nod—it was a "go."

But it was already too late for me. His windup would start about the same time my brain was picturing a strike-out. I had already imagined the disappointed moans of the spectators. Mary Webster's face appeared—a vision of dashed hopes.

Then would come the *coup de grâce*: a slow ball. That ball would be coming at me so slowly, I could have run to first base and back to home plate before it reached me. I would stand there thinking that it would probably arrive next Friday during my piano lesson.

That's when seventy-nine year old Big Steve and his creaky rocker would reappear.

False teeth clicking and chair squeaking, old Big Steve would croak out his inevitable message of blame: "Remember the time you struck out in nineteen-and-thirty-two and cost the team the game *again*? Yessir, just like you did in nineteen-and-thirty-one, when you missed that pop fly out in center field."

I would swing my bat and strike out about ten minutes after the ball had smacked into the catcher's mitt.

Me 'n' Earl

The adults all worked in the family business, and I had become a sometime caretaker for my little brother, Earl. He was a cute little guy. Ruth could not force herself to cut his beautiful long curls, and he looked as much like a girl as a boy. Earl's hair was the envy of every mother in town.

My brother and I would take long walks together. Earl loved it when I could name the make of a car or show him my latest baseball card, or when I told him stories about my cowboy heroes. I felt I was his teacher and his protector.

Back then we weren't worried about child molesters or kidnappers. The few cars on the roads traveled at reasonable speeds. Half the streets weren't paved, and it was bad form to startle a farmer's horse with a noisy car. About the most serious thing that could happen to a couple of kids was to step in a pile of horse poop.

Summer vacation was half over. A bunch of the neighborhood kids had played a game of baseball the day before on the baseball diamond that Gramps had staked out in a field behind our house. We played there a couple of times a week during the summer. Earl, as usual, had been watching the game.

My brother had a small kid-sized baseball glove he always wore to watch the games. Earl was my staunchest fan. If someone hit a ball to the outfield within a hundred feet of my spot, Earl would pound his small fist into his undersized glove, stand up, and yell at me to "Catch the ball, catch the ball!" The kid was a real embarrassment.

This day dawned with the Midwest sun so fiercely hot, it stoked a wind like the Devil's breath. Earl had lost his glove somewhere in the makeshift ball field behind our house. We were looking for it when Earl spotted Big Steve's baseball bat lying in the dirt. Big Steve had forgotten it. Earl recognized it from the **BS** carved on the bat's handle. He said, "I'll take it across the street to Big Steve."

The less I had to do with Big Steve, the better. I said, "Okay, but hurry up. Mom just came home to fix us a special lunch." I kept on looking for Earl's glove.

I heard the screech of the tires skidding on the pavement in front of our house. I looked that way in time to see my brother flying through the air like a rag doll, and I heard Big Steve's bat hit the pavement with a bang that seemed as loud as a cannon shot. My world exploded along with Big Steve's bat.

I ran to the house yelling, "Mom! Mom! Earl's been hit by a car!"

My mother and I ran to the street to find a tangled mess of bloodied curly hair, with twisted legs lying in the gutter. Ruthie picked up the limp body of her second born. She sat on the curb and moaned softly as she cradled Earl. She rocked him back and forth until the heat of the day caused sweat to stain the back of her dress and the blood of her son formed a brown-red pool in the gutter beside the street.

And I felt nothing, except the devastating knowledge that "the protector" had let his baby brother cross the street—alone—to be killed.

The neighbors had called the doctor and the ambulance. Doc Kindly was the town's only doctor. The doctor's office and the three-bed hospital were in the same building. A hearse was housed next door and doubled as an ambulance when needed. Doc Kindly was in his office when the phone rang. He could tell from the call that this was a serious accident and he drove to the scene with the hearse.

When the doctor arrived, he laid the unconscious Earl on the gurney. He looked at my brother's injuries. Blood leaked from Earl's head. His skinny legs were twisted and odd-looking. Even I could see that his breathing was sporadic.

Doc Kindly's skill was as limited as his empathy was limitless. His expressive eyes looked at my mother and he said, "I don't think he will live, Ruthie. Let's get him to the hospital right away."

My mother said in her soft voice, "I want to take him to St. Louis, to the Jewish Hospital."

The doctor said, "I don't think he can live long enough to get there."

Raising her voice a notch, my mother said, "I'll keep him alive! I want to take him to the Jewish Hospital."

The ambulance driver said, "I don't even know where the Jew Hospital is."

I could see frustration building and determination flashing in my mother's dark eyes. She grabbed Big Steve's baseball bat from the gutter and walked to the front of the hearse. With the strength born of a mother's desperation, she smashed the bat down on the hood of the hearse and faced the doctor and the driver. She commanded in a voice I had never heard, "This ambulance is not going to be a hearse for any member of my family. Driver, load my son in the car and get your ass behind the wheel. I'll tell you how to get to the hospital. Drive, or I'll take this Goddamn ambulance myself."

They loaded Earl in the hearse/ambulance. My mother joined my injured brother in the back of the car, and they set off for St. Louis. I remember seeing wavy fingers of midday heat rise from the road, blurring the vehicle as it disappeared on its 125-mile, three-hour journey.

I sat on the steps in front of our house and watched the ambulance drive away. I was aware of the neighbors, still hanging around talking about the terrible accident and speculating whether my brother would live or die. They wondered what miracle the "Jew Hospital" in St. Louis could perform that old Doc Kindly couldn't.

Looking back on that moment, I think I must have been numb from the sheer magnitude of the tragedy. I just sat on the steps leading to the front of our house and looked up the street, as if waiting for the ambulance to re-appear.

I heard one of the neighbors say, "His brother doesn't seem to be too affected." It made me think I was probably expected to cry, so I squeezed out a couple of tears. It seemed to satisfy the bystanders. They told me not to worry, that everything would be okay. After a while, they all went home.

After the ambulance left, someone thought to call the store and tell John and Sarah what had happened. My father was on a buying trip out of town. My grandparents contacted Ben. He would meet Ruth at the hospital in St. Louis; my grandmother came home from the store to be with me. In our separate locations and private hells, we all waited for the news of my brother's death.

There was no air conditioning in the 1930s. The ambulance was a stifling sweatbox hurtling through a suffocating desert of heat. My mother sat in the back of the ambulance bathing Earl's head with wet towels that steamed from the stifling outdoor temperature. She barked instructions to the driver. She told stories to try to keep Earl conscious. My brother lingered between life and death.

When they arrived at the Jewish Hospital in St. Louis, they were greeted by an emergency crew that Doc Kindly had called for. They wheeled my brother into an operating room and worked on him for four hours.

At eleven o'clock that night, we got the call. Earl would live.

Earl stayed in the hospital for a long time before he could come home. My mother got a hotel room next door to the hospital and was with him as much as the hospital would allow. Ben stayed with Ruth a couple of days until the doctor was sure Earl was out of any danger. Then he came home to go back to work.

Back in Bullneck, Preacher Spud's wife brought us a couple of apple pies. The neighbors came with their home-cooked offerings and their prayers. I spent most of my time moping down at the store and reading books I had checked out of the library.

A couple of days after Earl's accident, I went to return some books. I was feeling sorry for myself and walking hangdog to the library when I noticed Old Charlie sitting on his usual bench in front of the library, his nose stuck deep into a book.

I said, "Hi."

Charlie gave me an appraising look and mumbled, "Hi, I heard what happened to your brother. You look to me like you took a trip, too."

"Whadya mean? I never went anywhere."

"Maybe not, but I think maybe you did. You may still be there."

"Whadya talking about, Charlie? I'm right here talking to you."

"Sure you're not on the Isle of Guilt?"

"Oh, Charlie, I don't feel like one of your stories today."

"You certain? I think you'll like this one."

With that, Charlie scooted over on his bench and motioned for me to sit beside him. He waved his arm wide and began his story.

"Somewhere out there lies the Isle of Guilt. The main industry on this mysterious island is the manufacture of Guilt Sacks.

"Guilt Sacks are woven from a unique and special cloth. It's tougher—it's tighter—it has a specific design, and each one is made for only one owner. True genius is woven into the fabric of every sack: elastic! A Guilt Sack can stretch to dimensions unknown even to its creator. Finally, the makers add a little stickum, and it's ready to go. Once the designated owner touches it, it's like flypaper. You can't get rid of the thing.

"When you visit the Isle of Guilt, your own sack is already there, waiting for you. It's free for the taking. But believe me, nothing in this world is ever free. As always, there is a major catch to this 'free' gift. You have to fill the sack with guilt.

"Nobody gets through this life without visiting the Isle of Guilt. We each get our special guilt sacks to carry around. Some people stagger around with a fuller sack than others. Some have gigantic sacks. They keep loading their sacks, bending over with the size and the weight of the burden. Finally, they bend so low that their backs start to hurt and their shoulders ache, their muscles cramp, their stomachs don't function, they have dandruff, and they can't sleep. It's just too much. So they dump a part of their guilt on someone or something who doesn't deserve the burden—like a child, a neighbor, even a dog.

"A better way is to take the stuff out of the sack and look at it every now and then. Show it to a friend. You may decide it doesn't really need to be carried around any longer. If it doesn't, throw it away, before it grows bigger."

"Charlie, do you think I have a Guilt Sack?"

"What do you think?"

And right there in the middle of Charlie's story, I took some stuff out of my sack and shared it with Charlie.

I told him how bad I felt and that I didn't mean to hurt my brother. I told him it was my fault that Earl was in the hospital. I told him I had let my brother cross the street when I should have known better. I told Charlie I wanted to die, and that I didn't deserve to live.

Charlie looked at me and said, "Never say that. You're just a kid. You did the best you could. You are not perfect—nobody is! But you loaded your Guilt Sack with some pretty heavy stuff all at one time. Wouldn't hurt for us to take a look at what you got in there every once in a while, just to see if it all really belongs."

Right then I felt like crying, but I knew Buck Jones or Tom Mix would never cry. So I just bit my lip and looked at Charlie.

"Charlie, did you ever kill anybody in the war?"

I saw a single tear run down Charlie's wrinkled cheek. And my eyes got moist. Charlie and I just sat there for the longest time and didn't look at one another.

It took Earl a long time to fully recover. He was in a leg and body cast for months. He couldn't sit and he couldn't walk. He was miserable. The cast itched in places he couldn't reach. He needed help to eat, and someone had to tend to him in the bathroom. When they cut off his cast, his left leg looked like a broomstick, and it took over a year to regain its normal size and muscle.

Despite Charlie's story, the stickum on my sack was put there by experts, and its contents were not so easy to discard. I needed a little something extra to comfort me while carrying my new load of guilt. Food seemed to help. I gained a lot of weight during the time of my brother's recovery. It was the beginning of a lifelong struggle with my weight—and my guilt.

Even the small things had changed forever. The doctors had shaved off Earl's resplendent curly hair. When it grew back, it was straight. I thought that was my fault, too.

Go North, Young Man, Go North

Elijah "Spud" Hall was a real fire-and-brimstone preacher who believed in All Mighty Gawd, the sanctity of the Church, and the love of his country. He could find an explanation for anything in his beloved Bible, and he led his congregation over the tortuous road from heaven to hell and back again every Sunday.

When Spud preached, his parishioners could feel the heat building up in their bellies. Even his rendition of the Sermon on the Mount was a standing-room-only event. One year, Preacher Hall threw so much fire and brimstone that the pulpit burst into flames. People started running from the church screaming that Armageddon had come.

Bullneck's fire department roared up to the church to extinguish the fire. Fire Chief Moishe Grimsley discovered the fire had started when a bad speaker wire caused a spark. The spark had ignited some papers the good preacher had left under the pulpit. There was never a dull moment in Preacher Hall's church.

Spud had the largest and most affluent congregation in town. On the Halls' tenth wedding anniversary, the adoring congregation got together and raised the money to send the couple to Hawaii for a ten-day vacation.

The flock felt their money had been well spent when Mrs. Hall gave birth to a beautiful baby girl nine months after she and Preacher Hall returned from Hawaii. The proud parents christened the baby Independence.

Independence Hall lived across the street from me in the parish manse. The church grounds were a jungle of fruit trees, flowers, and exotic plants. Independence and I spent our summers playing and dreaming in innocent bliss on the reverend's church grounds. Independence was about the most beautiful girl I had ever seen, and sometimes she would tell me that she loved me. We had our own Eden in Spud's church garden.

One day my mother was in the kitchen making those mottled beige cannonballs she put in the chicken soup, and I was working on my homework. I asked her where north was.

She pointed across the street toward Independence Hall's house and said, "That's north." As long as we lived in that house, no matter where I was, I could find north with the accuracy of the finest compass.

Then we moved to a new house.

After that, I would close my eyes, mentally place myself in the kitchen of the house where we used to live, and picture Independence across the street telling me she loved me. The summer sun was always shining, and Independence Hall was always calling me out to play. North was where Independence was. My sense of direction was infallible.

When I started driving a car, my process of finding north became more difficult. Closing my eyes for a minute or two at a busy intersection to conjure up the image of my lovely forest sylph was becoming life-threatening.

Like most modern Americans, I've moved again and again over the years. After each move, it takes a little longer to get my bearings. If someone asks me for directions, I go into a sort of trance. My eyes glaze over and I transport myself back through my various residences until Independence, beautiful and sunbaked, is once more beckoning me north.

By the time I am ready to give directions, the questioner is usually long gone, having concluded that I was either having a seizure or had somehow escaped to nirvana.

A few months ago, I dreamed I was back in that first house. I could smell Preacher Hall's wife cooking Sunday morning bacon. Independence was running around the front yard yelling for me to come out and play.

Spud was outside doing his usual thing before Sunday morning services. Every Sunday morning just before devotions, he would take out his rifle and shoot at the crows in the trees. He hated the noise they made when he was giving a sermon.

In my dream, I said, "Which way is north, Preacher?"

Preacher Hall fired off a shot at the crows, and said, "Don't know, son. I have enough trouble guiding people up and down. Never had time for north and south."

Since that dream, I can't locate north anymore. I can get about as far back as my last three moves, and then I get stuck.

Maybe if I went back to that old town and looked up Independence, I could tell her my problem. I could pick a nice sunny day, and we could play in the church grounds as we used to do.

When she told me she loved me, I would know I had found north again.

The Fire Man

A fire alarm clanged its angry bell in my Uncle Harry's bed-room. It was the middle of the night. Harry's bell rang at the same time as the one in the main St. Louis fire station. A fire in St. Louis before World War II was a fairly frequent occurrence.

Uncle Harry would sigh and heave his substantial corpulence out of bed. He would call his driver, who lived only minutes away. It was nearly impossible for Harry to maneuver into position be-hind a steering wheel, so he had a full-time chauffeur. The driver would bring the car around, and off they would go to the fire. Uncle Harry never told anyone how he got an official fire alarm installed in his bedroom—or how much it had cost him.

My Uncle Harry was an insurance adjuster for "the people." He represented the victims of fire casualties. He was on the side of the little guy against the insurance companies. Harry had his private alarm installed so he could get to fire victims before an insurance company showed up waving a quick settlement check. A quick insurance settlement would usually be written for about half the amount Harry might negotiate at a later date.

Most of the time, Uncle Harry beat the fire department to the scene. He would haul his 300-pound bulk out of his chauffeured car, place his trademark white Fedora on his head, and you knew he was ready to challenge the world. The victims of the fire would be frightened and downcast. In shock, they would lament their lost possessions, wondering how their things could ever be re-placed. Uncle Harry would listen with sympathy and patience, his white hat held politely in his hand. Low-key and sincere, he said he knew how they felt. He would ask who carried their insurance, and they would usually tell him.

He gave the victims his card and told them to call him if their insurance company did not treat them right, or if they felt they were not getting a fair settlement. He explained that he would represent them against the insurance company. He charged a percentage and guaranteed to get his clients a larger settlement than they could possibly get for themselves.

I guess you might call him a first cousin to an ambulance chaser—and maybe he was. But you should have seen him when one of the victims he had contacted would come to him, despondent and beaten. A family whose business or home had gone up in flames, and who were on the verge of settling for a paltry amount because they could no longer fight.

Uncle Harry would start educating them. He would point out losses covered by insurance that the victims had not even thought of. As he talked, you could see a glimmer of hope replace their sense of defeat.

Harry promised to get them every penny they were entitled to collect. Sometimes he offered to loan the family some money until the settlement came through. Occasionally his clients would cry. Mostly, they would just sigh with relief that someone else was picking up a fight they didn't have the will to continue. Harry was one of the good guys. He really cared, and it showed.

Insurance companies are not all bad guys, but they fight hard to keep their payouts as low as possible. Fire victims are not all good guys. But insurance companies are in the power seat against a family broken with grief. Those fire victims took great comfort in knowing that Uncle Harry's 300-pound bulk was backed by a compassionate heart and the savvy to go head-to-head with the big guys.

Every time I hear a fire engine, whenever the news team films a crowd watching a burned-out home, whenever I see the tears in a victim's eyes, I can't help but look for Uncle Harry's massive mound of righteous advocacy to step from his car, put on his white Fedora, and quietly wait for someone to look his way.

A Writer's Best Friend
is his Wastebasket

I don't know how it is today, but when I was in high school and basketball season started, the players on the school basketball team were kings of the world. Team members would all sport the big orange school letter 𝔹 on their sweaters to identify them as members of the Bullneck Buffaloes. The whole town would fawn over them.

The girls would giggle with delight if a basketball player looked their way. The townspeople were certain their team would win the championship—though the chances of the team becoming a winner were about the same as our country *not* electing Franklin Roosevelt as President.

The Buffaloes would play a home game every couple of weeks in the high school gymnasium. The gym was always filled to capacity with a wildly cheering crowd. On weeks they didn't play at home, the team traveled to a neighboring town to oppose a hated rival. The cheering hometown throng would usually journey with them.

Bullneck's local paper, The Bull Horn, was the clarion for town happenings. It wasn't much for world news, but it was an invaluable source of information about weddings, church meetings, and the latest doings of the National Rifle Association and the KKK. A vital feature of this indispensable news was the front-page, play-by-play coverage of the Buffaloes' latest basketball game.

The Bull Horn was proud to have its own basketball sportswriter with his own column and byline. This basketball paragon was selected yearly from an essay contest judged by our school's English teacher.

At this time, there lived in my town a very nearsighted, but talented, teenager who thought the game of basketball should never have been invented. This teenager, whose expertise in basketball didn't extend beyond the certainty that he would always be chosen last for any team, entered the annual essay contest. He won the contest, his own weekly column, and his first byline in one fell swoop.

There were many benefits to being a basketball sportswriter beyond the column and byline. The sportswriter got to wear one of those big orange Bs on his sweater. It was the same as those worn by the athletes. No one could really tell the difference—except for some reason, the girls didn't giggle with delight when this sportswriter looked their way.

The sportswriter went to all the games and sat at a special sports desk right on the gym floor. He also got to visit the locker room after the game and listen to the cool talk about which girl was hot and which one was not.

This was long before girls were allowed to interview the players in the shower. That's the reason Bullneck's sportswriters were always boys. I thought I would add that before I started getting hate mail.

As an integral part of his job, the sportswriter was also the designated basketball statistician. His official duties were to keep score during the game and log who made the shots, who committed the fouls, and what penalties were imposed. Those duties were simple enough for someone who could see across the length of a gym. Not so simple for a seriously nearsighted boy who was too self-conscious to wear his glasses.

Our optically challenged scorekeeper had problems all season, but he usually muddled through by asking the official next to him what had just happened. It was during the regional championship game when things really came apart. The game was a hard-fought, fast, and crucial match between the Buffaloes and their most despised cross-town rival, the Panthers. As fate would have it, our intrepid sportswriter had no one sitting beside him.

The action was so fast and ferocious that the nearsighted scorekeeper was completely overwhelmed. He couldn't tell whether the last shot had swished or bounced, who had committed a foul, or if the action had stopped because of a foul or a time-out. The score and statistics were in complete chaos. The game had to be halted in the last minutes of the fourth period.

All hell erupted in the bleachers. Three fights broke out. Trash was thrown like confetti onto the gym floor. The noise was unbearable.

Francie Anne Tate got so agitated she went into labor and popped out twins, right under the bleachers. Coach Beldon had a face-off with the rival coach that promised blood. There was so much booing and stamping, it took almost an hour to straighten things out.

In the scuffle, the offending sportswriter disappeared and a new scorekeeper from the rival school took over.

The Buffaloes lost the game.

Everybody in town swore we lost because our team never got credit for two baskets. The mood of the town got pretty mean. A vigilante group proposed to kidnap the Panthers' whole team. The idea was abandoned because only three people were carrying shotguns in the back of their cars.

Preacher Elijah "Spud" Hall called a special prayer meeting. Coach Beldon broke into a hysterical crying fit in the middle of Preacher Spud's sermon on tolerance and fair play.

The next day's Bull Horn came out with a black border. The vital column on the losing game was given its usual front-page spot.

In further endangerment of his life, the sportswriter had suddenly become a basketball critic. Knowing absolutely nothing about basketball, he criticized two of the Buffalo players in his column when he reviewed the losing game. It was the last straw.

The town's wrath was so intense, the kid's parents were afraid to let Mr. Myopia out of the house.

A few days later, the sportswriter was summoned to the editor's office. As the kid entered the news room, the paper's only staff reporter looked up from his typewriter. He threw the kid a menacing look and an uncalled-for finger gesture. The thought occurred to our intrepid sportswriter that maybe things were not going too well.

In all fairness, I must say the editor fired me with a great deal of class. He admitted that never in fifty years of publishing had the Bull Horn received so much mail.

He gave me personal credit for that.

Is it Colder in the City in the Winter?

In the days before World War II, the most exciting thing that happened in our family was when Uncle Raymond stopped by for a visit.

Uncle Raymond sold ladies' dresses that were manufactured in the city. He traveled the countryside all year long and peddled his merchandise to dress shops in small towns throughout the Midwest. When he came by Bullneck to sell his wares to our family store, he was required to have dinner and spend the night with us. Everyone loved Uncle Raymond.

The routine was always the same. Uncle Raymond would burst through the front door just before the evening meal. With laughter and a great shout, he embraced everyone.

He would take one look at my brother and me and say with machine-gun delivery, "Tell me boys, is it colder in the city in the winter than it's warmer in the country in the summer?"

My brother and I would both say, "C'mon, Uncle Raymond, say it slower."

He would repeat it again, usually faster, and the whole family would fall down laughing at our confusion. He would give us each a quarter, laugh, and begin telling us all about his latest adventures.

Uncle Raymond painted word pictures of his experiences while traveling the Midwest countryside. Through his tales, we visited a farmer whose barn had burnt down. We were with Uncle Raymond when he ate his sandwich while parked beside a dairy farm or a quiet meadow stream. We listened to his stories about small town merchants and their customers.

Uncle Raymond especially loved wheat fields. He claimed the wheat stalks spoke a secret language. He said when the wind blew just right and the wheat waved in a gracefully hypnotic rhythm, it seemed that the wheat was speaking to him. Sometimes, he just liked to sit in his car and listen to the "gossip of the stalks."

Uncle Raymond could mimic any accent in the world, and he told stories in Irish brogue or guttural Germanic or with a country twang. We met all sorts of people—sad and funny, angelic and reprehensible. We changed tires in the rain and square danced in the town square. The entertainment went on for hours, and Uncle Raymond always left us wanting more.

One day Uncle Raymond burst through the door as usual. The family gathered around, he hugged everybody exuberantly, looked at my brother and me and said, "Tell me boys, is it colder in the city in the winter than it's warmer in the country in the summer?"

Earl said, "Uncle Raymond, that's a silly question." My brother had grown up.

There was dead silence. My mother was the first to recover with a "Hurry up, everybody, dinner is ready."

Uncle Raymond's stories were not as entertaining that night. He said he guessed he was tired, and went to bed early. Maybe my brother's remark was a portent of things soon to come. It was 1934, and Hitler had become Chancellor of Germany.

It was the beginning of the end of silliness.

Uncle Raymond's ritual query was a silly question in a more innocent age. But I sometimes find myself feeling colder in the city in the winter, and I wonder if it's warmer in the country in the summer.

You Can't Eat Soup With a Knife

In our family, nothing went to waste. When my grandfather won a set of drums in an all-night poker game, they had to be used. That's how I became a drummer.

My required practicing on the piano had already destroyed my social life. Why couldn't Gramps have won a pony or a bicycle or a sack of marbles? Or better still, why couldn't he have made a bad bet and lost the piano?

Now I had two things to practice: the piano in the living room and the drums in the closet. Because no one could stand the noise of my pounding, I was banished to the closet under the stairs to practice the drums. The slanted ceiling was just high enough to allow me to stand at the far end. My drum set shared the closet space with ice skates, rain gear, and boxes of long-forgotten content. A single light fixture, its glass cracked by some misguided coat hanger, shone dimly.

Once closeted, with the doors closed, little light, and less air, I stood between the raincoats and the overcoats. With sweat pouring down my face, I thought of how I would like to pound on Big Steve the bully, and I would beat the hell out of those stupid pieces of stretched animal hide.

I beat on "Big Steve" every day for almost five years. I went through four teachers, two raincoats, and six overcoats before the family finally agreed it would have been better if Gramps had not held the winning hand that night.

My father traded the drums for a saxophone for Earl. It was

mysteriously "stolen" within the first week. My brother had learned from my experience. Earl never wasted an opportunity to learn from my bad examples.

My reward for being a failure on drums was a sentence to practice the piano twice as long. As horrible as I was on drums, I was a drumming genius compared to my talent on the piano. After months of torturous practice, I could eventually learn a simple piece by rote. I didn't even know what I was playing—my fingers had learned the movements. Like an evangelist who preaches his message door to door, if my memorized recitation was interrupted, I had to start again from the beginning.

The piano teacher was instructed to teach me my father's favorite piece of music, Hearts and Flowers. Dad claimed it was his favorite but I always thought it was the only tune he knew by name. It was a sappy old ditty, the perfect match for my level of talent.

After months of practice, my fingers memorized Hearts and Flowers. My mother and father were very proud. I had finally mastered the difficult instrument! They insisted on displaying the talents of their elder son to any unsuspecting victim who wandered into our living room.

How I dreaded those fearsome words: "Burton, sit down and play the piano for our guest."

If nothing interrupted my recital, necessitating a start-over, the ordeal was mercifully short. I could resume breathing and disappear until the next unfortunate guest arrived.

I remember one beautiful springtime Sunday. It was one of those days that inspired my Uncle Raymond and his family to take a country drive and visit us "down south." Uncle Raymond arrived with his daughter, Audrey, an awesomely beautiful girl a year older than me.

How I loved that girl.

Raymond also brought his son, Horace, who was his pride and joy, and his wife, Clara, who never stopped talking. Poor cousin Horace, whom we called Horse-Face behind his back, was in a life-long struggle to overcome the stigma of his unfortunate moniker.

After a sumptuous lunch served with plenty of lively and argumentative conversation, the families retired to the living room and I heard the dreaded words, "Burton, sit down and play the piano for our guests."

I sat down, and my trained fingers started playing Hearts and Flowers. It took a little longer than usual because Aunt Clara interrupted the concert several times to ask questions or to gush about the song choice. I had to start over each time. Finally, the ordeal ended.

Uncle Raymond said Horace had been fooling with the piano for a couple of months, too. Instantly we all wanted Horse-Face to play for us.

After a little embarrassed posturing, Horace shuffled to the piano. He adjusted the seat. He sat down. He squirmed, he wriggled. After about five minutes of this, he went into a sort of reverie and started to play. He did a riff up and down the keys, and then launched into a popular tune. He modulated from ragtime to waltz. He bounced up and down to the rhythm until I thought the piano bench would collapse. Horace was lost in his music, and it looked as though the keys and his fingers were one. He played nonstop for over an hour. We were entranced.

Uncle Raymond and his family left early so they could get home in time to hear Jack Benny on the radio. We said goodbye. I got to kiss Audrey on the cheek. Damn, she was gorgeous.

How I loved that girl.

Later that day, my mother told me I didn't have to take piano lessons anymore.

The Bewildering Machine

I got a memory jolt today when my collection of home brew started exploding. I keep the bottles down in the cool of the basement while they age to a golden ripeness. Once in a while the mixture gets away from me, and bottles of almost-beer explode and shower their tart goodness in a magnificent cloud of liquid and glass. There is nothing quite like being engrossed in a televised period drama when suddenly, World War III erupts in your basement.

My beer explosions always jerk me back to my memories of our high school chemistry instructor, Dr. Henry Whipple. Bullneck was the envy of the surrounding communities for having acquired this paragon of educational excellence as our chemistry instructor.

There was one slight problem: Dr. Whipple could never get a chemistry experiment to come out right. Educational credentials aside, no matter what the experiment was supposed to show, Dr. Whipple always managed to screw it up to the point of explosion. His best efforts would culminate in a burst of steaming rainbow colors mixed with shattered beakers, the whole mess streaking skyward with awe-inspiring speed. The ensuing boom would be accompanied by the oohing and aahing of his worshipful students. That man could mix water and ice and get an explosion.

Inspired by the intrepid doctor's example of a willingness to fail, I set out to invent a telephone answering machine. I didn't know that Mr. Willy Muller had already invented the first automatic answering machine five years earlier. Willy's device had not been an overwhelming best-seller. It was a very complicated three-foot tall machine popular with Orthodox Jews who were forbidden to answer the phone on the Sabbath.

Not having the slightest idea of what I was getting into, I began my first adventure into the wonderful world of inventing. I knew the worst thing that could happen was that my creation would blow up—and maybe then Dr. Whipple would hire me as his assistant.

As I built the machine, each problem I solved created a new one. A few feet of wiring graduated to a few yards, and then kept going. The answering device became a labyrinth of wires, switches, relays, tubes, needles, and buttons. My invention had taken on the complexity of some diabolical necessity to the well being— or the destruction—of mankind.

I had placed my machine on the kitchen table for its final test when the catastrophe occurred. The ringer on the phone was supposed to vibrate a thin wire that contacted a solenoid. The solenoid then activated the recording disk. I decided I needed a tool from the storage shed to make an adjustment. I left my machine hooked up to the phone while I went to the shed.

My mother was in the kitchen heating some chicken soup for dinner when the phone rang. The lights on my answering machine flashed and the recording disk started to revolve. It scared the hell out of her. Thinking the "crazy contraption" was going to explode, she grabbed the pot of chicken soup from the stove and drowned my machine before it could destroy the house. Sparks showered the table top, and my machine ground to a smoking, shuddering halt.

It never worked again.

My machine, with its lingering odor of chicken soup, may have laid an egg in the kitchen, but it was a persistent feature in my bedroom. I moved it up there and for years to come, I would look at that mass of wiring and circuitry with amazement at the perseverance that had created it. I had gone beyond myself.

I began to see it as a model of how we build our lives: wire by wire, switch by switch, buttons on top of relays, until we have something that works, or does not work, or that works only sometimes. We build the convoluted contraption ourselves, and then spend the rest of our lives trying to decipher how we did it.

If You Intend to Bite,
Don't Bare Your Teeth

It was Uncle Harry's fatness that fooled everybody. He moved his 300-pound bulk slowly and groaned a lot. He groaned when he got into the car. He groaned when he sat down and when he got up. He groaned when he went to bed and he groaned in his sleep. He groaned when he was hungry—which was most of the time—and after he finished one of his gargantuan meals, he groaned.

I loved to go to my uncle's business meetings when they promised to be adversarial. Harry was an actor of the first magnitude—and the show was always good. He would sit down at the conference table with a loud groan and proceed to withdraw behind his large bulk with half-closed lids. You could see his opponents relax. What possible threat to them was this sleepy bag of beef?

Uncle Harry never had much to add to a business conference until the closing minutes. He would sit and listen and nod—half-asleep and showing profound disinterest, the picture of flabby complacency. Sometimes even insults were directed at him, but nothing seemed to penetrate those fleshy layers of insulation. But if, like me, you looked below those half-closed lids into his eyes, you could see them darting like flashes of lightning from one person to another. He didn't miss a thing.

About two-thirds of the way through the meeting, when the conversation was getting repetitive, Uncle Harry would emit one of his bigger groans and pull himself upright in his chair. He would search his pockets and find a torn envelope or piece of crumpled paper to use as a prop. Then a small miracle would take place.

Uncle Harry transformed from an amorphous bag of fat to a formidable man with a stentorian delivery. His eyes snapped and his manner was imposing. His fat seemed to ripple into muscles. A shock wave would reverberate around the table. The sleepy elephant was talking, and what he had to say usually devastated the meeting. He had done his homework. He could add columns of figures in his head and never be off a penny. He could page through masses of material and recall any line when needed. He revealed a mind like a rapier and wielded it with the adroitness of a fencing master.

Everyone (but me) would be in a state of shock. This was the show I had come to see. Once the transformation took place, no one ever interrupted him.

The odd thing was that he could fool the same people over and over. They saw the slow-moving obese man with the sleepy eyes and the soft body who groaned a lot. They fell for the facade and ignored the reality. As a result, they lost the contest—every time.

Uncle Harry reminded me of a big fat frog sitting, harmless and sleepy, on a lily pad. Until an insect came too close. It would be over in a flash. The insect would be gone. The frog would croak in pleasure, innocent and benign, until the next victim came along.

Desiree

When oil was discovered hidden under the farmlands of Southern Illinois, the oil drilling pros from Texas descended upon Bullneck. These flamboyant Texans brought their cowboy boots, their Stetson hats, their hard-drinking drillers, their muscled roughnecks, and the spectacular gem of Desiree.

She was a roughneck's daughter and made an impression on our small high school as big as all Texas. I would bet that seventy years later, each and every male student still remembers the girl named Desiree. With our hormones roaring at peak capacity, our imaginations spun day and night with visions of this lovely creature.

If Venus had been prone to violence, she would have killed for Desiree's five feet four inches of delectable eye candy. Desiree had natural (it didn't occur to us country boys that maybe it was not natural) light blond hair down to her perfect shoulders. She had big blue eyes that reminded you of the blue in the county reservoir on a cloudless day. She was vivacious, curvaceous, and delicious.

True to her Texan heritage, Desiree wore cowboy boots. I wondered if Texans really wore cowboy boots in their home state, or only when they left Texas so people could identify them as genuine Texans.

Desiree's cowboy boots sure showed off her legs. Her walk was the personification of the word sashay, and her boots made clicking sounds when she sashayed down the school's tiled halls. Traffic between classes would come to a standstill while we males watched Desiree's tight little ass wiggle its way along a passageway. Her trips up and down stairs in her swishing skirts were ecstasy to watch.

Desiree never wore a brassiere. She either didn't know what a brassiere was, or she knew what it was, and didn't like what it couldn't do. What a brassiere could not do was allow those perfect breasts to bounce in time to the tune of her clicking cowboy boots. I guess Desiree must have had an innate sense of rhythm that cried out to be expressed.

After a while, all the boys started wearing jockey shorts to hide their teenage reactions to Desiree. Unfortunately, much to the disappointment of her male schoolmates (and the delight of the females), it wasn't long before Desiree was taken off the market. She started going steady with Big Steve, the school's uncontested prime jock.

Steve and Desiree went steady for about a year, and then broke up early in their senior year. I think most jocks are decent guys. Steve wasn't. He fancied himself a lover and a storyteller, and he would entertain any group who would listen.

There was no detail too intimate for Big Steve's bragging. He enthralled his immature male audience into raptures by recalling his explicit sexual experiences with Desiree—while Desiree, the object of his stories, suffered the hurt and humiliation of a love affair gone wrong. And much worse: the realization that someone she had once loved was a mean and vindictive child.

I don't know how Desiree survived the pain and ridicule of her senior year. She changed from a vivacious and delightful blond beauty into a quiet and subdued D student. She gained weight. She lengthened her skirts. She started wearing a brassiere. She traded her boots for saddle shoes and bobby socks. She lost her Texas accent and Texas manners.

She tried to blend into Midwest blandness. It didn't work that well.

Her father, a Texan first and foremost, missed his home turf. He moved his family back to Texas before Desiree could graduate from high school. That's the last I ever saw or heard of her. But

I will never forget the beautiful Texan who enthralled a school and made my male classmates dream of things that might have been.

I wish I had been a fighting man so I could have beaten the hell out of Steve. He spoiled a hundred dreams and destroyed a young girl's joy in life. I wish I had been able to shut him up and give him the punishment he deserved.

Who knows? I might have ended up with Desiree. We could have moved back to Texas together. I could have become an oil man with a collection of cowboy boots to wear whenever I left Texas.

The Hero

The Fourth of July was a better holiday for me than Christmas ever was. Fourth of July was when my cousin, Horse-Face Horace, would blow himself up. You could count on Horace to hurt himself as surely as you could count on Independence Day arriving on the Fourth of July.

About the middle of February, my brother and I would start lobbying to get Horace and his family invited over for the Fourth. We would speculate for months about how Horace would hurt himself this year. He never disappointed. He had a reputation to build.

Horse-Face was fearless. The bigger the firecracker, the louder the rocket, the greater the blast—the happier he was. He would hold a firecracker until the last possible minute and then fling it into the air, trying to see how close he could cut it. He blasted cherry bombs from a board on his head. There was no end to his ingenuity when it came to fireworks. Inevitably, each year he pressed his luck too far.

This Fourth was no different. Horse-Face had been at his antics for about an hour when he strolled calmly into our house to get his mother. "Mom," he said, "I've had a little accident." Horace never cried. He was a master of understatement. A four-inch firecracker had exploded in his hand.

His mother, the normally bubbling and talkative Aunt Clara, took one look and said, "Crud, Horace, if the doctor doesn't cut off your hand this time it will be a miracle." She turned to my mother and said, "Call Doc Kindly and tell him we're on our way. Horace did it again."

This was always the best part of the holiday. We all piled into the car—dogs, kids, mothers, even the neighbor's kids. We all crammed ourselves into the doc's office. Doc Kindly was there waiting for us. He took one look at the scene and said, "Hello, Horace. It's almost 2 p.m.—you're late this year." He set to the task of cleaning up Horace's hand. We all knew what was coming and surreptitiously, we watched Aunt Clara. She started to turn white.

We all knew Horace was allergic to tetanus, but the doc had to give him the shot anyway. Just before the shot, Doc Kindly would say, "Horace, I hope you don't have a bad time with this." Horse-Face's mother would ask faintly, "What's the worst that could happen?" The doc pulled no punches. He would reply, "He could die."

Then, in would go the needle.

That's when it generally happened. Aunt Clara would keel over in a dead faint. The doc would get out the smelling salts and mumble something about how if the kid *did* die, maybe Doc would be able to spend a whole Fourth with his family for a change. Then Aunt Clara would revive, and we would all troop home and spend the rest of the holiday watching to see if Horse-Face would die.

Horace never did die. He became a decorated hero in World War II. He went through the whole war without a scratch.

The miracle is that his mother survived.

Bernie

It was one of those scorching Midwest summer days. The weather had been mean for almost two weeks. No rain, no cool breeze at night, no relief from the relentless heat.

My best friend, Bernie, had just lost his week's wages flipping coins and shooting pool after work. It generally took him about an hour after he was paid to become flat-ass broke. Bernie was never very lucky. He worked every Saturday during the school year at a little grocery store on Main Street. The owner, Clarence Leary, was a hard-working Irishman who expected his help to work as hard as he did. Bernie was his ideal employee. Clarence made Bernie responsible for taking care of the airless storeroom at the back of the grocery.

Bernie was the youngest of three brothers, so his family called him "The Babe." But there was nothing babyish about my good friend. He was built like a weightlifter and handled anything life threw at him with a good-natured smile.

Clarence Leary was merciless in taking advantage of The Babe. In addition to storeroom duties, Clarence had Bernie rearranging heavy boxes of canned goods, doing general store cleanup, and lugging things weighing up to a hundred pounds from one end of the store to the other.

Good-natured Bernie would give a smile, say, "Okay boss," and sweat through his shirt about twenty minutes after he reported for work. It took almost an hour for his pants to get as wet as his shirt. After ten hours of backbreaking work, Bernie would emerge from the storeroom wringing wet and ready for a trip to the local pool hall. Its dank underground basement gave him his first respite from a long, hot day. I worked in my father's store, and we met at the pool hall almost every Saturday night after our shifts ended.

It was the summer before my senior year of high school. Any teenager who had any sense at all knew you didn't graduate high school without having been drunk at least once, and without having been laid, also at least once. Bernie and I were virgins in both areas. We decided to take care of the drinking first. The girls were a bigger problem we would have to tackle later.

I don't know which one of us brought it up first, but we decided that this Sunday—hot, schmot—we were going to get half of our high school "diploma" and get drunk. To teenagers, it doesn't make a damn bit of difference how hot it gets. Life's prime directive is to do something stupid.

First we had to get the booze. Bernie was broke, as usual. He turned to me. I didn't have the slightest idea what kind of booze to get, and I was too young to buy it anyway.

Like every small town, Bullneck had its classic drunk. Old Dutch knew everyone, and everyone knew him. We would all wave and say hello when he swayed harmlessly down the street. Who else would know more about drinking and booze than our own local expert? Besides, we needed a front man to buy the booze. Bernie and I decided to have a conference with Old Dutch.

Old Dutch, Bernie, and I had a long confab on the bench in front of the courthouse. We asked Old Dutch what kind of booze would be best for a first drunk. He went deep into thought for a while, and then Old Dutch started wheezing and slapping his knee. He finally spewed out, "By God, this is a case for apricot brandy."

We found out later that apricot brandy was Old Dutch's favorite drink of all time. It was also so cheap, I could afford two quart bottles. One for Old Dutch, and one for Old Burt and Old Bernie. Old Dutch went to Don's Likker Store and bought our tickets to drunkville. He handed us our booze. He unscrewed the top of his bottle and grabbed a couple of quick swallows. He smacked his lips and started to deliver a beginners' course on drinking.

I didn't know there were that many nuances to becoming a drunk until Old Dutch started his wheezy litany. We tried to absorb as much as we could before his voice kind of drained down to a watery whisper and he fell asleep, his head hanging at an odd angle while he snored away. We left him alone at his favorite hangout—the bench in front of the courthouse—and went to Bernie's house to stock some provisions for our big adventure.

You couldn't open the fridge at Bernie's house without something spilling out. There were four behemoth men to feed, and a mother who loved to cook. Their oversized refrigerator housed every food known to man. If what you needed was not in the fridge, it would be somewhere in the generously stocked kitchen. Bernie nabbed a few pounds of hamburger, some onions, buns, lettuce, tomatoes, ketchup, mustard, four ears of corn, and an apple pie for dessert. I brought the apricot brandy. We were off on our drunk.

Bernie's family loved to fish. They had a favorite weekend spot on the Fox River about twenty miles out of town. It was off a deserted road, and Bernie said there was a small copse of trees on the bank of the river. The trees would give us shade from the heat that had threatened to melt our tires to the road.

By the time we got to our destination, we had forgotten whether Old Dutch had told us to drink before we ate, or after. We decided to do both. As soon as we got out of the car, we opened our bottle and took our first gigantic swig of apricot brandy.

I thought I would throw up. Bernie did throw up. It was the worst stuff either one of us had ever tasted. If Old Dutch had been there, we might have killed him. But we were determined. We had another drink. It wasn't as bad as the first one.

We dug a pit, started a fire, and put a wire grate over the top. We threw on four hamburgers and had another drink. This stuff wasn't bad at all. Our attitude toward Old Dutch started to soften.

We each ate a hamburger and had a couple more drinks. We looked at each other and said, "Shit, this booze must be bad. We can't even feel it." So, we had a couple more drinks.

We decided our expert, Old Dutch, didn't know what he was talking about. It was amazing how he had become the town drunk. Nobody could get drunk on the junk he had talked us into. We laughed a little as we downed a few more drinks.

We had decided not to cook the corn, so we threw on another round of burgers and had a couple more drinks and some pie. The drinks weren't affecting us anyway, and we noticed how the apricotty taste of the brandy went pretty good with the pie.

I walked down to the river to take a leak and stumbled on a rock. Bernie had to drag me back to the bank because I was gurgling facedown in the water. Bernie started laughing about losing his pay every week. He said, "How come I lose my pay every week and you double yours?" We both decided Bernie just didn't have any luck. Then I fell in the river again, and Bernie had to drag me out.

We took another drink, laughed, and said Old Dutch was a pretty good guy. We decided we would give him a bottle of our favorite booze—apricot brandy—for Christmas. Even though nobody could get drunk on the stuff.

Then Bernie sang Yankee Doodle Dandy and did an Indian war dance around the smoldering coals of our fire.

Bernie's mom, Mama Kruger, was caring but straight-laced—a schoolteacher and firm taskmaster. She enforced her family's moral code with an iron will. Bernie was especially worried that his mother might discover that The Babe, her precious youngest boy, had been drinking. He had gotten his clothes pretty messed up rescuing me from the river. We decided we would stay where we were until nightfall and then, under cover of darkness, Bernie could sneak back into the house before his mother missed him.

Having established our plan, we fell asleep. The mosquitoes woke us up around ten or eleven, and we were both pretty wobbly. We decided the hamburgers had made us a little dizzy. I managed to drive Bernie home, rolling the car quietly up his street with the headlights off.

Bernie silently closed the car door and I watched as he tiptoed up the front walk. I kept my fingers crossed that Mama Kruger was already asleep. Then all of a sudden Bernie started singing

Yankee Doodle Dandy again, and taking off his clothes! Then he started to dance. He scattered his clothes all over the front yard until he stood stark naked. He opened the front door and yelled, "Hello everybody. I'm home!"

Bernie was grounded for six months.

At Christmas, we gave Old Dutch a quart of that delicious apricot brandy. We knew it couldn't hurt him. There wasn't a kick in the whole quart.

I Never Met a Potato I Didn't Like

It was a potato that did me in.

I weighed 220 pounds when I was fifteen. 220 pounds is not bad if you play football and happen to be six-foot-five. I didn't play anything except bad piano, and I was just over five and a half feet tall.

I had an appetite that could never be sated. When everyone else had finished eating—when there was no one left to down that last slice of bread, those last two forlorn potatoes, that last piece of pie, that lonesome hunk of cake—that was when I did some of my best work.

Every morning I would get on the scale and say, "Two more pounds and I'll go on a diet." Fifty pounds later, I was still giving myself two more pounds.

When Mary Webster turned me down for a date because "the two of us couldn't fit in the back seat of your dad's car," I decided that—two pounds or not—the time had come.

In those days, we didn't know about complex carbohydrates or polyunsaturated fats. The grapefruit pill hadn't been invented. We didn't know you could lose weight while you were sleeping, or that you could eat as much as you wanted as long as you took four MeltRx LipoRids after every meal. All we knew was that some foods were fattening and some weren't.

The potato was fattening.

Potatoes were my favorite food of all time. Potatoes smeared with butter and piled high with sour cream. If I couldn't eat them, I would have been happy to rub them all over my body and digest them through osmosis. Baked, au gratin, mashed, fried, creamed, buttered, boiled, roasted. . . raw, if that was the only way I could have them.

I knew it would be embarrassing to explain to people who knew my eating habits that I had started a diet. So I decided simply to say I didn't like whatever it was I was not supposed to eat. We were unsophisticated in those days and could make decisions like that without the aid of psychotherapy.

When the potatoes were passed around the table, I said, "No thanks, I hate potatoes." My family was immediately concerned. My mother thought I was sick, and my father was convinced I was trying to aggravate him by allowing half a dozen potatoes go to waste. He was always certain that whatever I did was a scheme either to cost him money or give him a heart attack.

The first few weeks were the toughest, but I stayed the course. Finally, everybody was convinced that I really did hate potatoes. They couldn't understand it. No one hates potatoes. People would introduce me by saying, "This is Burton. He hates potatoes."

My father was the only one who never believed me. He would say, "Meet my son. He thinks if he says he hates potatoes I'll have a heart attack."

My hate list grew as the pounds fell off. I decided to hate bread, then ice cream. Candy, whipped cream, and desserts went on the list. I became a picky eater and a born-again hater. My weight went from 220 to 150. All because I had started hating potatoes.

This went on for thirty years of skinny bliss. Then it happened. I had been dining with friends in a fancy restaurant, celebrating a big event. The party had broken up and left me with the check. Suddenly, I felt something staring at me.

I looked down into the most gorgeous eyes I had ever seen. A potato—its oiled skin reflecting the candlelight, its perfectly rounded bottom resting seductively on its china plate. Its eyes, promising exquisite pleasures, beckoned me.

I ate it.

That was the beginning. My hate list evaporated as rapidly as that provocative potato had. This morning I got on the scale and weighed in at nearly what I did when I was in high school.

Two more pounds and I start hating potatoes again.

The Man Who Could Disappear

Uncle Raymond, storyteller extraordinaire, could make himself disappear. In times of stress, he just concentrated on making himself a part of the surroundings. He was convinced that no one could see him, and it seemed to work.

Uncle Raymond would disappear and reappear all the time. Just ask his wife, Clara. If you could get a word in. Aunt Clara talked like a machine gun. When she was awake her mouth was never closed, and I'm sure she talked in her sleep as well. She dominated every conversation with her endless stories about dull people and boring events. Stories that had been tiresome in the first telling became stultifying by the tenth.

When Aunt Clara was "on," Uncle Raymond could never squeeze in a word. He didn't even try. Clara would be talking and you could see the color start to drain from Uncle Ray's face. He would start to fade just as soon as Aunt Clara opened her mouth. He would get more and more transparent until finally he was gone.

Sooner or later someone would say, "What happened to Uncle Ray?" His wife would usually answer—if she could interrupt her storytelling long enough—"Oh, you know Ray, he just disappeared again."

Uncle Raymond would usually reappear right after Aunt Clara went to bed, a moment we eagerly anticipated. Once Uncle Ray got a chance to talk, he was a very entertaining man. He would keep us up late, sharing his experiences as a salesman. You wouldn't think that would be a very fascinating business, but Uncle Ray could make it sound like an adventure the astronauts would envy.

One day Aunt Clara called up and asked if we had seen Uncle Ray. She was worried. It was Sunday, and Aunt Clara had been talking to him over breakfast. When she turned around to pour him more coffee, he was gone. Disappeared into thin air. We didn't think this was especially remarkable, but Aunt Clara said it seemed different this time.

Aunt Clara went to bed early that day. She must have been completely worn out from all the calling and talking about Uncle Raymond's disappearance. We were all happy that at least she was talking about something we hadn't heard before. We figured Uncle Ray would reappear sometime after her bedtime, as he always did.

But he didn't—not ever again.

My mother was sure he had found a soul mate who only spoke in sign language. My dad said he must have run off to the exotic island featured in last month's National Geographic. He was probably selling brassieres to the beautiful half-naked female natives. Aunt Clara was convinced that Uncle Ray had wandered off and caught amnesia. She knew from her soap operas that amnesia was contagious, like the measles.

I always figured that Uncle Raymond was parked in the countryside somewhere, gazing at one of his beloved wheat fields and listening to the "gossip of the stalks."

The Killers

Pearl Harbor had been bombed a few months earlier. My friend Bernie Kruger and I were still too young to serve, but Bernie's oldest brother, Ernst, had joined the Army the day after the bombing. The middle Kruger brother, Karl, joined a few weeks later. Ernst's new Chevrolet convertible was on blocks in the garage, waiting for his return from the war. Sometimes Bernie and I would open the garage door and just stare at that car's red elegance and wish it belonged to us.

On this particular day, Bernie and I were planning a crow hunt. We went crow hunting a lot. We were both experts on the rifle range. We could hit a bull's-eye at 100 feet nine times out of ten, but we couldn't ever hit a crow.

I had developed this non-skill when I was about ten years old. I saw a pigeon strutting on the roof of the garage, as only pigeons can do. I picked up a rock and threw it at the bird. I hit the pigeon and it tumbled off the roof. I walked over and saw that its head was at an odd angle. The pigeon was dead.

I was surprised and distraught. Remembering how God had bailed me out when I lassoed the cat, I tried to make a deal with God to restore the bird to life, but I guess I must have missed a helping or two of green beans since my last deal. God was unresponsive. I dug frantically for worms, hoping that maybe food would revive the pigeon. Had I known what I know today, I probably would have been able to bring the dead bird back to life with chicken soup. However, at age ten I didn't have that expertise, and the bird refused to be revived. I buried it in the garden under my grandfather's favorite tomato plant.

Ever since that day, I have been unable to shoot or kill any living thing bigger than an ant. I also avoid anticide, if possible. Bernie must have had a similar experience, because no matter how proficient he became with a gun, he never managed to hit anything living.

On our crow hunts, we would tramp into the woods for hours until we located just the right place to hide. Bernie would take out his crow call and begin to caw for crows. That guy was a real Pied Piper. He would no sooner put that crow call to his lips than the place would be surrounded by hundreds of birds. We would both start firing our weapons. The woods echoed with the sounds of gunfire. There were hundreds of targets. It was impossible to miss. Spent shells would litter the forest floor.

Not one bird would fall from the sky or the trees. It was the most amazing display of misdirected fire since World War I.

I would look at Bernie; Bernie would look at me. We wouldn't say a word. Bernie would take out his crow call, and we'd repeat the entire episode until we ran out of ammo.

Then we'd make a date to go crow hunting again the next month.

When the U.S. entered World War II, Bernie and I were both called into the Army Infantry. After our basic training and just before we were to go overseas, we managed to get leave together. We'd gotten plenty of rifle training from the Army, and we couldn't wait to go crow hunting.

We tramped into the woods, and Bernie pulled out his crow call. The birds came flying and the shooting started. When the smoke cleared and the ammunition was all gone, we hadn't hit a single bird. I looked at Bernie and Bernie looked at me, and we were silently afraid for ourselves and each other.

He Had a Dream

My father had his dream. He was second-generation American, not far removed from the old-country expectation of seeing the family sons inherit the business their father had worked hard to establish. The next generation would grow the business to the grandeur of the father's dreams.

Unfortunately for Ben, his elder son chafed from his father's bullying and derision. I was as defiant and rebellious as my father was stubborn and uncompromising. Early in life I had learned that passive aggression was the best revenge against my raging father.

My arsenal was a job half done, or done too slowly. A forgotten promise. A mumbled innuendo. A perpetual frown. A half-hearted and meaningless apology for a "wrong" I felt justified in committing, and would commit again.

As my father's whipping boy—and I was just one among many—I fancied him the devil responsible for all the heartache in my life. We played a continual game of victim and verbal tormenter until he died.

As a backdrop to this private war, Ben's public persona was one of jovial affability. He was a paragon of civic responsibility. He was well-liked and respected by the community. He was always good for a drink or a free lunch at the golf club. He never missed a Rotary meeting. Only his family and his employees, whom he felt he owned, saw the real Ben in action.

Ben died at the early age of 57. His heart, something else out of his control, attacked him on Thanksgiving Day. It seemed appropriate to me. My brother cried at his funeral. I always wondered why.

Kaddish is a Jewish prayer for the dead. The Kaddish prayer is said for eleven months after the death of a loved one. Aware of the effect of his overpowering and negative personality, Ben often lamented, "No one will say Kaddish for me when I die."

I *did* say Kaddish for my father, every day during the year after his death. Every morning as I shaved, I mumbled the sacred Jewish prayer.

Many years later, I realized I did not say it to honor my father, but as my last act of defiance.

In spite of all his anger and malicious bullying, and my own hurt and retaliation, my father taught me a great deal. I learned, or inherited, his natural ability for merchandising and promotion. This talent earned me the "good life" I have enjoyed for many years.

My father also taught me many truths about living and life—as well as many untruths. He showed me how to be and how *not* to be. As I matured enough to tell the difference, the lessons were all invaluable.

During my high school years, I was expected to work at the family store after school and on Saturdays. I lived for the time when I could muster enough courage to move away. I hoped college would be the magic bullet that would end my servitude, but as I was beginning to realize, my father's dream dictated that I come into the business full time as soon as I graduated from high school.

Ben's knack for promoting had continued to serve him well in the retail business. In spite of our daily "trips" to the poorhouse, the pared-down family business was thriving. It seemed that my father's dream would truly become my nightmare.

My mother tried to take a stand. One of the few desires she persisted in voicing was for her sons to go to college. My father always replied, "Ruthie, if the boys go to college, you will lose them. Especially Burt. He will never come home again."

Almost all my peers were college-bound. Families had saved

money since the birth of their children to ensure giving them a college education. Earl and I were both excellent students. My father's friends, our neighbors, our teachers, all knew Ben could afford to send his sons to college. They were surprised when they heard college was not in the plan. The school principal scheduled a meeting with my parents to discuss the value of a higher education for me.

Whether from fear of damage to his public image by the disapproval of the community, or the pressure of my teachers, or the lecture from the principal, or the insistence of my mother—Ben finally caved.

He coughed up some financial help to send me to the state university. There were strings. I don't even remember what they were, but I didn't care. I was college-bound!

The Pinnacle

I roomed with Bob Weisman in 1942 in the Sigma Alpha Mu house at the University of Illinois. He was the prior of the Sammies, and I was a pledge. The difference between a pledge and a senior—especially the head of a fraternity—is unfathomable. They are like people of different races and languages in different time frames.

Despite this gulf, Bob and I had an unusual bond. I have thought about him often in the years since we last met.

1942 was a terribly wonderful time. The bombing of Pearl Harbor had thrown the U.S. into World War II. Events seemed to be condensed and moving too fast. The country's mood was fear mixed with exhilaration. The future had never been so hard to predict. In this troubled time, Bob was my guiding light. If it is possible to be a wise man at twenty-two, Bob was surely a candidate.

With wisdom and foresight, the fraternity leaders had stretched the fraternity's capacity to bursting. We had the largest pledge class in our history in expectation of the members who would leave school to join the war effort.

The policy of the fraternity was to move pledges into different rooms with different roommates every few weeks. That way we could get to know the house members on a more intimate basis. My first roommate was Bob. He must have liked his innocent country-boy roommate; he refused to have me moved. We remained roommates for the entire semester.

A fraternity pin has the initials of its owner engraved on the back. On the final night of pledging, when the pledges officially become fraternal brothers, the Sammies had a time-honored tradition. A brother could present his worn and cherished monogrammed pin to his favorite pledge as a symbol of honor.

The officers of the fraternity were not allowed to participate in this ritual. I wanted Bob's fraternity pin more than anything else in my young life, but he was the fraternity's highest officer. I knew there was no way he could break the rules and give me this honor.

With the solemn ceremony characteristic of time-honored fraternal rituals, the pledges were ushered into the hushed and dimly lit "sacred" Chapter Room. Secret vows were exchanged, cryptic tomes were opened, passages of import were recited.

Finally, the pledges were welcomed into the fraternity as full-fledged brothers of Sigma Alpha Mu. The fraternity pins were handed out to the lineup of proud and awed new members. I received my pin and looked on the back.

Two initials were engraved there: R.W.

Screw the rules—Bob had given me his pin!

What is important to an eighteen-year-old might seem trivial to a man of thirty, and idiotic to one in his seventies. But it's easy for me to transport myself back in time and realize that becoming a frater at SAM and getting that gesture of regard from my wise friend was the most important event in all my eighteen years.

If God Lived on Earth,
People Would Break His Windows

A plaintive—first quiet and then increasingly louder—melody floated to the closed windows as fifty voices were raised in song.

The first snow of the season was falling on the University of Illinois campus. We had just won the homecoming football game. It was the era of boogie-woogie, jive, and jitterbugging to big band music. The romantic wartime movie, "Mrs. Miniver," won the Academy Award for Outstanding Motion Picture. "White Christmas" was the song of the season. It was "love conquers all" and "marriage is forever." We were fighting for the American way and Mom's apple pie. America was invincible and might was right.

Clichés were in style.

It had been a happy and eventful weekend, full of the excitement and pageantry of the big homecoming game. We were on a high we thought would never end.

Melly Bernstein had pinned Jackie Blum, a sorority girl from Sigma Delta Tau, on Friday. Congratulations flowed freely when the match was announced at Saturday's house dinner.

Pinning was a solemn matter. If not a promise to marry, it was close. The gesture was treated seriously by the fraternities and sororities and by the two people involved. Each fraternity brother treated the newly-pinned girl as a sister.

It was serenade time. Sunday was the one day no meals were served at the fraternity, and the men had individually filtered back from dinner and dates. We had planned a late-night serenade at the $\Sigma\Delta T$ house in honor of the pinning of one of their sisters.

Our conversations were hushed as we tramped through the snow toward the ΣΔT sorority house on the other side of campus. The sidewalks were deserted and the drifts were high. The tires of the infrequent cars crunched slowly along the streets. The air was clean and crisp. Ice glistened from the trees and snow was falling—silent, soft and steady. The scenic beauty was, in itself, a Christmas card cliché.

We quietly arranged ourselves beneath the windows of the sorority house. Most of the girls were in bed or getting ready for bed. Part of the joy of the event was the fact that we had managed to keep the serenade a secret—a special surprise for the newly-pinned Jackie and her sisters.

We began to sing.

A window opened. Then another—then all. The faces of the girls appeared, lit by the candles they were holding. The luminous faces at the windows looked like angels to the men below. We became inspired and sang as never before. Our voices swelled with the melody of our collective love for the one girl who was honored and for all women we held in honor.

We sang song after song, each one more lovely and more heartfelt. Melly had ambitions to be a cantor, that most beautiful and stirring singer of Jewish religious songs. During a particularly haunting love song, his voice rose in a solo to his true love.

It soared above the group. Spontaneously, we all gave way to the purity of the individual voice and became a background accompaniment to Melly's superior instrument. A great crescendo of emotion filled us all. Then—

"*GO HOME, JEW BOYS. SHUT UP, KIKES!*"

It came from across the street.

Our fraternity was scholarly, but we also had our share of athletes: a couple of football players, a wrestler or two, and a few mean Chicago hood types.

Rosen was one of our football players, standing about six-five and weighing over 250 pounds of solid muscle. He was a massive man and he was tough.

Rosen whispered, "I know those bastards." He wandered off with four or five other men in the direction of the noise. A few minutes later there were some muffled shouts, a little noise, and that was the last we heard. Rosen and his crew quietly rejoined us.

We looked up as voices sounded from the windows of the sorority. A response to our love call! The sweet melody grew in strength and volume as the girls joined each other in answer to our serenade.

As the song ended, echoes of the girls' voices seemed to haunt the white stillness. The girls' angelic faces grew dimmer as the candles were extinguished one by one. We all felt there could be no further high than this.

We left, as silently as we had come.

— Los Angeles Times, March 22nd, 1986:

USC SUSPENDS TWO ORGANIZATIONS FOR ANTI-SEMITIC ACTS

— Global News Service, April 8th, 2009:

SWASTIKA PAINTED ON FLORIDA JEWISH FRATERNITY HOUSE

A Road Best Not Traveled

— *November 11, 1942*

DRAFT AGE IS LOWERED TO 18

World War II was a roaring inferno in Europe and Asia. With the bombing of Pearl Harbor, U.S. sentiment was finally united behind the effort to defeat Germany and Japan. Our fraternity was becoming decimated. It became a regular ritual at the "Thank God It's Friday" weekly dinner to read the names of those members whose number had come up in the latest draft.

We all knew our turn would come soon enough.

I was just a few months older than Bernie, but a year ahead in school. I had left Bullneck for the University of Illinois a year before Bernie was to graduate from high school and begin his own college career. I had two fantastic semesters of college life before the Army grabbed me. The Babe, true to his history of rotten luck, didn't even get that. His draft number was one of the first to come up when the draft age was lowered. He was in the Army a few weeks after his high school graduation.

As in all small towns, the major entertainment in Bullneck was gossip and other people's business. I write of a time long past—of shared lives, when neighbor knew neighbor, and troubles and joys were a community affair.

World War II had united the townspeople even more. We were one like-minded group with a single goal. Neighbor clung to neighbor in shared misery and patriotism to fight a common enemy. I don't think we have had another time like it before or since.

The Krugers, Bernie's family, were third-generation pure German. Papa Kruger was a beer-drinking, gruff and tough man. He had his own coal delivery company and worked long, hard days. It was muscle-straining work, shoveling coal to fill the town's basements with heating fuel. Mama Kruger was a gentle, caring, and God-fearing retired teacher. Mama and Papa Kruger were polar opposites, but they had raised a close and loving family.

The elder Kruger boys, Karl and Ernst, helped in the family business while Bernie worked for Clarence Leary to bring in a little extra spending money. All the boys developed into beautiful physical specimens—tall, muscular, likeable athletes. Heroes on the football team and scholars in the classroom. They epitomized the type of man the Army most needed. Karl and Ernst, older than The Babe by a few years, had both been raring to go to war.

Papa and Mama Kruger were united in asking their sons to wait, but it didn't do any good. The boys were filled with the invincibility and energy of youth. They were sure the big adventure would all be over soon, and it would be too late if they didn't get into the action right away. They both volunteered.

First Ernst, the oldest son, shipped overseas to join the battle in Europe. A little later the middle son, Karl, joined him. Then the biggest tragedy for me—The Babe, my big gentle friend, was called to war.

This was a time in World War II when things were not going well. The U.S. and our Allies were fighting Japan in Asia, and Hitler had overrun most of Europe. England was in dire peril. The three Kruger men were all sent, in separate Army units, to an area on the European front where the fighting was especially vicious.

About a year after The Babe entered the war, an unimaginable tragedy shocked our town. Papa and Mama Kruger received word that all three of their magnificent sons were missing in action and presumed dead. A few months later, two returned—wounded but safe. When the war ended, Bernie was returned in an Army coffin.

Today, I see The Babe in the faces of the troops that go off to war, and I remember. I feel the stirring of rage inside me, and I try to suppress it. I think of the bravery and the sacrifice and the hurt of that wonderful family from my past, and I wonder if we will ever learn.

You would think at my age, I would know the answer.

Fulcrums

All my life, luck has followed me like an obedient dog. But my family and my culture taught me to conceal the good things. What if God should find out? What if Someone said to God, "Have you read Burt's book? How come you let Burt have all the luck, when there are so many bad things that happen to other people?"

Would God say, "Someone, you are right. I didn't notice. I'll have to fix that."

I am trusting that God will not read my book and that "Someone" will keep his damn mouth shut.

I spent three years in the Army in safe duty behind the lines. Three years without an incident or an accident. After my discharge, I was eager to resume the good life at the University of Illinois.

But the campus had changed, and so had I. The University was stretched to overcapacity with returning GIs and the newly affluent post-war undergraduates. I didn't fit into fraternity life any longer. I went into a deep depression. The GI Bill for returning war veterans allowed me enough money to move out of the Sammie house. I rented an apartment on campus and spent more time playing bridge than going to class. My mind wandered.

The tales my grandmother Sarah had shared with me began to tickle at the fringes of my mind. I recalled her wondrous stories of California's glistening oceans, sandy beaches, sunsets that color the horizon and fall into the sea, snow-capped mountains, restaurants in the shape of hats, and smiling, golden-skinned sunbathers.

I thought of the program for my life: finish school, go back to Bullneck, work for my father. I couldn't settle back into Ben's business in that tiny town without experiencing Sarah's odyssey for myself. I talked my old buddy, Frank, into leaving the University of Illinois. We set out together to conquer the University of Southern California, playboy training ground of the West.

I still marvel at that decision. Like the lever long enough to move the earth, it changed my life in ways I could never have fathomed. Thank you, lovable Sarah.

■ ■ ■

On a typically sun-washed late California afternoon, Frank and I were driving from L.A. to Long Beach to pick up our dates. We were doubling for the evening. I was the designated chauffeur. As friends will do, Frank and I had fooled around all day and time had slipped away. We were running very, very late.

I rang the doorbell. My date, Annie, answered—shot me one nasty look—and slammed the door shut without a word.

I stood at the threshold for a moment gathering my thoughts. It was true we were very late. It was true we could have stopped to call her. It was true Annie had a right to be angry and disappointed.

It was also true that I had driven over an hour and a half from Los Angeles to Long Beach. I felt I deserved an opportunity to explain. I had my bullshit story all prepared. Any decent person would have let me talk, and *then* slammed the door.

Frank and I had suspected we'd be in big trouble before we got there. As a peace offering, we stopped at a neighborhood market to buy celery sticks and carrots. We bought the prettiest vegetable greens we could find. We got some violet-colored paper and fashioned the vegetables into bouquets for our dates. Those bouquets were violet, orange, and green works of art. Preparing the gifts made us even later, but we figured the laugh would make it worthwhile.

As soon as the door opened, I offered my bouquet. I don't think Annie even saw it. She slammed the door so damn fast, its edge sliced a celery stick right out of the arrangement.

So many thoughts ran through my mind as I stood there and nibbled at that broken celery stick. I wondered, did I even *want* to date someone this volatile? Was she worth the effort? How humiliated was I? Annie hadn't even given me a chance to offer my carefully concocted bullshit excuse.

Hadn't I tried to be a gentleman? I had even brought her a bouquet. Maybe she didn't have a sense of humor. I mean, really, what kind of a person couldn't laugh at a bunch of celery and carrots?

Maybe I should have added beets.

I didn't have to take this kind of treatment from anyone. I should walk away. Dump the broad.

Yet... Annie was a sexy little thing. She had a face like an angel and a body to die for. She was a drop-dead beauty. The first date had been a good one...

I decided to give it one more chance. I knocked on the door. Annie opened it. I told her my bullshit story.

She bought it!

It could have gone the other way. I came within a hair of walking away. If I had left, I never would have come back. On the other hand, Annie could have refused to answer the door the second time. Two destinies, forever changed.

Six months later I saw the Taming of the Shrew. Too late for me: I had already married that lovable ball of fury.

A Man is Incomplete Until he Marries; Then he is Finished

There are two basic reasons why people marry:

    1) A male reason;
    2) A female reason.

The male of the species sees a great pair of legs, his juices start to flow and he is off for the chase. He is like a puppy with his tongue hanging out. He pants around the female, shows her how fast he can run, how many bones he has stored around the house. He jumps and cavorts, he licks and barks—he has no idea he is flirting with serious consequences.

The female of the species doesn't see the actual man at all. She sees the man that is to be. She sees the clay she will mold into the perfect father, lover, and husband.

And so the battle is joined—for better or for worse, in sickness and in health...

Most of the time, the male does not even know he is fighting a battle until he has lost the war. The ladies are clever. And, of course, they have a goal. The male sometimes never recovers from his puppyhood, which really is a blessing for both of them.

Personally, I think it is nice. I never recovered from my puppyhood. I have been stretched, molded, washed, ironed, and steam-pressed so many times I lost count. Most of the shaping was done painlessly.

When you stop to think about it, the arrangement makes a

great deal of sense. When I was young, I used to worry that when all the older people died, there would be no one around to tell me what to do.

Then I grew older, and I realized that my wife would be there. She would tell me.

Honey Mooned

The azure of the sky was mirrored in the calm sea that day. Annie and I were sitting on the sea wall that stretched along the sand of Long Beach. We held hands as the ocean lapped at the sand. As the gentle sounds spoke to us, both our eyes filled with tears.

Annie's parents lived a few blocks from the ocean, and Annie had been a body-surfer since she was a child. She felt like a part of the sea.

I had long ago fallen in love with the ocean; Sarah had given me that gift years ago.

But we were going to leave it all behind.

I had explained my life plan to Annie before we were married. I was to return to Bullneck to take my place in the family business. We knew it wouldn't be easy, but it was a solid start, and once we had enough money saved, we could return to California and "resume our lives."

After our idyllic honeymoon weeks on the California coast, it was especially wrenching to think of leaving this paradise for the flatlands of Bullneck, Illinois. But we had a job to do.

My father had taken advantage of our trip to snag himself a good deal on a new Buick, so Annie and I were driving it across country for him.

On the third night of our long drive, Annie was taking her turn at the wheel. Suddenly, we found ourselves looking directly into the headlights of the only car we'd seen for two hours. It was coming straight for us. It hit our fender and spun us out of control.

We spun and veered on that Kansas highway like a missile in a tailspin—my new bride frantically turning the wheel of the car in one direction and then the other. Then that sickening slide. Our car flipped over four times, finally coming to a stop upside-down in a ditch beside the road. We both ended up in a small hospital run by the nuns of the local convent.

It was July of 1948. The temperature was around 105 degrees. There had been no rain for months. The perpetual Kansas wind was blowing yellow-brown dust in miserable gusts. The mood of the locals was about as nasty as the weather.

The hospital nuns were fit to be tied because Annie, a born and bred Southern California girl, was brought to the hospital "shamelessly dressed" in a short, strapless sundress and sandals. They wouldn't allow the doctor to examine her in such a "provocative" costume.

Instead, they gave her a hospital gown split in the rear from neck to ankles. Evidently, rear ends weren't provocative in Kansas. Before Annie could cover her naked posterior, she took one look at the bleeding leg that was to keep me on crutches for two months and passed out. The nuns carried her, exposed rear end and all, to a bed in an isolated hospital room. They didn't want her spreading her wanton California ways to the other patients.

The hospital staff had put me in a hallway. They told me that was considered the VIP ward: it was the only place with cross-ventilation. Later, I found out why I got the special treatment. When the ambulance driver had demanded money before taking us to the hospital, I had told him I was Clark Gable and that the studio would be sending him a check. I explained to the star-struck (and gullible) driver that my moustache must have been ripped off during the accident. He had spotted my California license plate and incredibly, he bought the story.

The country doctor almost killed himself getting to the hospital. He had heard that Clark Gable was in the emergency ward with a bum leg. He took one look at me, snorted, and said, "This man isn't Clark Gable—he's Gary Cooper!" I explained in a confidential whisper that he was right. I always traveled under the name of Clark Gable because I didn't want special treatment.

Annie and I fully recovered. I have a ten-inch scar on my leg that I like to expose when I sit down. It adds to my rugged appearance. Annie was afraid to drive a car for over a year. When she did take up the wheel again, her top speed was thirty miles an hour.

Maybe the most important thing we both learned was how quickly life could go from happiness to tragedy. We knew on that hot day in Kansas, the gods had blinked and let us escape.

He Ain't Heavy

What kind of irony is it that I am twenty years older than my grandfather was when he died, and I still think of him as an older, and certainly wiser, man? How old do I have to be before I'm a grown-up?

What a strong and noble gentleman my Gramps was. He made claim to lifting a 500-pound safe and carrying it down a flight of stairs. He did admit that his office was on fire at the time, so he probably had an extra charge of adrenalin working in his favor.

When he talked about it, it seemed as if the tale might have been cut off the same snowshoe as the one that all parents love to tell. You know the story: how they tramped five miles to school, uphill both ways, through the snow, in a perpetual blizzard...

I always thought I should ask him why he didn't empty that safe and carry just the contents down the stairs. Of course, I never ever would have asked him that. I wouldn't have embarrassed that paragon of justice and wisdom and love for a lifetime of trivial truths. So, I just listened, and worshiped him.

When I left the hospital after my unfortunate honeymoon-ending traffic accident, I returned to Bullneck to recuperate. My leg was badly damaged and several dozen stitches closed the extensive wound. I was unable to walk. I couldn't even stand for more than a few seconds without severe pain.

I arrived home a wreck from a wreck. The bedroom in our family homestead that had been designated for me and Annie was in the attic, two stories up. Just the thought of negotiating that staircase brought tears to my eyes. The only way I could have done it was by crawling, backwards, one step at a time.

Mr. Goodman, that marvelous man, was there to welcome me. He took one look and picked me up in his arms. I protested, but he didn't even answer. He cradled his twenty-five-year-old, 160-pound grandson like a baby and began to carry me up the stairs. He wasn't the young safe-carrier anymore. He was an old man. He didn't show it—he wouldn't have—but I could feel him laboring as we went up those long steps. But we made it.

I never doubted his stories again. I think maybe he lifted the safe with the help of adrenalin fueled by the fire, but I knew I had been carried up those stairs with the strength of love.

Adjustments

The accident had happened when a drunken driver swerved across the line and hit our car. The fault was not in question; the drunk's insurance company would pay. True to form, my father never did forgive me and Annie for totaling his brand-new Buick. With Ben, everything was always about Ben. Never mind that Annie and I had almost been killed. What about Ben's Buick? And how about Ben's ten-year-old Samsonite luggage that had been stolen from the wreck? (He conveniently forgot that he had already handed down the luggage to us, so technically the bags weren't even his.)

To add insult to our considerable injuries, my father decided that this would be a good time to pull a power play. He produced a long-worded contract for Annie and me to sign, requiring us to stay in Bullneck for the next five years. If we agreed, he would reward us with ¼ ownership of the family business. The other fourths would be owned by my dad, my grandfather, and my brother.

It really was a pretty good deal, except for having my father as a partner. The odds of that working more than a day were a million to one. The two of us couldn't be in the same room without having a fight, and I always lost.

I let the proposal sit on ice for a few days.

That's when we got the call from the insurance company's adjuster, Mr. Hoffman. He was making a special effort to arrange his schedule, traveling down from Chicago especially to talk to Annie and me. He could only spare a day, and it would be next Wednesday.

It was time for my personal insurance adjuster, Uncle Harry, to come to the rescue! Uncle Harry would give that insurance company an adjustment they would never forget. He could turn any adjuster into mincemeat. I made the call.

As it turned out, Uncle Harry had already scheduled one of his "emergency" hospital operations. I knew he wouldn't change it, even for me.

Whenever Uncle Harry was fed up with the world, he would pay a visit to his doctor and ask to have some internal body part removed or repaired or examined. He would complain and rag until the doctor gave up and said, "Okay, Harry, if you are in that much discomfort, we can do an exploratory operation. We'll just look and see if we can find out what's going on."

Harry loved exploratories. Exploratory operations were fairly common before today's sophisticated X-rays, CT scans, and ultrasounds. Uncle Harry had already set the record for the most operations on a single patient in the history of St. Louis. Another exploratory would probably clinch his title for all time.

After Harry and the doctor had set the operation date, Harry would inform all his relatives and friends that the doctors had found something seriously wrong with him. He made sure we all knew the date he'd be surrendering himself to the hospital, and the likelihood that he'd never survive.

Uncle Harry would check into the fanciest hospital in town and set up residence in a huge suite of rooms several days before the operation. As he registered at the front office, the nurses and attendants would greet him as if he were a returning potentate. It was, "Hi, Harry, what are they taking out this time?" The hospital staff knew there would be fun and games with Uncle Harry coming back to visit.

Harry would have a refrigerator delivered to his suite. His chauffeur would stock it with exotic foods and drinks. He would don his favorite felt house slippers with their little doggie faces and shuffle his corpulent bulk around the hallways. Like an official greeter, his generous behind showing through the slit in his hospital gown, he would laugh and welcome each arriving patient. He would visit every room on his floor. He would pinch the nurses and shamelessly flatter any sick lady on his floor who was alert enough to pay attention. There would be a continuous card game going on in a corner of his expansive suite.

The day of Harry's operation would arrive. Relatives and friends would crowd into his suite for drinks and hors d'oeuvres. They came with good wishes for Harry, and to await the outcome. Harry would be high as a kite for his operation, cracking jokes about his terrible illness and his imminent demise. The women would cry and the men would clap Harry on the back and tell him everything would be okay. Harry was in his own particular heaven.

The hospital attendants would finally wheel Uncle Harry into the operating room. We would sit around eating and drinking for a couple of hours until the doctor came into the suite to say, "The old bastard will outlive us all—he's fine." The attendants would wheel a peacefully sleeping Uncle Harry back into his suite.

Harry would wake up in a few hours with a big smile on his face. In a day or so, he would be exposing his ample ass again as he shuffled down the hallways, pinching nurses and making his rounds. In a few weeks he'd be completely refreshed and ready to go back to work.

Unfortunately for me and Annie, this regular ritual conflicted with the arrival of our adjuster. The schedule just couldn't work out. We decided to proceed on our own. Big mistake.

I was still on crutches when we met Mr. Hoffman, the insurance adjuster. He was one of the nicest and most pleasant men we had ever met. He took us to lunch at Oscar's Diner, the best restaurant in town. He bought us martinis before lunch and drinks after lunch. He refused to discuss the settlement until after we had eaten and had our fill to drink. He wanted to "get acquainted" first. We seemed like such "gosh-darn cute kids, just starting out on life's great adventure."

Sylvester, as he insisted we call him, said he had a few questions to ask before he gave us our settlement check. Questions like: How fast were we going? How long had we been driving before the accident? Where were we coming from? Did we ever fool around a little while we were driving? (Hearty laugh.) After all, we were newlyweds. Had we celebrated with a little champagne along the drive? (Hearty laugh.) After all, we had plenty to celebrate. Old Sly was just full of questions. He knew we wouldn't mind if he took a few notes while we talked.

Good old Sly must have ordered a Dr. Jekyll cocktail before lunch, because after lunch, his drink was definitely a Mr. Hyde. Sylvester started twisting all our innocent words about the accident into the most damning tale of two wild honeymooners hell-bent for trouble and getting exactly what they deserved.

We had done nothing wrong, but Sylvester's intimidation worked. By the time he finished with us, we felt grateful to him for offering to pay just a part of our hospital bills. Our claims for lost wages, stolen belongings, post-injury physical therapy, and punitive damages were never even discussed.

My father, bless his mercenary heart, thought the adjuster was a very fair man. He and Sly had hit if off pretty well. Sylvester offered to replace the wrecked Buick for a more luxurious model. They both laughed that his luggage was "irreplaceable." They just didn't make bags like that anymore. They settled for a matched set of Italian leather luggage as a replacement.

That was my first personal experience with what insurance "adjusting" was all about. I learned first-hand what I should have already known: adjusters do what the name implies. They adjust what you deserve down to the least the company thinks it can get away with. I got another lesson in intimidation, and how it feels to be its victim. But unlike the lessons I got from my father, this lesson seemed to flip a switch in me. Even though I had been defeated, I felt stronger and less vulnerable.

Meanwhile, Annie had seen enough of Ben. She was suffocating from the stifling Midwest heat. She was tired of batting away the summer locusts. We both longed for the ocean every day and most of the night.

My grandfather, seeing our pain, passed us some money Ben would never know about and said, "Get the hell out of here."

I got my crutches. Gramps took us to the train station. We boarded the red-eye to Long Beach, California, to take our chances with Annie's folks.

I left my father's contract, unsigned, on the kitchen table.

His Just Desserts

300-pound Uncle Harry knew more about eating than anyone in the world. There were four refrigerators in his house, three in his office, and one in the car. The 20-minute trip to his office always took him a minimum of an hour. Uncle Harry could never make it without at least four stops for food.

Having a personal chauffeur had some rewarding side benefits for my uncle. It allowed Harry to be dropped closer to his beloved food markets, and it enabled him to eat on the road.

Uncle Harry had one fear in life: he was afraid of high blood pressure. His father had died of a heart attack, and it was something he wanted to avoid at all costs. He had read somewhere that garlic lowered blood pressure. He loved garlic so much, he decided garlic was the cure-all for anything that would ever ail him.

The finest restaurants or the greatest gourmet cooks never used enough garlic to satisfy Uncle Harry. He carried a special monogrammed golden garlic cellar filled with pungent ground garlic. It was attached to his vest by a gold chain. No matter where he was dining, out would come the garlic cellar. With grandiose gestures he would sprinkle the garlic crystals liberally over his entire meal.

When Uncle Harry started tipping the scales at over 300 pounds, he decided to get a checkup. The doctor put down his stethoscope, looked Uncle Harry in the eye, and said, "Harry, I got good news and I got bad news. The good news is: I don't know why, but you have the blood pressure of a seventeen-year-old. The bad news is: if you don't quit eating so much, it'll kill you."

Uncle Harry replied, "Then I'll die. At least I'll die with the blood pressure of a seventeen-year-old. And to make you happy, Doc, I'll go on a diet. I'll cut the desserts down to three per meal."

It was always fun to go to a restaurant with Uncle Harry. He would place his Orson Wellesian bulk in the most comfortable chair available, snap two napkins open with an accomplished flourish, and fasten them securely under his several chins with a diamond stickpin. The restaurants he frequented were well prepared. As he walked in the door, loaves of bread were immediately heated for his pleasure. Butter, cheeses, myriad spreads and hors d'oeuvres were placed before him. He always ordered at least two meals for himself, but after that day in the doctor's office, he kept to his promised diet. He never ate more than three desserts.

On his seventy-ninth birthday, Uncle Harry died peacefully in his bed. The remains of a corned beef sandwich and a half-finished kosher pickle were by his side.

We buried him with his monogrammed garlic cellar in his hand and two napkins under his chins, pinned securely by his diamond stickpin. On his tombstone were chiseled a double dip ice cream cone, a chocolate decadence quadruple layer cake, and a box of chocolates.

Three desserts.

Taking Myself to the Cleaners

When Annie and I got back to California, I had no idea how I was going to make a living. I had an honorable discharge from the Army, a freshly-minted degree in business, but no experience in the real world. The war was over and the country was filled with veterans—like myself, all looking for work.

My father had convinced me I was worthless. When I gave up my share of the business and left Bullneck, I had turned my back on what most people spend their lives trying to attain. I felt like a frightened fool who could never succeed, yet part of me was convinced I was where I belonged.

The ocean, only a few blocks from where Annie's family lived, was my solace. Annie's parents, Tillie and Murray, accepted me as their son. Murray, an ex-cab driver and ex-professional fighter, was a model of courage and determination. He convinced me I could do anything I wanted to do.

Murray gave me his unqualified support. I felt like I had found the West Coast version of my grandfather. Right or wrong, successful or not, Murray was always on my side. Annie knew she had married the brightest and most wonderful man in the world. My new family was a treasure.

However, my newfound support could only propel me so far, so fast. I was cautious—wounded inside and out from my journeys back and forth across the country, my traumatic accident, and my rift with my family.

I got a temporary job riveting airplane parts for Douglas Aircraft. It was a place to hide, to recover, and to rebuild myself—and as close to being back in the Army that I ever experienced. The work was mindless and repetitive. The only thing that made it bearable was Milton.

Milton had a Ph.D. in psychology. He had been fired from his job with the local hospital because he felt his supervisor had no feeling or insight concerning the patients. Milton was a thinker. He had questioned the policy of medicating a veteran suffering from shell-shock without trying the new "talk" therapy first. His supervisor refused to discuss it. Milton called his supervisor "a damn dumb shit" and was fired on the spot.

After the strain of treating mentally and emotionally wounded Army veterans, Milton felt he needed a brainless job for a while. Douglas Aircraft was his hiding place as well as mine.

Milton and I worked side-by-side assembling the small parts that went into aircraft. We talked about our problems. We talked about psychology and politics and how the rain would affect the crops. We talked about the problems of integrating ourselves back into the real world now that the war was over. We talked about what we would do if we had a million dollars. Milton made my days at Douglas not only bearable, but something I could look forward to.

Milton loved to drink in the morning. His feet no sooner hit the floor after a good night's sleep than he would reach for the whiskey bottle beside his bed and down a quick one. He had been doing this for years. Just one shot in the morning, and he was finished drinking for the day.

When he reported for work at Douglas, his breath sometimes smelled of liquor. He did his work quickly and accurately and was named Most Valuable Employee two months in a row. He often worked overtime to earn a few extra dollars.

One day the district manager was inspecting the assembly plant and happened to bump into Milton as he was leaving the men's room. Milton coughed, begged the manager's pardon, and went happily on his way. It was 10 a.m. The district manager was appalled. He had smelled whiskey.

The district manager shot into the supervisor's office and told him about the scandalous discovery. The supervisor was stunned. Milton, his most valuable employee two months running, was a drunk? He ran down to where Milton was carefully and expertly assembling a tricky part scheduled to go into the newest aircraft. The supervisor stuck his nose close to Milton's face and said, "I'll be damned."

Milton was told that since he had a drinking problem, he would have to be placed into the Employee Betterment Program, the vice-president's latest pet project. Milton was a trained psychologist. He knew he wasn't an alcoholic. He didn't understand what the supervisor's problem was, but since his job depended on his being "bettered," Milton decided he should go.

The psychologist in charge of the program explained to Milton that drinking in the morning was one of the sure signs of alcoholism, and if that wasn't enough, drinking alone was the capper. Milton was clearly a certified drunk. Milton remembered the last time he had called a psychologist a "damn dumb shit," and kept his mouth shut.

Milton told the psychologist that he liked the taste of liquor better than coffee, and that was the reason he always had a jolt for breakfast. The psychologist laughed heartily and said he was used to this type of explanation. He said that if Milton wanted to help himself, he would have to quit making these silly excuses for his behavior and admit he was an alcoholic.

Milton shrugged his shoulders and toed the line. After a few months of "betterment," he was released from the program by the psychologist.

After that, Milton would take a beating before he would drink alone or in the morning. He would sometimes sneak a beer to drink with the boys at lunch and he always packed in a few blasts at the local bar before going home, but he knew better than to drink in the morning or to drink alone.

I overheard the district manager wondering why Milton didn't produce like he used to, but he seemed pretty happy about Milton's cure.

While Milton was in rehab, I kept my eye out for a business opportunity of my own. I met a quirky guy selling draperies in a storefront business. His name was Cluck. Seriously. That should have told me something, but I ignored the red flag.

Cluck needed company on the road to bankruptcy. Since Milton had been cured, he wasn't much fun anymore, so I quit Douglas Aircraft, invested my meager savings, and became Cluck's partner. Between the two of us, our knowledge of the drapery business would have fit on the head of a drapery pin.

The partnership lasted six angst-filled months. I was lucky enough and quick enough to pull most of my investment out before Cluck realized he was headed down the drain. That put me back on the street—a little wiser, but still confused and frightened. I couldn't even go back to my safe hiding place. Douglas Aircraft wasn't hiring any longer.

I nursed my wounds for a while, and then Annie and I decided to follow in Uncle Raymond's footsteps. We tried a short stint "on the road." We didn't want to invest our savings in a sample set of ladies' clothing, so we scaled it down a bit. We decided to sell women's hosiery to retail stores. After all, I was qualified: I didn't I know any more about hosiery than I did about draperies. Annie drove while I practiced my spiel. We would park in front of a ladies' ready-to-wear-store and sit in the car for about ten minutes while Annie pumped me up with a pep talk. Then I would run into the store and deliver my spiel while the pep was still ringing in my ears. Sometimes it worked.

When Annie ran out of pep, we quit the road and opened a store-front laundry in Long Beach. It wasn't long before a sailor came into our store. His ship was anchored in Long Beach harbor for repairs, and the ship's washers and dryers were inoperable. He asked if we could wash and dry the crew's laundry.

Annie and I looked outside our window at a truck overflowing with sacks of navy whites. We had been in the laundry business for almost two months. We were seasoned laundrateurs! We knew we had lucked into a bonanza.

We both said, "Sure, bring it in."

The sailor adjusted the jaunty slant of his cap. "The Chief Officer says I got to have a price per pound before I let somebody have it."

We charged by the machine load and didn't have the slightest idea how to charge by the pound. Annie and I huddled. She said a penny a pound sounded like a nice round figure. I said three cents a pound sounded like a nicer rounder figure. We split the difference and told our sailor we would wash, dry, and fold his truckload for two cents a pound.

He gave us a strange look and yelled to the two other sailors in the truck, "Okay guys—drop 'em off."

That truck must have had a false bottom. When they finished unloading, our store looked as if it was buried under a giant snow-drift. As Annie and I sat bleakly on one side of the drift, we faintly heard the sailor's last words from the other side: "We're shipping out in twenty-four hours. If you want to get paid, I need the whole load done by 1600 hours tomorrow."

We had twenty Bendix washers and two commercial dryers to do a shipload of laundry. In our haste to quote a price, we hadn't realized that we'd have to do the ship's laundry in individual batches to keep the identical uniforms, towels, and sheets separated by owner.

The machines ran for the full twenty-four hours, and we ran right along with them. Through the hot and sultry night we load-ed, carted, and folded. By the time we finished that load of white misery, Annie was crying with fatigue and I was tired and mean.

We finished folding and weighing with a half-hour to spare. The Navy's bill came to a grand total of $150. After expenses, we had lost money on the deal.

The laundrateurs had been hung out to dry.

We kept the laundry for about six months of hard work, and then put it up for sale. The new owner changed it to a self-service operation. He showed up a few times a day to stock the detergent and rake in the coins while his customers washed and dried their own clothes. Our only consolation was that we'd made a small profit on the sale of the business.

Through all our trials and errors, Annie and I lived frugally and always managed to keep our precious "go into business" money in-tact. She still believed in me, and in a strange way, my various fail-ures were building my confidence. I was surviving, and learning.

Ribs

Ribs can be delightful or painful. It depends on whether they are barbecued or cracked.

(Please pardon the rib.)

When I was young and foolish and unused to pain or physical hurts, I was careless and acquired a cracked rib. Over the years, it has become an old friend. He (or she—who knows?) tweaks me with pain at odd times to remind me of the tragedies and foibles of my silly past.

We were at an especially delightful party by the bay. At that stage of my life, "delightful" meant there was plenty of booze and the host was generous. I was blotto enough to be having a good time, yet still upright and steady. Annie was off somewhere, also probably upright, but one could never be completely sure.

We were living in Long Beach, Annie's hometown. Annie's mother, Tillie, owned a small but classy ladies shop. She catered to a group of women who were gearing up to participate in the nascent Miss Universe Pageant, which originated in Long Beach. Annie worked at Tillie's shop and dressed some of the most fabulous models in town. They all hoped their appearance in the Pageant would net them the big prize. On a daily basis, they all acted as if they had already clinched the deal.

We found ourselves joining this "fun" group every weekend for drinks, dinner and other activities. This was about as close as a small town guy was ever going to get to the Hollywood "A" crowd, and I was in heaven.

I love pretty girls. I don't have to sleep with them. I don't have to touch them. I don't even have to talk to them. All I want to do is admire and wonder at the miracle that nature has created in the form and face of a beautiful female.

I think my fascination with pretty women first developed in fifth grade, when I met Mary Webster. She had stayed after school to console me, a shy kid who had just humiliated himself at a spelling bee. She let me collect her books and walk her home.

I'll always remember Mary. I only kissed her once, but I remember the kiss as if it were yesterday. I wish I had kissed her more than once.

So, anyway, here I am at a riotous party in Long Beach and this girl—model, of course—looks down on me from her six-foot tower of delightfully sculpted flesh and says,

"How about a run on the beach?"

Up to this point in my life, a "run" meant "run away." Run away from danger. Run away from home. Run away from Dad. A run was no fun. But this run didn't seem to have the same odious connotation.

So, we held hands and I ran.

I ran right off the cliff surrounding the bay. I fell fifteen feet over the edge into shallow shore water, where I wallowed like a wounded walrus. I was hurt—unable to help myself to an upright position. The paramedics hauled me off to be X-rayed and prodded and taped, and I was diagnosed with a cracked rib. That's the same rib that periodically torments me with pain and memories of things that could have been.

I have never run since that day. I don't think anything could ever make me run again. Unless, of course, a gorgeous hunk of female were to appear and say,

"How about a run on the beach?"

Where Did All the Oranges Go?

I like to think about California as it was sixty years ago...

Our dinner reservations were for 9 p.m. and we took the coastal route from Long Beach to Los Angeles. We traveled through the sparse traffic and marveled at the beauty of the hills. The fading light turned the suburban homes into canvases of individual shadows and lights. No sameness here. Each neighborhood had its own stamp of individuality and independence. We waved to the late-working gardeners and the children playing in the yards, and we marveled at the tranquility of the simple scenes.

When I moved here, it took me a long time to get over the fact that cars stopped for pedestrians. For me, it set the tone for the whole polite, fun-loving place. It became my singular ambition to make this my home.

On our way to dinner, we took a detour. We drove over the dark roads to the top of the ridge that overlooked the entire city. Lights sparkled in the crisp, clean air, and the ocean in the distance gave a black backdrop to the scene. We got that familiar breathless feeling when we reached the summit and saw the amazing world stretched out before us.

Los Angeles, the beautiful city. That wonderful, vibrant place that promised so much and delivered it all. The street artists and the flea markets. The food bazaars and the strange build-ings. The lovely women with their long legs and open faces, their hair blowing in the salty ocean breeze. The noisy bars and the crowded restaurants. The hurried gait of the suits and the shuffle of those who have nowhere to go. The readiness to help and the friendly looks. Once in a great while, we would get the special treat of seeing a movie star shopping alongside us in the supermarket.

It's too bad we couldn't have built a "Great Wall" around L.A. sixty years ago to keep the new people out. I would have been all for it—just as soon as I had staked out my spot.

Southern California has changed since the old days, but so has the world.

Why are Southern Californians so disliked? Even San Franciscans live in fear of being "Southern Californicated." But the facts belie the noise. The pattern seems to be intense hatred, followed by emulation. Why? Don't we all know that the "Californication" of any area is driven by the universal seduction of greed?

There is no one true Californian or Los Angeleno. If the United States is the most diversified mixture of nationalities, races, and cultures in the world, California is probably the most diversified state in the USA. We come from everywhere. We represent every culture and facet of society.

We don't Californicate anyone or anyplace. We are just a little ahead of the curve. Where and how California goes, so goes the world.

Until we all find a better way.

Partners

We were the best of friends. Annie's cousin Eldon and his wife, Lucinda, hung out with us almost every night watching TV and sipping martinis. We discussed politics, how to raise our children, and whose turn it was to help clean out the mess in the garage.

Annie adored Lucinda, and the feeling seemed to be mutual. Eldon was a good-natured and likable fellow, but he was failing in his retail jewelry store. I had been consistently training for failure in business; it seemed like the natural order of things for me to proceed directly to the next failing venture.

The four of us were like fun-loving children, taking our cue from a favorite Judy Garland/Mickey Rooney film. In the happy blur of martinis and television one night, we made what seemed like an obvious choice: "Let's do a play!" Our play was titled "Burt Joins Eldon's Jewelry Business."

For my investment share, I used my carefully hoarded stash of "go into business" funds to buy the stock of a nearby bankrupt jewelry store. We paid fifty cents on the dollar for the failed retailer's merchandise and moved it all to Eldon's store.

We were partners.

Partnerships always hang on fragile hooks. They usually work in the beginning, when times are tough and both partners are more concerned with the survival of the business than with each other's participation. If the partners are lucky, the combination works and they are successful.

That's usually when the egos start stirring and partnership

relations start to unravel. The partners have time to think about things other than survival. They begin to wonder why they need "the other guy." You know the one, the guy who never does his share. The one who never was too bright and who now claims he's the partner who does all the work and is responsible for the success of the firm. The loudmouthed partner with no talent.

Funny thing, they both think the other guy is "the other guy."

It was no different with us. But despite the inevitable problems, Eldon and I hung in there and worked them out. For the thirty-odd years we were in business, Eldon was the perfect partner for me. We respected each other and we never actually fought, but the strain of operating the business did cost us our close friendship.

Our store was the cash cow that generated high living standards for both families, and it financed my ventures into real estate. As partnerships go, it was a good and successful one.

I don't know when my business mind graduated from thinking in hundreds of dollars to thousands, and then to hundreds of thousands. It was a process that grew from hard work and experienced judgment.

The fear that I could never make it in the real world, that I could not live up to the faith of those who believed in me, was becoming less a part of my life. But like a California river that sometimes goes underground, only to reappear without notice in an angry, terrifying burst of power, my fears would never be completely gone.

RK Enters, Not Laughing

After Gramps died, Annie and I both had the same thought. It was time to have a baby. We would name it John, in honor of my grandfather. Boy or girl, I didn't care—it would be a John. We wore ourselves out for six months, and nothing happened except that we had a great time. About the time we decided we were too tired to keep trying, Annie got pregnant.

Now that I was working with Eldon at the jewelry store, it made sense for Annie to stay home while she was "with child." Bored and antsy, she traded her martinis for salty snacks and developed a penchant for watching football on TV. All during the week she studied the sports pages and picked her favorite teams. Then every weekend, slurping from an ever-present jar of sauerkraut, she'd plant herself in front of the TV and scream at the myopic referees, the incompetent quarterbacks, the stupid coaches, and the fumble-fingered pass receivers. She developed an uncanny knack for picking winners. But her rages were really starting to scare me.

I decided to find her a shrink.

We found a psychiatrist with a Jewish-sounding name and an opening in his schedule for a new client. We scheduled an interview. Dr. Fritz Geisenberg listened to us for about thirty minutes, leaned back in his chair, adjusted his glasses and his paunch, and said, "I sink you are both a couple of vehrry sick cookies. I can arrange to treat ze two of you, zeparately."

A declaration like this, uttered in a foreign accent by a Jewish shrink, was gospel.

I said, "I can't afford for both of us to be in therapy."

With the benevolent brevity I would come to recognize as his trademark, he said, "Zen go out and make zome more money." I had heard similar commands before, so zat's what I determined to do.

A few months later, Annie's water broke in the third quarter of the NFL Championship game and we rushed her to the hospital. Then we waited two days for the labor pains to start. That kid wouldn't move. Finally, the doctor gave up and said he would induce labor with some shots. Still nothing happened.

I left the hospital for lunch, and the baby took that opportunity to shoot out of the womb like one of cousin Horace's Roman candles on the Fourth of July. She has never moved that fast again. Both she and her mother loved to tell the story of how "Burt would have been there, but he asked for his hamburger to be well done."

There was nothing in the world we could do to make our baby daughter smile. She was frowning when we brought her home from the hospital, and that frown stuck to her face like dried milk. She was interested in two things: sleep and food. Once in a while, if we were lucky, we could get a burp. Right away, we took to calling her "Rotten Kid"—RK, for short.

Personally, I could understand it. Life is tough after the womb. I have a theory that right after she was born, she took quick assessment of the situation and decided it wasn't worth a smile. She knew she should have stayed where she was. Even at that age, she was super bright.

When we first brought her home, we looked on her as kind of a challenge. We would tickle her ribs. Annie used a feather on her face. Grandma Tillie made noises. I told her my funniest jokes. Nothing worked. That frown was making permanent creases in her face.

She became a project for the entire family. No one could make any headway. Dr. Geisenberg said she was suffering from acute depression, probably arising from some forgotten incident in her past. Her "past" was only about two months. Dr. G mumbled something about the need for intensive analysis and that three sessions a week should be enough for the beginning. I told him we would get back to him in twenty years.

Several months into the kid's depression, we decided to wallpaper the hallway leading into the nursery. The phone rang just after I had cut a wallpaper strip, and I placed the strip over the rail of the crib to answer the phone. When I came back into the room, RK was laughing hysterically. That kid was beaming from ear to ear. I yelled for my wife. We both stared at the kid and laughed right with her.

I called the family and told them the good news. Grandma Tillie said it was the chicken soup she'd sent over that did the trick. Dr. G claimed it was his interpretation of her burps that was responsible.

The entire family gathered around the crib to witness the smiling baby—but the frown was back, and back to stay. Nobody could budge that rotten kid. They all finally left. The consensus was that it had probably been a gas pain. In complete and utter frustration, I picked up a piece of the wallpaper from the floor and threw it in the crib.

Instant laughter.

It was the wallpaper that had made her laugh! That hideous wallpaper we had inherited from my mother-in-law because no one would buy it at her garage sale. The paper with the ugly cabbage roses that were balanced crookedly on a sagging bush and painted a greenish-reddish color that defied description.

We tried other papers, but no other would do. Only that paper. It was the only thing that would make our kid laugh.

Instead of a baby blanket, RK carried around a roll of that wallpaper until she was ten. What kind of a childhood would she have had if we hadn't stumbled on that particular wallpaper?

Our shrink said it probably reminded her of something she had seen in the womb.

We still have a piece of that wallpaper today. RK is fifty-two years old now, and we always like to keep that piece handy. It brings her right out of any depression.

The Night of the Killer Worms

We lived in some strange houses over the years, and some pretty odd things happened, but the saga of the killer worms was one of the weirdest. Our friends claimed we were deep in Martini-ville that night. But it really happened. My mother-in-law, Tillie, was there and she will testify on our behalf. God knows mothers-in-law don't make up stories. They don't have to.

It was an odd house anyway. There were thumps in the ga-rage and creaks in the attic. Doors slammed by themselves. One gloomy old room had been added to the house about thirty years before we moved in. We made it our den and spent most of our martini time there.

On this night, admittedly, we were on our third, or maybe our fifth martini. Those were the days when martinis were in fashion. That sophisticated time when we all dressed for dinner at 9 or 10 p.m. and the pre-dinner cocktail *de rigueur* was the dry martini.

Too bad for those of you who were never rewarded by the pleasant world that the third martini opens for the enjoyment of the imbiber.

We had none of that sissy wine-sniffing nonsense with the ritual tasting, requiring funny faces and mouth gargling and cer-emonial cork examination. By the time today's wine connoisseur could finish assessing his first sip as "amusing" or "intellectual" or "grassy," we would be well into the bliss of our third martini.

We had worked for weeks to construct a padded bar that fit per-fectly into the corner of our gloomy den. We outfitted the bar with wheels so we could move it outside in good weather. I made some of my greatest creations behind that edifice to good cheer, working under the glow of the hanging neon light that spelled out "Budweiser."

The room also had the dubious advantage of being built on a sinking foundation. It was especially gratifying when the bar would seemingly make its own decision and slowly glide down from the far end of the room to where we were sitting, as if beckoning us to have another drink.

Annie saw the first worm. It had to be her: she hated bugs. Moths became hornets. Ants were scorpions. Every spider was a tarantula.

"Snake!" Annie screamed, as Tillie and I serenely watched the half-inch worm crawl across the floor.

I got up to build another martini and carefully stepped around the worm. The world was too harmonious to destroy any of God's creatures. If the worm had not traversed the length of the room by morning—perhaps then. It seemed the sporting thing to wait.

"Snake!" screamed Annie again. We all watched as another worm made its way across the floor.

"Snakes!" screamed Annie for the third time. To our glazed astonishment, worms appeared on the walls and on the floor. They dropped from the ceiling. They were crawling everywhere. We silently picked up our martinis and stepped gingerly to another room. Needless to say, Annie had preceded us.

To those disbelievers among you, I should tell you something about my mother-in-law and star witness, Tillie.

Tillie lost her husband, Murray, to cancer in the prime of life, but she never wasted one day in mourning. She turned her attention to her yard, her hobbies, and her extended family.

When she wasn't covering an object in beads, knitting a sweater for her granddaughter, or whipping up a batch of *kugel* to tempt her family to come over for dinner, she worked tirelessly to create a lush paradise in her back yard that we all called "Hawaii"—arid California climate be damned.

Backyard family feasts in "Hawaii" were regular events, and we always warned the uninitiated: "Don't stand still at Tillie's house—she's likely to bead you, plant you, or throw you in a pot of soup!"

Frequently Tillie could be found sitting on her carefully manicured lawn, cursing and waving a pair of long scissors. She would move her blue-jeaned bottom from weed to weed on that luminous green patch of dichondra and snip, pull, and blaspheme with the ferocity of a pit bull. She always had a pitcher of martinis within easy reach to replenish the martini glass she balanced in her free hand. This activity would go on for hours. She was perpetually lubricated, and never, ever drunk.

A person with a character as weed-free as my mother-in-law's could never tell a lie. And on this night, as usual, she was completely lucid.

I called Mr. Sheldon, our landlord, and he promised to come over first thing in the morning.

Predictably, when Mr. Sheldon arrived, there was no sign of the worms. There were not even any dead worms. The room was as clean and deserted as it had been before the invasion. The only sign that the room had even been occupied was Annie's broken martini glass.

Mr. Sheldon adjusted his spectacles and spotted the broken glass. He said he had owned the building for thirty years and never had a complaint like this before. He wondered if maybe we had imagined it, "under the influence."

Annie told him she wasn't in the habit of "imagining worms as big as snakes" no matter how many martinis she had. Then she said something about a falling-down building, and then he said something about eviction. I had to step in and use my irresistible smile.

We stayed in that house another year. We spent the entire year looking for those worms to come back. Each time we saw Mr. Sheldon, he made some snide comment asking if we'd had a repeat of the "invasion of the killer worms." Some of our friends still remember the great parties we had, trying to reconstruct the scene and entice those sneaky little bastards out of the walls again.

But no matter how many drinks we served up, those worms never did come back.

The Manly Art of
Recognizing and Passing Love Tests

A while into my marriage, I discovered that women have a variety of love tests they like to throw at their men. Annie had one I called the football test. If I remembered to bring home a copy of Wednesday's Football Digest for her to read, then I really loved her.

She had another one I called the blanket test. On a cold night, Annie would place a blanket on the floor at the foot of her bed, "just in case" she needed it. She could just as easily have put it on her bed, but in order to set up the test she would place it on the floor. If I got up in the middle of a cold night and covered her, then I really loved her. The colder the night, the deeper my love.

Then there was the pimple test. She would grow a pimple. If I noticed it, then I still loved her. If I noticed it and kissed it, I had not only passed the test, but I got an 'A.'

These exams were all performed very surreptitiously. I didn't realize I was being tested until about the fifth year of our marriage.

I couldn't understand why, all of a sudden, old pimple-face wasn't speaking to me. No matter what I said, I couldn't get a word out of that woman. I finally looked at her and said, "What the hell is the matter with your face?" Annie broke into a big smile and said, "It's only a pimple—it will probably be gone tomorrow." And it was.

That's how I passed my first test.

I grew to understand that these tests have certain rules. For instance, if Annie made this comment over breakfast: "It's been a long time since I've seen the Football Digest," and if I brought the Digest home that night, I had passed the test. On the other hand, if Annie called me just before I left the office and asked me to bring home the Football Digest, it was not a test.

Unless, of course, I forgot to bring the Digest home.

Let's take a moment to analyze the aforementioned blanket test. The blanket can be placed on the floor, without comment, while I am in the room. It is also okay for Annie to say, "The weather has certainly turned cold the last couple of days, especially at night." But God help me if I hear a breakfast complaint like, "I froze my ass off last night."

That's real trouble. I had failed again.

In discussing this phenomenon with other men, I have isolated over 300 common tests used by women in the United States alone. This does not include the exotic tests favored by women in other countries.

The final test I would like to discuss is the broken heel test. This test usually crops up when you and your loved one are hurrying to an important business affair that will probably determine the direction of your career for the next thirty-five years.

She looks gorgeous. You are equally breathtaking. The two of you haven't had a fight for almost a week. Things have been going fantastically well at the office.

After walking ten steps away from the limousine you have rented specifically for this evening, she breaks the heel of her shoe.

If you say to her, "Hell, woman, that's the third time this week," you have not only failed the test miserably and completely, but I would appreciate it if you would read no further. You haven't learned a thing. You are hopeless.

The proper response is, "Darling lady, to hell with this affair. Although our future for the next thirty-five years depends on it, I know you don't want to go. Let's forget it."

That earns you a passing grade. She knows you love her.

There is, however, an even better response. The truly sophisticated and dedicated test-taker will recognize this as an opportunity that may never come again. He will be prepared. After all, he has had two preliminary tests earlier this week.

Sweeping his loved one into his arms and carrying her gracefully back to the rented chariot, he says, in a low and breathy voice, "Don't worry, my darling, I have another pair of shoes in the trunk. We can go inside or forget it, and just the two of us will go out and have a great time."

If the replacement shoes are the right color. If they are not the ones that you know damn well pinch her toes. If they have the correct heel height. If you kneel gallantly and replace the broken shoe with a grand flourish and perhaps even a gentle kiss on her lovely instep.

Then, you not only pass. You not only get an 'A.' But you probably will never have to take another test again. She truly knows you love her. She would follow you anywhere—on crutches, if need be.

Unfortunately, these opportunities are very rare.

Remember, love tests are made to be passed. Your loved one is pulling for you. She really wants you to do well.

Will the Real Jimmy Stewart
Please Stand Up?

When I was younger, I used to be Jimmy Stewart. You remember me—the actor with the Midwest accent who used to fight all the good fights. If that seems hard to believe, you have to realize that I was much thinner than I am today, and about ten inches taller.

Remember when I went to Washington and stood up before all those United States Congressmen and staged that great filibuster to save the land for the Boy Rangers' national campground? I saved it all right. You bet I did. Me and that pretty girl, Jean Arthur. We did it together. We licked all the bad guys. What's more, we did it in less than two hours.

After my triumph over the U.S. Congress, it should have been a snap to stand up to the City Council of Orangeville. Those two-faced turncoats wanted to allow a gas station on a residential corner where they had promised to allow only houses. Promised in writing and promised in speeches. Promised with conviction ringing in their voices and their eyes raised to heaven as God shined His benevolent light to illuminate their divine intentions. That was two months before the election.

Now, the election was over and God had sent the Councilmen a new message: Orangeville needed another gas station. Needed that station exactly where the candidates had stood and proclaimed in ringing tones, "We will never allow a commercial development on this, or any corner zoned residential."

Obviously, it was a job for Jimmy Stewart.

Jimmy recruited the neighbors. The neighbors recruited more neighbors. Orangeville was a buzzing camp of dedicated warriors, an angry beehive of rebellion against petty politicians and greedy developers. Petitions circulated, money was raised, phones rang nonstop. Children were sent to school with signs proclaiming the dignity of man and the fact that there were already ten gas stations within three blocks of the proposed station.

Leading this dedicated group, I—the Jimmy Stewart of Orangeville—was the resolute and inspiring general. I led my moppets, moms, and would-be military attack dogs to City Hall for the final day of reckoning: the public hearing for the Consent Agenda of that august body, the City Council of Orangeville, California.

The hearing room was standing room only. I had prepared well. My soldiers stood in readiness. We had submitted our petitions to City Hall days ago. Our letters had flooded the mail. My three-page speech was full of logic, pathos, and persuasion. I had rehearsed it for weeks.

Our item was next on the agenda.

Suddenly, the P.A. system started to malfunction. Unintelligible sounds and static filled the room. I thought I heard the mayor say something about three minutes remaining for refuting the resolution to allow a service station. There was some yelling in the front rows. The gavel hit the desk. I stood up and yelled, "I have something to say about the resolution concerning the building of a gas station on my corner." The mayor said, "That resolution has just been passed. This meeting is adjourned."

The Jimmy Stewart of Orangeville had been gaveled.

Several years later, three members of the City Council were indicted for accepting bribes. As I remember, they were sentenced to become members of the City Council of nearby Garden Glen.

The Jimmy Stewart of Orangeville hung up his shield, boxed his General's uniform, and moved away. The rest of the Councilmen moved on as well, to carry on the mission of ensuring that other cities have plenty of gas stations. Perhaps they came to your city.

As we all know, the price of gas skyrocketed. The oil companies decided to close many of their unprofitable stations. The gas station we fought over is still there, abandoned on its island of cement, its inoperative pumps standing erect like metal grave markers.

A-HA!

Poor Freud. No one pays much attention to his genius any longer. We have traded his analysis for pills. You can have your pills—give me the thrill of a good A-HA.

> *A-HA: The medical term employed by psychologists and psychiatrists when a significant discovery has been recognized in psychotherapy. These discoveries are often signaled by the involuntary expulsion of the word "A-HA" from the patient being analyzed—or as they say in the trade, "the mark."*

Let me illustrate: during a particularly stressful session of psychoanalysis, I had a breakthrough while relating a story I had told maybe ten or twelve times before.

After finishing my story, I said, "A-HA!"

This exclamation roused my shrink, the good doctor Fritz Geisenberg, from his customary coma as though a cannon had been fired next to his good ear. His bad ear had come to my attention early in therapy when I asked him for a pen to write a check. He didn't respond. I knew then that he had either died or lost his hearing. Then he changed positions. On my second request, he offered me his pen with an amazing burst of energy. I realized that when the good doctor felt like tuning out his patients, he would turn his head so that his good ear was flat against the back of his chair, and contentedly nod off.

This time his ears were in "hearing" mode. At the sound of my

A-HA, Dr. G shifted his considerable bulk and murmured over the groaning complaints of his reinforced chair, "A-HA, vee may haff zomsing here."

The astute reader will note a salient point: the A-HA can be used by either the shrink or the mark.

This particular A-HA arose as I was recounting a tender story of motherly love.

When I was six years old, my mother slammed the car door on my middle finger, mashing it into the lumpy-looking digit it remains to this day. Any therapist in the world would give up his "I Love Freud" T-shirt for a shot at analyzing a mother smashing her male child's middle finger. It's what the learned, well-trained psychologist calls a Freudian slam-dunk.

As soon as the good doctor Geisenberg heard this choice morsel and instinctively echoed my "A-HA," he entered his own world of Teutonic analytical bliss. He mumbled broken and half-finished sentences of undecipherable German with sprinklings of Yiddish. I heard words like penis envy, emasculation, and masturbation. He was A-HA-ing his way into shrink nirvana.

I tuned out the mumblings of my therapist and veered off into my own A-HA reverie. My mother had been handing me a guilt trip ever since I had moved to California. She wanted me to come home to Bullneck. If not that, then come for a visit. If not that, then call her every few days. My guilt sack was really starting to weigh me down.

I suddenly realized that I'd been passing up my heaven-sent opportunity to impress upon my mother how deeply her careless act of finger-mauling had traumatized my young psyche. I could turn the tables and make my mother feel guilty. I could challenge the champ!

This delectable turn-about would take place on the phone. That's how she gave me her best guilt trips—why not give her the same? I would speak to her in a voice cracking with emotion. "Mom, do you remember when I was six years old and you slammed my finger in the car door? It was my mangled finger that kept me from becoming the concert pianist you always wanted me to be. God knows, I had the talent."

I dialed the phone. "Mom, remember when I was six years old—"

She cut me off quicker than my wife could say *no*.

"Remember! How could I forget? That's the year you ran to the car and stuck your finger in the door just as I was closing it. I remember your father saying, "Now maybe the fool can tell his left hand from his right." You kept using that hurt finger as an excuse for not practicing your piano. You could have become a concert pianist! God knows, you inherited the talent."

And that's how my mother and I came to a complete understanding concerning guilt.

I have it; she never did.

I hope this illustrates the potency of the A-HA as a weapon in the arsenal against mental illness.

Sam the Sword

There was an ear-shattering scream and the pounding of running rubber-booted feet. I shot a frightened glance at Annie. She looked back at me, shrugged her shoulders and said, "I guess Sam found another garter snake."

Sam Nakamura had been our gardener for about ten years. We kept buying and selling houses and moving, but Sam stuck with us. He was a terrible gardener. He was afraid of insects and all animals large and small. He was allergic to most plants. At least three times a year, he was bedridden with a debilitating case of poison ivy. He was terrified of garter snakes.

The weather could be over 100 degrees and he would come to work in the same uniform:

— Rubber waders to his waist, to protect him from the evil pests of the fields;
— A surgeon's mask, to filter out the pollen and dust;
— Elbow-length gloves, to protect his hands from poison ivy or nettles or thorns;
— Samurai sword strapped to his side, to behead any snakes he couldn't outrun.

Sam always made our house his last stop of the week. He would finish his gardening in about fifteen or twenty minutes and knock on the back door. He would then peel off his elbow-length gloves, remove his mask, and we'd break out a six-pack. The four of us (my gardener, my pre-teen daughter, my wife, and I) would sit down and enjoy a Thank-God-It's-Friday break.

The only time in ten years our yard ever looked well-tended

was when Sam took a long vacation to Japan. He set us up with a substitute gardener, and in two weeks the place looked like a park. The new man cleared away the weeds and planted flowers. He trimmed the trees. He fertilized and tilled. We had forgotten that the natural color of grass was green—not brown.

Sam came back and took one look at the place, mumbled something about "crazy old-country fool," and knocked on the door for his beer.

Eventually, we got tired of the brown grass and the tall weeds. Then, when the neighborhood association ordered us to clean up the place and stop frightening the locals with those bloodcurdling screams every Friday, I figured things had gone far enough. We had a family meeting where it was decided I would fire Sam and get a new gardener.

I fired Sam the next week, right after our last TGIF beer.

The new gardener got to work, and in a couple of weeks the place looked great. He came on a Monday early in the morning, and he worked like a demon for four hours at half the money I had been paying Sam.

About a month after the change, late on a Friday afternoon, I came home to find Annie and RK huddled over a six-pack, wailing and crying. You would have thought the world was ending. Tears streaming down their faces, they told me what a miserable person they thought I was. They didn't like the yard anymore. It was too neat. The new gardener didn't scream and run from snakes. He wore Levis and regular shoes. And worst of all, where was the new gardener's samurai sword? They wanted Sam back.

I finally found Sam, working in a weed-filled yard a couple of blocks from our house. I asked him to please come back. I told him the place just wasn't the same without him. He said he would come back for "the wife and the kid."

Of course, he would need a raise.

And if I said anything to him about the brown grass, he would have to quit.

And he banned me from the TGIF beer sessions for life.

137

If Yer Time Ain't Come,
Even a Doctor Cain't Kill Ya

In the early '60s, my family was being treated by a doctor who was a font of arcane misinformation. Dr. Dolt knew only enough to be dangerous. He would try any medication that was in vogue. If he read about a newly discovered illness, it would become his diagnosis of the week. His favorite patient was the "second opinion patient," sent by another doctor who had failed to make a diagnosis. He would open his Physician's Handbook and start with the letter "A."

At that time, we believed that our doctors were infallible and not to be questioned. They always had our best interests at heart. Today, with the limitless resources of the Internet, we all think we know as much as the doctor. She just has a more expensive blood pressure machine.

Annie was born predisposed to exhibit the symptoms of every illness that has plagued mankind since Adam choked on Eve's apple. Her repertoire was enormous. Like Doctor Dolt, she had a voracious appetite for reading medical articles. Annie's union with this incompetent lunatic was a coupling made in heaven. She would follow his instructions to the letter, and she invited Dr. Dolt to give her every test known to man and machine. He could prescribe those new medications that the pharmaceutical salesman had just pitched, and Annie would take them eagerly.

Annie became Dr. Dolt's dream patient. When she came in with her latest symptom, the doc would concoct some weird theory to substantiate his preconceived conclusion. He would convince her she was suffering from the most controversial new ailment or exotic bug. He would page through a thick book from his shelf, give a grunt of satisfaction, remove his horn-rimmed glasses, gaze at Annie sincerely—and write an unreadable prescription.

It was a case of mutual trust. Dr. Dolt trusted his own judgment because he was an arrogant fool. Annie trusted the doctor because he gave her the attention she craved. I was trusted by both of them to pay the bills.

The meds never did any good, or they made Annie sicker, so doctor and patient would meet every couple of weeks and redo the protocol. They would start over, or Dr. Dolt would increase the current medication dosage, or he would re-prescribe a medication he had tried earlier and forgotten.

The doctor's routine was no different for my daughter and me. Dr. Dolt finally increased my daughter's dosage of (unnecessary) thyroid medication to the point where the school nurse called us into the office. The nurse reported that RK was vibrating like a violin string. She thought it unlikely that a twelve-year-old would develop palsy, and suggested that we have our daughter's health checked.

About this same time, during a routine physical, Dr. Dolt astutely discerned that I was in need of treatment for my lupus. He prescribed massive doses of cortisone. I didn't know I *had* lupus—I thought the roses in my cheeks were signs of good health. Coincidentally, that very day, a pharmaceutical salesman had left some samples of the new wonder drug, cortisone. The doctor had never prescribed that particular drug, and he was eager to give it a try. Why not on me?

Fortunately, Annie and I were seeing our shrink, Dr. Geisenberg, at the same time we were being treated by Dr. Dolt. Dr. G heard these stories of physical distress and had the good sense to suggest we seek a more learned opinion for some of the illnesses our doctor had diagnosed. We were able to get appointments with a respected internist in Beverly Hills.

Dr. Fantastic took one look at my daughter and took her off all the thyroid pills. He examined Annie, studied her extensive portfolio of test results and her meds, took her off all medications and told her to write a book. He looked at me, examined my "lupus" and said, "Get off the booze and those red spots will disappear. And, oh yeah, dump the clown that's medicating you people."

He was my kind of guy.

He became a permanent friend and our trusted family doctor until he retired.

He cried tears large when Annie died, and I loved him for that.

So, beware the clown and find the healer.

And for God's sake, get off the booze. If that doesn't work, write a book.

King Kong and the
Japanese Tea Room

As soon as we walked into the house, we knew something serious had happened. Annie said the bookcases were all falling over. I thought the floor was caving in.

Our housekeeper, Tonika, had arranged all our books in ascending order of height. Like little soldiers, they stood in perfect alignment, each one exactly one step taller than the next. We knew our reading selection would now involve choosing books not by author, but by height.

Over the years, we had five different housekeepers. All of them thought they had been hired as decorators.

The mistress of a house may think she knows what she is doing when she spends a lot of time, effort, and money for new drapes, furniture, or accessories, but any housekeeper worth her dust pan can improve on the most carefully thought-out decor. What is more, her hand will never leave her vacuum cleaner.

Chairs are moved to different angles. Pictures are exchanged. The pillows and lamps are pushed to different spots. Do not believe for one second that these items are cleaned and then misplaced by accident. These subtle "corrections" are gestures of disapproval.

Bedrooms were where Annie and I did our most expressive decorating, generally reflecting the particular phase that our marriage was in at the time. One of our most successful bedrooms was inspired by a ten-foot replica of King Kong. (I was in my macho period in therapy.)

We were living on the twenty-first floor of an apartment building in Los Angeles when we visited a Hollywood movie prop store. In the corner was a ten-foot stuffed King Kong gorilla. We decided it was perfect for our apartment. We bought it and placed it on a small patio just outside our bedroom window.

We artistically broke the window and stuck King Kong's big hairy arm through the hole. You do things like this when you start making a little money and you want to impress your friends. We decorated the walls with movie posters of Fay Wray cradled in the arms of the beast. We picked up some ratty old animal skins, a couple of spears, and twenty-five African jungle drums that were on sale at the local African Artifacts and Moldy Animal Skins shop. That bedroom was our masterpiece. I got myself a leopard loincloth. Annie perfected her screaming, and I practiced using my spear.

Some of my greatest memories revolve around that fantastic room.

When we moved from the apartment, we had a party and auctioned off King Kong. Our shrink, Dr. Geisenberg, was the highest bidder. He knew what that animal had done for me, and he was determined to have King Kong for himself.

We used the money to repair the artistically broken window.

In the meantime, we set about planning our bedroom in the next house. We decided to reward Tonika for her many years of loyal service. We designed a room in a way we thought she would appreciate.

Tonika had hated King Kong, but she had been a pretty good sport. She did insist on stacking the small jungle drums on top of the big ones. No matter how many times Annie and I arranged those drums, the following week Tonika would pile them one on top of the other, like an African totem pole.

Every week, we would have to rearrange them so we could use them for our fertility rites.

But Tonika was entitled to these gestures of defiance. After all, we had not consulted her prior to decorating the bedroom in 20th-century Gorilla. That's why we decided this time, we would show her how much we appreciated her. We decided to decorate the new bedroom as a Japanese tea room.

It took us a long time to coordinate that room. Finally, we proudly escorted Tonika to see the finished product.

She hated it. We found out later we had done it in Chinese instead of Japanese.

Different flowers look good to different people.

(Chinese — or Japanese — proverb)

Better a Coward for a Minute
Than Dead for the Rest of Your Life

I saw the wave. It was big, and it was coming fast. I yelled to the man next to me, "Look what's coming—what should we do?" He shouted, "I don't know!" Then it hit.

I was in the ocean about fifty feet offshore, my feet in the sand and the waves rocking me back and forth like a giant hammock. The other man, about fifteen feet away, was enjoying the day as much as I was.

I wasn't really a swimmer. I might swim to save my life, but never for pleasure. I could manage to keep my head above water and navigate a few hundred yards—then my athletic prowess would run awater, so to speak. I would surface and sound like a hyperventilating whale.

Just before that monster wave hit me, you could say I was frightened. You could say that, if you were a master of understatement. I was petrified. I couldn't move. The wave caught me and turned me over and over.

I banged into the ocean floor with a couple tons of force behind me, and when I surfaced, I was gasping for breath...only to see an even larger wave almost upon me. Three gargantuan waves hit me, leaving me gulping saltwater and sand, shaking and barely able to make it to shore. My nearby companion struggled to shore beside me.

My heart was pounding so hard, I was sure God had saved me from drowning just to kill me with a heart attack. I lay in the sand trying to catch my breath and waiting for my heart to give out. I knew the people on the beach had seen my dilemma and I was humiliated, overcome by the knowledge that I hadn't been very brave.

I lay there on the sand thinking about bravery and cowardice. What seems like a brave act is often a result of reflexes: don't think, just act. That's what they tried to teach me in the Army. But despite my training, I was right back on that baseball diamond, looking into the laughing face of Big Steve.

I saw the wave coming but instead of acting, I started thinking. I was supposed to jump instinctively *into* the wave—not away from it. But I had too much time to think, and I let my cowardice take control.

A well-trained hero would have reacted without thinking. He would have jumped into that wall of water. Then he would have swum to the rescue of his swimming companion, the one gasping for breath beside him. He would have labored to the side of that drowning man and clasped him under the arms, struggling to keep both their heads above water.

That way they both could have drowned.

The afternoon paper could have run the headline:

BRAVE MAN DROWNS IN ATTEMPT TO SAVE BUDDY

I could have been that "brave man."

I love that kind of non-thinking, reactive bravery. But there's another kind of everyday heroism that just doesn't get the recognition it deserves. The above-and-beyond valor that surrounds us everywhere, when people have plenty of time to think about what to do—and they choose the courageous route.

For example, I am terrified of the dentist. Most people are, to a certain extent—but not like me! My hair starts falling out a couple days before the appointment.

But bravely, I show up.

I never actually sit in the dentist's chair. I levitate one foot above the seat. My dentist's hygienist tells me the dentist always takes tranquilizers on the day of my appointment. The last time he tried to shoot me with the novocaine, I made him so nervous he stuck himself in the thumb. He was out of commission for the rest of the day.

But bravely, he still sees me.

I thought about these things while lying on the sand, somewhere between dying and recovering. Right about then I realized my swimming trunks were missing. The same people who had sympathetically witnessed my brush with death were now smiling with glee at my unfortunate nakedness. I wished I were back facing death again under the merciful cover of salty waves.

Annie had no patience with abstractions or shades of gray. Naked people should be covered. Almost getting killed is no excuse. "Almost" is too vague. If I had actually been killed, it would have been okay to lie there naked.

She came over to me and said, "First you roll around in the ocean like a five-year-old, and now you're lying naked on the sand. Don't you think you're a little old for this kind of baloney?" With a disgusted gesture, she threw a towel over me.

Another act of pure bravery.

She had revealed we were together.

Dishing it Out

Though we lived in more homes than I can recall during our years in Southern California, one particularly stands out in my memory. When we bought the place, it had an Olympic-sized pool and two full-time housekeepers. We told the housekeepers we wouldn't need them any longer. I was learning that the more help we had, the harder Annie would work to please them. Her favorite phrase was, "What will the housekeeper think?"

Her next favorite phrase was, "Be sure to clean up after yourself so the housekeeper doesn't have to do it." It was much easier without the "help."

I also hated that money pit called a swimming pool. I never used it. I can hardly recall an encounter with water when I didn't end up facedown and sputtering. It would have been my pleasure to make a sunken garden out of every swimming pool in the world. But Annie had a different perspective. She'd say, "You never know when you will get the urge to swim, and I'll be damned if I'm getting into a cold pool."

We came home from dinner one cool October night and found smoke rising from the pool area. I jumped from the car and yelled to Annie that the pool house was on fire. I scrambled for the garden hose and my fireman's hat, which I always kept in the trunk of the car (along with an assortment of high heels) for just such emergencies.

The smoke was not from a flaming pool house. It was steam, rising from our overheated swimming pool.

That pool generated a roiling cloud of steam that rose like some misplaced volcanic phenomenon. It humidified the air for miles around and drew a steady stream of tourists looking for a close encounter.

I didn't know our swimming pool was destined to become California's second most popular attraction after Disneyland. We single-handedly turned our neighborhood into a steaming tropical micro-climate. The utility company offered to buy our house and let us live there free. All we had to do was to continue to heat the swimming pool, and promise to pay their astronomical gas bills.

Four o'clock in the morning is the coldest time of the day. I know this because precisely at four o'clock every morning, God would punish me. He would wake me and say, "Go. Go, my son, to the swimming pool."

Obediently, I would go to the pool. I would see the steam rising and cry, "My God, how much will it cost this month?" God never answered. Probably because He wanted to surprise me.

I tried to convince Annie that we had to turn off the pool heater. It wasn't the expense; it was a matter of public safety! The fog created by that pool could interfere with airline traffic and cause a terrible accident. I didn't want to be responsible for that.

My argument was ineffective.

If it hadn't been for our shrink, Dr. Geisenberg, we would have moved much earlier. It was Dr. G who introduced us to swimming pool therapy.

Annie was still having a bit of trouble restraining her anger. It got really bad around the time we bought the big house with the swimming pool. Dr. Geisenberg used a special formula to calculate that with three sessions a week, he might get her anger under control for our daughter's thirty-fifth birthday—about twenty years away.

Dr. G had started out as a pretty cutting-edge talk-therapist, but recently he had sunk into deep hero-worship of Freud. "Doctor F," as he wanted us to call him then, had grown a beard and was smoking cigars. He was perfecting a Viennese accent. He lost fifty pounds and took to wearing a vest, high button shoes, and a celluloid collar.

He moved his practice to Beverly Hills and was completely booked. We felt lucky to have found him when his accent was still Jewish. After he became Viennese, he doubled his prices.

Annie was not the most forthcoming of therapy patients. It was around her fifth year of therapy and the second year in our Orange County steam cloud when Annie finally admitted to "Doctor F" that she was having a bit of trouble keeping her temper. In his best Freudian impression he said, "Vat do you mean?"

"What do you mean, 'Vat do I mean'?" she shouted. "Can't you understand English, you Viennese creep?"

Dr. Geisenberg knew that Annie was on the verge of a breakthrough because she usually called him a Jewish creep. To mark the moment, he checked the time on his large pocket watch and leisurely polished his pince-nez glasses. Then he intoned in his deepest VienEnglish, "Mein Liebschen, vy don't you srow dishes in your svimming pool?" Not exactly a Freudian technique, but delivered in enthusiastic Viennese.

Annie kicked over her chair and threw a book, which Dr. F artfully dodged. She stomped out of the office.

But the seed had taken root. After dinner that night, instead of picking a fight with the neighbor and biting his dog (her normal routine), Annie took a stack of dishes outside and began furiously hurling them into the pool. I left her at this activity and went inside to watch "Time for Beanie" on TV with RK. We could hear Annie snarling and growling as she flung the dishes into the depths of the pool.

When I returned a half-hour later, I noticed a miraculous change. Annie had spent all her anger in furious dish hurling. Now she was smiling and trying to skim those dishes over the water. She was dancing around the pool like a wood nymph, humming a lilting ditty and tossing plates as if they were flowers.

Dr. F had done it! Maybe he really *was* Viennese.

Annie was okay after that. The dishes started collecting like algae in the bottom of our pool. We had a routine. I would don my scuba gear and retrieve the dishes once a week. Annie would throw them back into the pool the following week. Annie made up with the neighbor and let his dog bite her. She stopped calling the shrink a creep, and things got so quiet that RK threatened to run away from home.

After a few more years, Annie decided the pool's permanent steam bank was softening my brain and she suggested we move. We got a place without a pool. We were in the new pool-less house for about a month when Annie bit the new neighbor's dog. I called Dr. Geisenberg.

This was a time when all kinds of weird therapies were in vogue. The "est" movement was one of the strangest and most popular. It was a big hit with the shrinkees. It offered a cure in three days instead of three decades. Formally called Erhard Seminars Training, it featured extended lectures that held a large audience of devotees captive (if not captivated). The participants were not allowed to leave the auditorium for extremely long stretches. That included bathroom visits. The audience was ridiculed and demeaned, both as a group and individually.

Dr. G went with the flow and entered his est period. Instead of "Doctor F," he now asked his patients to call him "Doctor E." He also insisted his patients not relieve themselves for five hours before and after each of their sessions.

The est didn't work. Annie's anger didn't improve. But she developed a phenomenal bladder. That woman could go sixteen hours, mad as hell, without a trip to the bathroom.

Annie's anger got so bad, we started looking for another house with a swimming pool. Annie threw "test" dishes in the pool of every open house we visited. Knowing Annie, I lived in constant fear one of the real estate agents would step out of line and say something.

What if he couldn't swim?

We finally settled for a house on the ocean. Annie had a great time sailing her plates right into the Pacific. The only problem: once she threw them, they were gone forever.

I had traded my heating bills for weekly trips to the mall to buy new dishes.

A Masters Thesis for a Degree in Fights

Sometimes it's not so much *what* something is, but *how far it goes* that serves as the measure of its importance.

Let's begin with a simple example. The temperature is 80 degrees outside—tolerable. It's 90 degrees outside—uncomfortable. It's 100 degrees and still rising—I can't stand it any longer! Simple? It's not the temperature, it's the extremity that's important.

Now let's examine husband-and-wife fights.

80-degree fights are pretty common, because life is full of little setbacks and aggravations. An 80-degree fight is tolerable. It's not your fault that your wife is sometimes a little headstrong. But in time, these minor disagreements cool down on their own.

A 90-degree fight is uncomfortable. For example: Your wife just doesn't realize you don't want to join the Riblots for dinner. Mrs. Riblot never stops talking, and Mr. Riblot is so deaf he never hears anything. It's like having dinner at a rock concert while trying to converse with someone wearing earmuffs.

In the 90-degree fight, the husband feels he must make a statement. He tells his wife he hates going out with the Riblots. He knows he'll end up dining with the Riblots anyway, but he overheard someone at the office commenting that he was turning into a wimp. He has decided to give expression to his manhood.

Having expressed himself, he finishes getting dressed and goes out to dinner with the Riblots. The next day he will tell the crew at the office that he "really put his foot down last night."

His wife, however, will not even know they had an altercation.

A 100-degree-and-still-rising fight is the one that can't be ignored. This is when the husband offers a serious challenge, such as, "I am never going out to dinner with the Riblots again."

I am an old-timer at 100-degree fights. I can sustain one for about sixty seconds, and then my voice just kind of dies out and I start to marvel with unbelievable and envious awe at the vocabulary, the memory, the articulation—not to mention the faultless delivery—of that same person who was proclaiming undying love just yesterday.

I have found that the only thing that will save you during a 100-degree fight is to have a serious heart attack.

A minor heart attack will not work. It has to be serious.

Even though a Catholic priest shows up to administer your Jewish last rites, your wife, that paragon of truth and ruthless follower of righteousness, will pursue a 100-degree fight right up to the time they roll you into intensive care.

But after that, there is blessed peace.

The Riblots will have to dine alone.

You have won that one, old bean.

When Money Speaks,
the Truth is Silent

Two elderly women sat behind a large table, sorting mail by hand in a ramshackle building. The sun cast odd shadows on the walls as it shone through the broken roof shingles. I felt as though I had come home. The sophistication of Newport Beach was less than ten miles away. Bustling Los Angeles was a sixty-minute drive. But this scene seemed like one from my childhood. This was the U.S. Post Office in Laguna Beach, California, in 1971.

In the '70s, Laguna Beach was full of anachronisms and characters. Take the Greeter, for example: six-foot-six, bearded and raggedly dressed, with a booming cheerful voice. He stood at the corner of Laguna's main street and the Pacific Coast Highway every day and waved his long arms like wings. We expected him to launch his gaunt body into space. He gestured and wig-wagged and bellowed greetings at every passing car. Visitors were first frightened and surprised, then found themselves yelling and waving back to join in the contagious enthusiasm of the entire fun-loving town.

Annie and I had spent a year looking for land to build our dream home. One lazy Sunday morning, I took a leisurely exploratory walk with Rotten Kid in the town of Laguna Beach and along the Laguna sea bluffs. We discovered a vacant lot on a small cove at the ocean's edge. A paradise within a paradise. I bought the property the next day.

We found an architect with one bad eye and a God-given gift to visualize beauty on paper. We called him Eyeball Brown.

After listening to our dreams, Eyeball designed us a small castle. What a talent he was! His creativity was not only in designing—he also had an incredible talent for turning wealth into poverty. His genius promised us our dreams. Making it a reality put us further in debt than even my nightmares would have let me imagine. Nevertheless, we finished our little castle on the sea. We built a wall to shut out the world, and we built a platform over the ocean that seemed to reach out to forever. From this deck, we watched dolphins jump and fishermen haul crab pots from the ocean. The pelicans soared so close to the waves we thought they would surely crash—but they never did. I loved to descend the rocky cliff-side stairs to my private cove and sunbathe next to my beautiful topless neighbor.

Sometimes near sunset, a mermaid-like figure appeared. She seemed to materialize from the sea itself. She would sit serenely on a rocky point, playing a melancholy tune on her flute. She serenaded the sun as it lowered itself into the sea. And then, like the sun, she disappeared. I never knew when she would come or where she came from.

We settled into our castle amid the surfers and the sun worshipers and the social misfits. And we felt we belonged, with our mountain of debt and our bronzed skin.

And then modern reality invaded our paradise. "Mr. Big" purchased a building lot on our little cove.

Mr. Big was rich, and he was used to getting what he wanted. And what he wanted was to build a monument to himself. Like us, he had his own dream, and it was 15,000 square feet of bad taste. He felt contempt for the "shacks" that dotted the street he now felt he owned. All the neighbors hated his vision. If he got his, theirs would end. His massive structure would block their view of the sea.

We decided to fight him. He had a retinue: a team of lawyers and engineers, a staff of secretaries, and a corporate hierarchy of experts who knew how to fight dirty or clean, fair or foul—whatever it took to win.

We had no money, no skills, no experience—but we had God and righteousness on our side. Anyone who has ever been to the movies knows that's all we needed. We had one other thing. We had Burt, the Jimmy Stewart of Laguna Beach. The same Jimmy Stewart who had been so successful in blocking the gas stations in Orangeville. This was my chance to redeem myself.

I wrote letters of protest to the City Supervisors, the Planning Commission, and the State. I wrote persuasive prose to anyone who was anybody who had a mailbox. I gave speeches; I raised money. I had a silver pen and a golden tongue. Or maybe it was the other way around.

I marveled at my own brilliance. Annie thought I should run for President. Respected people raved about my eloquence. I was praised by the newspaper and asked to speak at public gatherings. I felt I truly was Jimmy Stewart—champion of worthy causes and talented orator, battling a corrupt enemy.

We fought hard, but we were losing. We won delays and promises, but the heavyweights were winning the decisions. Finally, Mr. Big got his city building permit. We had lost the last local battle. There was only one more chance.

We decided to appeal to the California Coastal Commission.

One of the prime objectives of the Coastal Commission was to protect the beauty of the California coast as seen from the sea looking landward. Mr. Big's proposed behemoth extended out over the cliffs, supported by a huge steel structure. No doubt about it, it was an eyesore from any angle.

Mr. Big had built a scale model of his proposed home. It sat resplendent on its own special wheeled display table. At every city planning meeting, with supreme and obvious pride, Mr. Big would direct two of his men to wheel out this monument for all to see.

The two wheel-men were artists. With the grace of bullfighters, they would sweep off the model's protective cover with a flourish of flying cloth. At the great unveiling, I always expected the members of the Planning Commission to break out in wild applause.

It was a beautiful scale model, complete in every detail, including the finished landscaping. Mr. Big had spent more money on his model than many people in Laguna Beach had spent on their houses.

But there was a flaw. And only I, Jimmy Stewart, could have

seen it. In Mr. Big's model, the vast and ugly steel understructure was cleverly hidden by bushy landscaping and large trees. They were pasted onto his mock-up of the rocky windblown cliff. The replica's landscaping looked as if it had been there forever.

In reality, his screening landscape was impossible to create.

Nothing would grow on that cliffside. I knew, because I lived a few hundred feet from the proposed site. I had tried for five years to grow nature's hardiest plants on that same cliff. They all died within months. There was no topsoil. The wind howled and battered the plants. The cliff was too fragile to support a retaining wall. To dig holes for planting would invite the danger of a landslide. Saltwater spray saturated the cliffside most of the year. Worst of all, the salt killed every growing thing. I had consulted a host of experts, and there was no solution.

The eyesore of Mr. Big's understructure and his monumental house could not be softened. It would dominate the view of the coastline forever.

At the Coastal Commission hearing, I knew all I had to do was rip off the misleading landscaping and expose that horrible tower of steel, cement, and wood to the Commissioners. My imagination played out the scenario: with movements as lavish as the flourishes of Mr. Big's wheel men, I would rip off the landscape piece by piece. As each side of that terrible understructure was revealed, the Commissioners would gasp in revulsion. I would explain that without the impossible landscaping, this cliffside blight would be forever visible from the sea. It struck at the very heart of the Commission's purpose: to prohibit anything from spoiling the natural beauty of the California coastline as seen from the sea.

The Commission would have no choice. Mr. Big's obscenity would die.

The day of the hearing was hot and humid. The crowd was expectant. Mr. Big's model sat covered, in readiness. I had polished my speech. I noticed with dismay that we were last on the agenda.

The morning agenda seemed endless. The pleas were long and repetitive. The Commissioners were inattentive and cranky. We returned from lunch to an even warmer auditorium; half the audience had disappeared. The Commissioners had degenerated from cranky to mean. They cut presentations short. They refused to hear some arguments altogether. They just wanted to end the day.

Finally, it was our turn. Mr. Big had brought his big guns, and they gave a lengthy discourse on the beneficent Mr. Big's research, his attention to engineering, to community welfare, to his design, and to his efforts to improve the environs of the great City of Laguna Beach. The speakers droned on and on. Mr. Big's magnificent model was displayed in all its glory.

At about 4:30 in the afternoon, my grand moment of revelation was finally at hand. I delivered my heroic speech and sat down.

Incredibly, I had forgotten to rip off the model's misleading landscape and fully expose the deception. I had completely forgotten my *tour de force*!

Jimmy Stewart, the savior, was so wound up in his own self-congratulatory grandiloquence that he forgot what the hell he was supposed to do. The cause was lost.

The California Coastal Commission gave its blessing to Mr. Big's project.

Mr. Big is long gone, but his blot still stains the coastline. The understructure and house loom, an ugly scar on an otherwise lovely cliff.

And I will never forget that I forgot.

The Schikker

The Yiddish word for a drunk is *schikker*. In my family, that word was said with great disdain. Old Dutch, the town drunk, was a *schikker*.

My grandfather drank sometimes. How much, I don't know. I do know that bottles of bourbon appeared and disappeared from the family liquor chest with regularity. My father considered himself "drunk" after one drink and refused to take more. My mother would have a cocktail or two and might get a little looped at a special social event. My grandmother would celebrate with one glass of syrupy Manischewitz wine about twice a year. Gramps and I would have dinner late on a working Saturday night, getting high on a few beers.

No one in *our* family would ever associate with or—God forbid—become a *schikker*. A *schikker* was below contempt.

I woke up from my 40th birthday celebration with a headache pounding in my brain. I was dizzy. My mouth was dry. I ached all over. My eyes were swollen and I was sick to my stomach. I didn't remember a single event of the previous night. I had the granddaddy of all hangovers.

I had never tried it, but I had heard that "the hair of the dog" could alleviate my suffering. I walked to the bar and downed a quick shot of scotch. Miracle of miracles—I felt better. My hangover was not only tolerable, but almost nonexistent. I tossed off one more drink to complete the cure.

Then the "cure" turned on me. A leaden lump began to form in my stomach, its molten heat spreading through my body. I had an intense feeling of overwhelming fear. In my brain a warning siren echoed. I had crossed the line.

I was a *schikker*!

It seems unthinkable to me now that I hadn't already realized it, but that's how it was. Shaken, I looked in the mirror at my bloodshot eyes and puffy face and promised myself I would quit drinking that very day.

I wish I could say I kept that promise, but that day was only the first of many similar days. Promises made in the morning were broken in the evening to come. One day, before a year was up, my promise stuck. I counted the hours and then the days and then the months. Finally, I stopped counting the years.

But Annie had lost her drinking buddy.

Nobody Ever Bet Enough
on a Winning Horse

Carmine Costello was a debonair, elegant Italian ex-mobster transplanted from New Jersey to California. Only two things gave away his origin: a Jersey accent, and atrocious taste in jewelry. He had done some small-time jobs for the mob in Jersey, but had decided early on that the life of an East Coast mobster wasn't for him. Before he got in too deep, he headed for the land of sunshine. But he took some of his gangster roots along for the ride.

It didn't take Carmine long to become a big fish in our town. His perfectly tailored Italian suits revealed a slight bulge that looked suspiciously like he was "carrying"—but no one ever asked. Carmine never drove his car over the speed limit. He didn't drink or use drugs. He knew every cop by name. He had lunch with the mayor at least twice a week. Carmine lived a good, respectable life. But he was funding this good life by booking bets on sporting events—then, as now, a completely illegal activity in California.

Carmine was a good customer at our jewelry store. Every few months he'd come in to buy a gift for his wife, one of his mistresses, or a politician friend. His own watch was a showpiece—a diamond-encrusted Rolex bigger than his wrist was round.

One day Carmine swaggered into my jewelry store looking for "Da mudda of all pinky rings." He wanted a five-carat diamond pinky ring to mirror his diamond-studded Rolex. And he wanted to buy the ring cheaper than he could have it stolen.

It so happened we had such a ring. It was part of the stock we'd purchased from the defunct jewelry store to augment our business. Every year I counted it at inventory time, and every year I put it back in the safe because it was too grotesque to display. The gigantic stone was mounted in an ornate, old-fashioned, heavy gold setting. The mounting looked as though it had been crafted by a maker of automobile hood ornaments instead of a goldsmith.

I took it out of the safe and placed it in Carmine's hand.

It was love at first sight. Carmine had to have that ring.

Meanwhile, back at home, Annie's penchant for football had become a mania. College, professional—if they had televised kindergarten games, she would have watched with fierce concentration. Everyone in the family called her "Sport."

She started betting—first with weekly combination cards, then she started handicapping the individual games. She won. And won more. Her problem was getting and keeping a bookie to place her wagers. It seemed as if every time she found someone, he would get busted—inevitably, just before he paid off on one of her winning bets.

In a stroke of genius, I made Carmine an offer he couldn't refuse. I gave him a steal on my five-carat "mudda of all pinky rings" if he would agree to take all Annie's football bets with no added vigorish—the commission the bookies charge whether you win or lose. Carmine kissed me on both cheeks, opened his briefcase, threw a couple stacks of big bills on the counter, and screwed his new ring on his pinky finger.

Carmine and Annie bet every week for 20 years. In all that time, Annie never met or spoke to Carmine. She was afraid it would break her luck. They made and settled their bets through me. Every Tuesday Carmine would drop by, pass me the week's football odds, and shoot the breeze while I cleaned "da mudda of all pinky rings."

Carmine's respect for Annie's betting skill became more obvious every week. He even asked for a picture of Annie to carry in his wallet. He said he wanted to see what his "favorite handicapper" looked like. He confided to me that Annie was the only client he'd ever had who consistently won at football betting. He said it was costing him a small fortune to pay up every week, but he was so cheerful about it that Annie and I were convinced he was making side bets using Annie's picks.

Annie's preoccupation continued to escalate. We needed more TV channels so Annie could watch more games. In those days, a home TV satellite dish was a strange and wondrous thing. We were early adopters: we decided to install a gigantic ground-squatting saucer on our lawn. Unfortunately, every time we wanted to change the channel, we had to run outside to heave the dish toward a different place in the sky.

We soon tired of wrangling that behemoth saucer to its new position a dozen times a night. We got it geared for mechanical rotation and wired for a remote so we could change channels from inside the house. When the job was finished, the technician handed the remote to a smiling Annie.

Annie was beside herself. She would grasp a remote in each hand and fire at the TV and the satellite dish as if she were Wyatt Earp doing his last shootout at the OK Corral.

From Saturday morning to the end of Monday Night Football, Sport peered at the screen, wielding her double remotes and scribbling in her notebooks. She knew every statistic for every player on every team and whether he was feeling good, had tweaked his ankle, or just had a fight with his girlfriend. The money poured in.

The day came when Annie had garnered enough money from her betting to buy herself a long-desired toy: a vintage white 1957 Ford Thunderbird convertible.

The T-Bird was the only thing that got her away from her games or her statistics. You'd see her riding that white steed through town with the top off, protected from the sun and wind by a wide-brimmed hat, gigantic sunglasses, and a scarf that flapped all the way past the car's taillights. She became a local celebrity, speeding through town on her way from the post office to the supermarket.

Sometime during the third decade of Annie's stellar betting career, a new mayor was elected on a "clean up the town" campaign. The cleanup was short-lived, but lasted long enough to force Carmine to trade his Italian suit for a striped set of prison denims. Carmine's booking days were over.

Annie got a letter from Carmine's wife, Fortuna, saying that Carmine was in jail. That's when Annie learned that what we had suspected was true. While Sport was betting hundreds, Carmine was using her handicapping skill to bet thousands. Fortuna confided that Annie's picks had funded half their house in Beverly Hills.

Be Careful What You Wish For

I was raised to be a money machine. Money, if not the most important thing in life, was certainly damn close. You can talk about love and caring and family and all the good things in life, but I have seen money make more people happy and destroy more people's lives than any other single thing.

My business partner Eldon and I were making out well in the jewelry business. I had finally found my niche, and I was damn good at it. My course was obvious: I would leverage myself into a chain of jewelry stores. We had already opened a second store, and I had found a location for our third. I made arrangements at the bank and special deals with my suppliers. I was ready to go. I told Annie what I had in mind.

"Open another store and I'm out of here. You work too hard, and we don't spend enough time together. I don't need any more money. I need you."

As quick as that, the third store had been torpedoed.

But the jewelry business was no longer a challenge for me. I didn't know quite what to do with myself. I took a couple of classes and spent many hours in the library. After about six months, I became convinced that my future was in real estate and that it was something Annie and I could do together.

I leveraged my house, my car, and my business. I went looking for the most expensive apartment building I could afford in the best area in the world—Beverly Hills.

Annie was in heaven. She was my full partner and we tackled

164

the project together. We only looked at buildings in Beverly Hills because that was the best location in the world. We couldn't afford to buy there, but I knew that was where we wanted to own and that it was the best possible investment.

We would look at a building in Beverly Hills, and the realtor *knew* we couldn't afford it. So he would insist on showing us a similar building just across the Beverly Hills line.

The sales talk was always the same. "This building is a hell of a buy! If it were in Beverly Hills, it would be twice the price." I wondered how much it would have cost if it had been in Malverne, Arkansas.

We got another realtor. She was less experienced and didn't know we couldn't afford a building in Beverly Hills, so she found us one, and we bought it.

It had taken us over a year to find our first building. It was the first of a series of exciting and challenging investments that would keep me engaged and financially healthy for the rest of my life.

Beverly Hills was notorious for its difficult and demanding tenants who felt their high rents entitled them to be coddled. Annie and I agreed, and we were determined to be the best landlords the community had ever seen. My experience in the retail business had taught me how to please the most exacting customers. Beverly Hills tenants would be a breeze!

Marbo was the first tenant to test our skills.

Marbo was the world's least satisfied tenant. The previous owner of our building, Hurd, had been the world's most cantankerous landlord. The Fates had done their worst in uniting these two as live-in landlord and tenant in the same building.

We heard the history from Scarlett, an observant and dramatic tenant on the third floor who became a great source of insider information over the years.

Six mornings a week, Marbo and Hurd rode down the elevator without speaking or even glancing at each other. Scowling from opposite corners of the lobby, Marbo and Hurd would plant themselves, lurking in silent anticipation for the postman to drop the daily mail into the tenants' individual mailboxes. They carried on a grim competition to retrieve their mail first each day.

Sometimes the mailman delivered Mr. Hurd's mail first. Triumphantly smiling, Hurd would pull out his key and, with a flourish, extract his mail.

If the mailman delivered the mail to Mr. Marbo's box first, Marbo would whistle a little tune as he extracted a gold key from his pocket. He would retrieve his mail and execute a little twirl as he left the lobby.

They never spoke. But each day written demands, refusals, threats, and warnings would spew from the mailboxes of these petty men. Marbo would complain that the central air conditioning was too cold. (Hurd would make it colder.) Marbo would complain about trash in his hallway. (Hurd would tell the janitor to leave his trash container outside Marbo's door.) Marbo would threaten to vacate his apartment. Hurd would threaten to have him evicted.

This unpleasant feud had continued for ten years. Then Annie and I bought the building, and Hurd moved out. We were determined to be as considerate and kind as the old owner had been difficult. We sent flowers to the tenants. We smiled and spoke with everyone. We listened to the tenants and vowed to do whatever they wanted with dispatch and compassion.

Marbo sprang into action! He wasted no time mailing his first list of complaints. Annie and I arranged a conference in Marbo's apartment. We gave him a special air conditioning control. We promised to clean his hallway three times a day. We satisfied his every complaint.

After a while, something strange began to happen to Marbo. He quit complaining. His health began to fail. He grew thin and became increasingly listless and tired. His doctors told him there was no cure for his mysterious malaise. Dejected and forlorn, Marbo decided he needed a change. He decided to switch apartments with his sister.

We took Marbo to lunch on his last day in our building. We had come to like the old curmudgeon. Marbo bid us a tearful farewell and moved from the building.

Marbo's sister, Elaine, told us the rest of the story.

Within a week of moving to his new apartment, Marbo encountered a familiar face in the elevator. His old nemesis Mr. Hurd had just bought that building and moved into the penthouse!

It was rage at first sight.

Elaine had been with Marbo when he spotted Hurd, and she described his miraculous transformation. Marbo instantly straightened to his full height for the first time in months. His eyes flashed fire. He snarled at Hurd. It was as if they had never parted. Marbo resumed his campaign of demands and complaints, and Hurd ignored them all.

Marbo returned to fighting weight and regained his health within a few months. His doctors were amazed at his miraculous recovery. He staked out a spot in the lobby of the new building, where he waited for the mailman every morning, scowling across the lobby at Hurd and fingering his golden key.

Dr. G and Abby Make a Plan

Annie and I had a problem: life was so good, it was depressing us. We had been very fortunate during our married life. After the first couple of tough years, we had always managed to live in beautiful places, each more exquisite than the last. We built or remodeled our houses the way we liked them. The one on the bluff in Laguna Beach was an architectural masterpiece, framing views that didn't stop and postcard sunsets, with the ever-present sound of the surf crashing below us.

But we were still seeing Dr. Geisenberg on a biweekly basis to root out the source of our lingering depression. One day, our shrink announced that while reviewing our situation during his weekly study session with Dear Abby, he had come to a conclusion. He and Abby had agreed that the cure for Annie and me was to move to an ugly house. It didn't make any difference where it was. The house just had to be really ugly. Our depressing problem was: we had nothing we wanted to get away from.

Dr. G said we couldn't spend our lives totally surrounded by beauty. We had to have some relief! Dear Abby had explained it to him. It was like eating ice cream twenty-four hours a day, or having great sex every time you try. Only sick people can function in that kind of perfection.

The two agreed that we needed to find a really ugly place to live—perhaps with mean neighbors who had vicious dogs and played loud obnoxious music. That would give us something we would be happy to leave.

I wondered what we were doing in the shrink's office. We could have written directly to Dear Abby and cut out the middleman.

But Dr. G did offer to housesit at our Laguna pad while we were looking for our ugly place. That counted for something.

We started looking in places we had never been—gloomy forests, polluted lakes, old gravel pits. Surely we could find at least one horrible house. We visited real estate offices and traveled to far places. Nothing seemed to suit.

We had almost given up when we found the perfect place. Believe it or not, it was in Pebble Beach, the exclusive golf course community just outside of Carmel, California. The house was a Chinese modern work of horror, around fifty years old. It stood silhouetted on a windy hill. The lawn was dead; weeds had taken its place. Air blew through the leaky windows in a constant gale. The roof needed replacing and the garage was populated with rats. The siding was rotten and the front door wouldn't close. Our real estate agent refused to go inside. She said she would wait for us in her car. We went in alone, and stood in awe at the collection of bats hanging in the closet filled with moldy old clothes. It was perfect.

We named it Windrush for the fog-laden gusts that penetrated those walls.

After the first night in our ugly house, we discovered we needed one more thing: a really mean dog to intimidate the neighbor's dog. Well into the wee hours, the infernal beast next door had howled a pathetic, ear-splitting song.

Annie decided we needed a Doberman to silence our neighbor's "wailing monster." I thought the breed was perfect. Both Annie and the dog could show their teeth and growl in unison.

When we bought our Doberman, there were two pups left in the litter. We were having a terrible time choosing between them when one came up to my wife, put his head on her sandal, immediately fell asleep, and started to snore. When Annie moved her foot, the dog bit her toe.

Annie was in love. No other puppy in the whole world would do but this one, and if she couldn't have it she would just *die.*

Mr. McPherson was a very conscientious and experienced breeder of puppies. He said, "Not for sale." He was keeping this particular puppy for himself. Not only that, he explained, this wasn't the dog for us. Too headstrong, with a temper to boot. The other pup was a "lover" and would make a fine pet for us. Mr. McPherson said he would be glad to let us have the "lover" for a week, and if we weren't happy, we could bring him back.

If there had been any doubt in Annie's mind which puppy she wanted, it was hereby dispelled. It had to be the one she couldn't have. The one who was buzzing away on her shoe.

I long ago realized that in situations like these, when Annie turned her penetrating brown eyes in my direction, it was time to buckle on my sword, mount the old white charger, and come to the rescue.

Being an experienced man of the world, I offered Mr. McPherson three times what he was asking for the puppy. For a minute, I could see he was wavering—between ordering us off the premises and setting his dogs on us.

I immediately explained to him that this was my way of having a little joke and that not only would we take the puppy he had recommended, but that it was the one we had really wanted all along. I said it before and I'll say it again: you've got to be very careful with dog people. I felt lucky to get out of there alive.

We took the dog home and named him Brutus. We eagerly anticipated the job he would be doing for us: facing down the howling beast next door to our new ugly house. But Mr. McPherson knew his business. Brutus was truly a lover. He was happy and carefree. I swear, that dog laughed. He adored everyone. Not only that, he was an ingenious diplomat.

About a month after Brutus arrived, the neighbor's dog was doing his infernal singing routine. Brutus got out of bed and gave us his "hungry" signal: he stood by the refrigerator and looked forlorn. Annie gave him a piece of leftover steak I was saving for lunch. Brutus took the steak in his mouth and scratched the door to be let outside. I could have killed that damn dog when he trotted over to the fence and gave my steak to the howling monster next door. But it worked a miracle: the neighbor dog clammed up, and Brutus had a pal for life.

I wondered if a piece of leftover steak would help with Annie.

Signals

It had been a very exciting week. We'd had the ugly Pebble Beach house scoured from guano-encrusted garage rafters to moldy basement, and Annie and I were just about set for our first major "relief" trip. The drive from Laguna Beach to Windrush is a total of 350 miles each way, for a grand total of 700 miles. That may not seem like much to some of you, but to Annie and me it was quite an adventure.

Annie had been packing her suitcases since February, and it was almost September. The seasons had changed twice, which necessitated a complete repacking each time. I thought we'd better hit the road before Sport got too entangled in her football wagering.

Taking a trip of this magnitude also required a training period. We took practice runs on the untraveled back roads for a few months prior to any "big adventure" such as this.

These practice runs gave Annie an opportunity to perfect her yelling technique. Frankly, I thought she yelled perfectly. But she felt a little fine-tuning never hurt when preparing to travel. It also afforded her the opportunity to refine her hand signals. You know, those various nonverbal commands that are so helpful on a long trip. If we practiced enough, we thought we could perfect the signals so that conversation was not even necessary.

— *HAND EXTENDED WITH OPEN PALM:* "Stop, you idiot, before you hit him!"

— *HANDS CLASPED TIGHTLY AROUND HEAD:* "Look out, narrow bridge."

— *FEET DRUMMING ON FLOORBOARD:* "You're going too fast."

— *HUMMING A DREAMY 1948 MELODY:* "You're going too slow."

— *PUSHING FRANTICALLY ON DASHBOARD:* "The horn, you fool, the horn."

— *SHOULDERS HUNCHED AND BODY CONTRACTED INTO SMALL BALL:* "Large truck approaching. Shrink car."

Those are all I can recall right now. We practiced these and several more for a couple of months before the big weekend excursion. Meanwhile, in between our practice runs, Annie had been doing her packing.

She considered having professional moving people move all her clothing. I wasn't sure they could get it all in one truck. It might have worked if they left her shoes at home.

In preparation for our trip, I reviewed the nonverbal signs in front of the big mirror. There was so much to remember that I was having difficulty retaining it all. My memory was not what it used to be, and the commands had become more complicated.

I suddenly realized I had completely forgotten the meaning of a closed fist with the middle finger extended.

Was that "Turn right," or "Turn left?"

Peninsula vs. Palms

The Monterey Peninsula and Palm Springs are two California destination resorts with a lot in common. Both communities boast a collection of golf courses visited by people from all over the world—at least those who have managed to weather the latest market crash. These fortunate folk celebrate by savoring gourmet meals, guzzling vintage wine, and forking over exorbitant greens fees.

The main difference between the two towns is that Palm Springs is surrounded by desert and has plenty of water, whereas the Peninsula is surrounded by plenty of water and suffers from perpetual drought.

I miss Palm Springs and the Monterey Peninsula the way they used to be: islands of suspended time. Before we entered the 21st century, these special places existed in a lovely and unchanging time warp, holding fast to their celebrity heyday of the '40s and '50s.

Until about 1985, the Palm Springs telephone operator would say, "The time is a little past 1945, Pacific Standard Time." In the background you could hear strains of the Ink Spots singing a medley of their last hits.

Monterey was much the same. The operator would announce the time in a melodic voice: "At the sound of the tone, the time will be four months and three days before the Bing Crosby Pro-Am Golf Tournament."

Citizens of the Monterey Peninsula cherished their quiet elegance. Modern-day glitz triumphed only once each year, when the celebrities came to Pebble Beach and played in the Crosby Pro-Am, affectionately called the "Clam Bake." Stories of their escapades in this quiet community gave the locals plenty to gossip about until the following year's tournament.

At the 1980 Clam Bake, you could have found Sean Connery, Clint Eastwood, Jack Lemmon, Efrem Zimbalist Jr., Arnold Palmer, Jack Nicklaus, Telly Savalas, James Garner, Gerald Ford, George C. Scott, and Willie Mays joking their way around the golf course. Everything was informal and in the spirit of fun. You could talk to the celebrities, and they would quip back in return.

I personally saw Sean Connery take a leak in the woods just off the fairway. He spewed out a stream of solid steel, broke it off, and tossed it into the rough.

James Garner's drive off the 10th tee at Pebble Beach hit a bystander in the head. When the man complained, it was rumored that Garner slugged him. He claimed the spectator was crowding the fairway and had it coming. All the locals sided with Garner.

Palm Springs had a different ambience. There, the Hollywood elite had huddled their Spanish-styled mansions in one prestigious colony known as Las Palmas. It was the Beverly Hills of Palm Springs, a neighborhood where the old actors would come to retire and to reminisce with each other. The colony remained virtually the same for fifty years.

I remember Palm Springs for having the greatest deli food west of New York. Deep fry was king, and cholesterol was as unacknowledged as a failed movie.

In the '80s, vintage automobiles still cruised the streets. The local radio station featured big band favorites of the '40s. You could tune to Jack Benny almost any hour. Charlie McCarthy was still cracking jokes with Mortimer Snerd. Frank Sinatra owned the airwaves. I wouldn't have been surprised if the broadcast had been interrupted for one of FDR's fireside chats.

The old stars came to Palm Springs to avail themselves of the local time warp. They would "retire" to the desert looking old and worn. Then they would reappear in Hollywood after twenty or thirty years, looking just like they did in their prime.

They would bask in newfound glory. They would be lauded and applauded, toasted and roasted, banqueted and awarded. Then they would make a picture or two before "retiring" back to Palm Springs. We would expect their reappearance in twenty or thirty more years, looking just like they did sixty years before.

But time has caught up with Palm Springs, and the old stars are gone for good.

The playful, lovable stars have also disappeared from Pebble Beach. The old Bing Crosby Clam Bake is now the all-business AT&T National Pro-Am Golf Tournament. Thousands crowd the fairways with their cardboard periscopes, just hoping to glimpse the shoulder of the latest 20-year old golf prodigy.

Can progress work backward as well as forward? That's certainly not a new question. I wouldn't attempt to answer it.

Would it be a kind of progress if we could have the old Palm Springs and the old Monterey Peninsula back the way they used to be?

Maybe not, but I think it would be a lot more fun.

RK and the Cops

Tillie, my mother in law, stopped weeding her lawn for a couple of days and hopped on a plane for Las Vegas. She was planning to win a fortune shooting craps. If she didn't win, at least she would have the satisfaction of spending three days saying "craps" in mixed company.

Rotten Kid, hearing that her grandmother's cozy hideaway was unoccupied, promptly planned a visit to the empty love-nest with her new boyfriend, Adrian. RK had a long history of break-ins at Tillie's house. In her youth, RK had made the trek around the block to Grandma's house countless times. She would shinny up the primordial vines in Tillie's lush back yard, climb through a bedroom window, and avail herself of the large stockpile of See's candy that Tillie always kept behind the bar.

Adrian had a contracting business with his dad. Always impressed by feats of derring-do, he was eager to see this vine-climbing routine. He also didn't mind chocolate, or the prospect of illicit love at Grandma's. The two adventurers drove to the empty house in the dead of night and parked Adrian's pickup in the vacant driveway.

As fate would have it, on this night at around 3 a.m. Tillie's nosy neighbor, Millicent Mincy, ran out of booze and couldn't sleep. Millicent headed for the local all-night liquor store.

Millicent was returning from the store with a bottle of J&B Scotch and three Mars bars when she noticed the strange pickup parked in Tillie's driveway. It didn't take her sleep-starved and paranoid brain long to decide it was time to call the cops and report a break-in.

RK and Adrian were sleeping off their chocolate and illicit-love orgy in Tillie's big bed when they heard a loud banging on the front door, followed immediately by the crash of a size-thirteen shoe breaking through the lock.

"POLICE! Hands up and knees down on the floor!"

Adrian and RK were petrified with fear as the muzzle of a police-issue revolver poked around the bedroom doorframe. Adrian tried to tell the officers about the innocent liaison, but no sound would issue from his throat.

Finally, hands held above the bed sheets, RK croaked out, "Naked person under here...can I get some clothes on, please?"

The police, suppressing smiles, allowed the pair to wrap themselves in the bedsheets. Meanwhile RK, affecting her most obsequious smile, explained to the cops that she was house-sitting for Grandma. When they contacted Tillie in Vegas, she reportedly said, "Make sure they change the sheets." The cops were finally satisfied when Millicent Mincy staggered over to give RK a positive I.D.

Adrian didn't get his voice back for almost three days. When he was able to speak, RK brought him over to "meet the family." I spent a few hours trying to warn him that this escapade was only a glimpse of his troubles to come.

When Tillie came back and found her candy gone, the shit was really going to hit the fan.

As Time Goes By

Retail stores are no longer what they used to be. Everything is based on price. Is it cheaper to buy an item at Walmart or Best Buy? How about online? Customer loyalty is a thing of the past. Even if you want to support your local merchant, a savings of 20% can sometimes be too tempting to pass up.

Brick-and-mortar stores are cutting costs in an effort to compete. That includes scrimping on sales help. Today's retail "help" is a far cry from being helpful. The careful training, service and ethics of years past have disappeared along with the smile and the tact.

We ran things differently in the old days. Sales help took their titles seriously. They always tried to please and never ignored you. They always told you what you wanted to hear. Today it is almost impossible to find a store that puts its customers first.

In our jewelry store, Eldon and I employed a wonderful English watchmaker. His name was Ian MacAllister, but we all called him Mac. Mac was the first person we hired when I joined Eldon in the jewelry business. Mac was an anchor to me. Rain or shine, sick or well, happy or sad, Mac would arrive promptly to the minute and take up his spot at the watchmaker's counter, his stalwart presence giving me the message that there was something I could always depend on. If Mac was there, the world was right.

I would often turn toward his counter, admiring his focused concentration as he worked with his tiny watchmaking tools. He seemed to be surrounded by a cloud of serenity even in the midst of chaos. His service ethic was beyond compare.

One day a customer brought her mantel clock in and asked for a repair estimate. As was his custom, Mac placed the clock on the watchmaker's counter and started to open its back to examine the mechanism. The customer watched Mac's skillful hands as the back of the clock opened to reveal its secrets.

Just inside the cover was a very large and very dead cockroach.

What do to? Both the customer and Mac were appalled. Years of tact and an unrivaled record of customer relations hung in the balance.

Mac didn't miss a beat. With no change of expression and with a haughty gesture, he merely brushed the dead bug from the back of the case, and with his most highborn English inflection said, "Madam, the motor man has obviously died. We shall replace him with a new mechanism and have your clock running again within the fortnight."

I am sure that to this day, that woman is not sure what really makes her clock run.

Mac worked for us for 29 years. When he finally retired, my jewelry stores were never the same to me. It wasn't long after he left that I decided it was time for me to retire and start another phase of my life. The jewelry business just didn't seem to be the place for me any longer.

The business wasn't the only thing that had lost its sheen for me.

The old character of Laguna Beach was gone. The climate had changed from perfect to oppressively humid. The hills were all populated with mansions. The coastline was a duplicate of the hills.

The town had become gentrified. As land became too expensive to justify the charming old ramshackle structures, they were replaced one by one with mega-mansions just like Mr. Big's. The main street had become choked with traffic. Nobody fished for crabs off my coast any longer.

My sunbathing neighbor had moved and my flute-playing mermaid had disappeared.

The ragged Greeter who had waved so cheerfully to tourists had died many years ago. He could never be replaced.

I sold my interest in both my stores. Annie and I sold our little Laguna Beach castle on the cliff and moved permanently to Windrush, the ugly house on the golf course in Pebble Beach.

The Married Man's Approach to Diet and Sex

I wrote to the Pope last month and asked him to ask God why he made losing hair so easy and losing weight so tough. I asked him to please find out if maybe God had just gotten things turned around. Maybe he had been too busy, or maybe his phone had rung in the middle of Creation and it made him lose his train of thought. I asked, did the Pope think it would do any good to bring it to God's attention? Maybe this little quirk had slipped through the chain of commandments.

I haven't heard from the Pope yet—I think he's busy covering up the evidence of an alien visitation. Or he may be having difficulty getting through to God. Maybe he is conferring with Jim Bakker, and Jim's probation officer is slowing them down.

About six times a year, I read about a "fabulous" new diet. They are all the same. I don't want to read one more breakthrough diet article about watching calories, getting plenty of exercise, or controlling your appetite. If I wanted to do those things, I wouldn't be fat in the first place.

Have you noticed that all the people who try to sell us diets look alike? There's this long, skinny body topped with a head of hair that would be the envy of any TV anchorperson. I feel like I'm listening to a talking hair tree.

These people are skinny because everything they eat goes directly to their hair. They don't gain weight—they gain hair. They pig out, cut their hair, and there go the extra pounds. They don't know a damn thing about dieting.

Well, forget the calories, the exercise, and the appetite. I have worked out the perfect diet. I'm not going to tell you what it is yet. I'll divulge it a little later on. You can consider this a test of your willpower. If you don't read any further and skip right to the diet, it'll never work. You don't have enough willpower to lose weight.

I also have some very subtle and little-known hints for attaining a fantastic sex life. You can consider this a test of willpower also. In fact, this is a double test.

If you skip to the diet first, not only is your weight loss bound to fail, but it shows where your priorities are. You would rather eat than have sex. Your wife is right about you.

If you skip directly to the sex information, this speaks for itself. We know what is always on your mind. Your wife is still right about you.

If you continue reading without skipping at all, you are not interested in the really important things in life. Like weight loss and sex. Your wife is right again.

You will note that whatever you do, your wife is right. If you don't learn anything except that your wife is always right, you will have taken the first giant step toward leading a fulfilled and happy married life. You can forget this entire article and proceed to get as fat as you want.

The first diet I ever went on was a simple one. I lost thirty pounds. This was before every diet had a name. Back then a diet was just called "diet." Now, I suppose we would have to call my old diet the Canned Soup Diet. Because that's what it consisted of: one can of soup three times a day.

A prescription for the Canned Soup Diet would read:

Eat one can of soup at each mealtime, until you don't have enough strength to open the cans, or until you are fainting regularly, whichever comes first.

The Canned Soup Diet worked. I lost weight. I was so weak that the only thing keeping me upright was the internal gas generated from downing so much soup. My advice to anyone trying to lose weight on that diet is to wear football padding so you don't hurt yourself when you faint and, if you want to keep your friends, hang out in well-ventilated places.

Dr. Henry Stoltz was a media doctor whose column regularly appeared in our local paper. I used to love reading it. His credo was that exercise broke down the body cells and was extremely hazardous to your health. He was a man of rare stature. A true genius.

Dr. Stoltz felt that even the *thought* of exercise was enough to damage the brain cells. He postulated that anything that could be done standing up, could be done better sitting down. Furthermore, if you could do it sitting down, it was best to lie down and just not think about it.

Dr. Stoltz died at age ninety-seven. In his favorite place: bed. He choked to death laughing, while watching a Jazzercize tape on TV. No one has picked up his standard until now. Although I can never hope to fill the giant shoes of this great man, I would like to champion his cause.

The thought of no exercise will disturb many people. Fallen joggers will retract their swollen tongues and croak out in pop-eyed, sweaty protest. But it has to be said. Exercise can kill. Ask any mountain climber. Even that purveyor of bone-jarring exercise machines, The Sharper Image, saw the handwriting on the wall. They went belly-up.

"Control your appetite" is a stupid edict that has been touted as a method of losing weight. If a person controls his appetite, how can he consume the amount of celery all those diets tell you to eat? This is obviously a case of fallacious reasoning. However, we just had an election, and all sorts of stupid things are being said.

Which brings us to the silliest admonition of them all: "watch calories."

I have been trying to watch calories all my life. There are probably four thousand calories in a nice thick, fat-marbled, mouth-watering, porterhouse steak. I can't remember the number of steaks I've brought home from the market, set down on the dining room table, and tried to watch for calories.

What a study in futility! Nothing ever happens. What are the calories supposed to do—perform a little song and dance? I keep watching for those ugly little bastards to appear, but they never show up. I finally figure, the hell with it. Calories don't deserve to be watched. I'll just broil the little monsters and eat them.

It seems to me that if they were really there in the first place, they could never survive that kind of treatment. So, where's the harm?

I've tried it with ice cream, too. I'll take a glob that's supposed to have at least a thousand calories. I'll watch for the calories until the ice cream starts to melt. If they don't show by then, it's down the old pie-hole.

Anyhow, I promised you a diet that would work.

I think the best way I can describe this revolutionary diet is to illustrate by example:

You wait until your wife disagrees with you about something. That should be about five minutes into the breakfast she's made for you. You let a little spittle trickle from the side of your mouth, kind of Humphrey Bogart-like. You squint your eyes in that threatening way you have. You put your face right up close to hers.

You look her right in the eye and mutter in a low and scary drawl, "Okay, sweetheart, if that's the way ya wanna play it, I'm not eatin' one damn bite a your cookin' till ya come around to my way a thinkin'."

And right there, at that moment, you have started The Married Man's Diet.

A Whisper Can be
Louder Than a Roar

Having lived in California for many years, I can truthfully say that I never missed Bullneck, Illinois. I never expected to see it again.

My mother, however, pulled one of her usual tricks. That woman was after me for years to come visit her. I kept telling her, "Who in his right mind would come to Bullneck unless it was to visit somebody sick, or to collect a vast fortune?"

The money part went right over her head. I figured it would. But the sick bit must have gotten to her. Two days later, she managed to fall off a bar stool, break three toes on her left foot, and get herself incarcerated in a convalescent home in St. Louis. I had to go visit her. While I was in St. Louis, I thought: I haven't been to Bullneck in years. It's only a few hours' drive away, why not go ahead and visit the town of my youth?

I fondly recalled the slow pace of the small country town. Friendly neighbors. The corner grocer who knows what you need before you know it yourself. The soft buzz of family talk coming from the front porches. The clink of a spoon stirring the sugar in the iced tea. The sound of children playing. Moms calling the kids in for supper. Sunday morning church bells. Crosses burning on the front lawns...

It turned out that Bullneck, Illinois, was a miracle of stasis in a world gone mad with change. It had the same library in the same Victorian building where I checked out my very first library book. The population—5,000, give or take a few animals—had not grown a bit over the decades.

I remembered the giant iron statue of a dog still standing majestically on the library's front lawn. (A dog? What's a city library doing sporting the statue of a dog?) I've never seen another statue of a dog, especially this size, anyplace, before or since. It looked like Paul Bunyan's dog. I remember thinking, if that dog took a pee, it would flood the town.

It seemed that the same old men in their faded overalls were sitting in the sun in front of the courthouse, whittlin' the same sticks with the same knives they used fifty years ago.

The old house where I played hide and seek was still there. It had been falling down when I was a kid, and it was still falling down. No wonder nothing ever changed. Even gravity doesn't work in Bullneck, Illinois.

The high point of my visit was when I saw Big Steve. Memories came flooding back: how he said my lips were thick, my smile was crooked, and my eyelids hung down too far. The only thing he was right about was that I deserved to be chosen last for a game of baseball. With the gullibility of a child, I had believed everything he said.

I ran into him in the town square. He had lost most of his hair, and he had a substantial paunch. I said hello, and he stopped and squinted at me for a minute. Then he said, "Ain't you the ugly kid who used to live across the street from me and couldn't play baseball for shit?"

Somehow, it seemed appropriate that, like the town, he hadn't changed a bit. Some things are just not meant to change.

Old Charlie had been dead for quite awhile when I returned to Bullneck. I thought of his great stories as I took a nostalgic walk to his old stomping grounds at the library.

I could not believe what I was seeing! There on the bench, in front of the big dog, slouched Old Charlie—just where he always had been. I ran up to say hello, but it wasn't Old Charlie at all. It was my old childhood friend, Bill. Bill sat with Charlie's old Indian book beside him. He eyed me over his rimless glasses, just as Charlie used to do. He said, "Hi, I heard you were in town. I wondered if you'd drop by."

I said, "Long time, Bill. I just drove up from St. Louis on the way to Palm Springs. Thought I might drop in."

Bill gave me one of Charlie's long looks and said, "Bet you didn't know I worked out in Palm Springs for a while. I worked on one of those golf courses they were always building."

And just like Charlie, Bill was off on and running on one of the craziest yarns I ever heard.

Bill said, "You surely remember the great lover, Rudolph Valentino, the cinema "sheik" of the 1920s. Maybe you remember that Valentino disappeared around eighty-five years ago during the filming of Sheik XII. Half the female population of the world went into mourning.

"Sheik XII was filmed in the desert right near where I was working. We were breaking ground for Golf Course #719. By the time I got there, Palm Springs had run through the list of Indian names for golf courses and had started using numbers. The architect of the course declared it necessary to move the adjacent Mount Kemosabi about a hundred feet south, so that the dog leg leading to the seventh green could angle off at precisely 23 degrees.

"It would take a crew of thousands, but we started moving Mount Kemosabi load by load. About halfway through the project, this wild-eyed horseman dressed in flowing white robes and riding a snorting beast attacked the bulldozers with a vicious-looking scimitar. He was a whirling dervish, sometimes roaring and sometimes screaming about dust and allergies and the rights of mountains to stay where Mohammed had put them.

"It was a really weird attack, and it terrified us all. The entire construction crew scattered in all directions. We summoned reinforcements in the form of the gallant and courageous Palm Springs Volunteer Fire Department. They promptly tear-gassed the sword-waving sheik and his Arabian stallion into submission.

"When the commotion ended and the gas masks were removed, a female fire fighter screamed, 'My God, it's Rudolph Valentino and his horse, Trigger!' and the pandemonium started all over again."

Bill took out a handkerchief and cleaned his glasses.

"Of course, it wasn't Trigger. Everybody knows that Trigger is stuffed and pawing the air in Roy Rogers' living room. But it was Rudolph Valentino. I saw him myself.

"We stopped construction on Golf Course #719. The Rudolph

Valentino Fan Club petitioned the state to designate the area as a national monument. They sent us all home, so I don't know what finally happened, but it sure was exciting at the time."

I thanked Bill for a wonderful story and we spent an hour or two reminiscing about old acquaintances and ancient adventures. As I was about to leave, Bill kind of plucked at my sleeve and said in a soft voice, "I'll bet you didn't know that Old Charlie left me his Indian book when he died."

Stunned, I thought back on the day we had tried to steal that most prized possession from the old storyteller.

"Yep," he said, "It was still blank, except for one page. That old coot wrote me a note. He wrote that the book had been given to him by an old Indian medicine man, and he was passing it on to me. He told me to write down all the 'bad medicine' that happened to me each day, and then to burn the pages over a sagebrush fire each night.

Bill continued, "I figured, what the heck? I've been doin' that for nearly thirty years now. I sure am glad we never told anyone about breaking into Charlie's place."

I took an appraising look at Bill and realized he had the same look of peaceful acceptance that I had admired so much in Old Charlie. Some things are just not meant to change.

I only had one more thing to do in Bullneck before I left. I closed my eyes and pointed myself toward the old church where Preacher Spud had set the fires burning in his parishioners' bellies. It was still there.

The Eden where Independence Hall and I had gamboled away our childhood days was overgrown and a bit unkempt. I found a place to sit under a grand old maple tree, now grown to twice the size I remembered. I lingered for a while and listened as the wind stirred the leaves of the big tree, thinking of the times that Independence had said she loved me.

And as the leaves rustled above me, I thought I heard the sweet whispering of her voice again. But this time she said, "Some things *are* meant to change."

The Perfect Car

Annie had been after me to buy a Rolls Royce for years. I thought they were pretentious and that no car could be worth the same amount of money as a house. Besides, I really didn't think I deserved to own a Rolls.

But she was patient. As usual, her good judgment won out over my stubborn resistance and we bought a Rolls Royce. God help the fool with the bad taste to call it a "Rolls" within listening distance of the British salesman, immaculately dressed, and standing in the glistening, superbly furnished showroom. He explained to me how the Rolls Royce should not be considered merely a "motor car," but an investment.

It was difficult for me to justify an "investment" that was going to cost me the equivalent of a new Cadillac every year in lost interest alone, but if someone with an accent like his told me it was so, it had to be.

For those of you who have never owned a Rolls Royce, allow me to say at the outset that it is a rare and perfect car. For example, there are only eight men who know how to assemble the grill. Mine was put together by Major Geoffrey Appleton. I knew this because his signature was engraved on the underside of the top plate of the grill just beneath the hood ornament. Should you doubt this, it could be viewed by holding a dentist's mirror just under the ornament and about an inch to the right.

The brakes on my new motor car squeaked. This was especially embarrassing when driving my Rolls Royce through the streets of Carmel. I returned to the dealer with my complaint and was given a gold card with an unlisted phone number to contact the warranty repair department. After making my appointment, I was ushered into the carpeted garage, where I stated my complaint in hushed tones to the Maitre d'Mechanic.

The Maitre d' introduced me to Head Mechanic Captain Horatio Greensprings. The British mechanic explained to me in his impeccable English—disdainfully, and flicking a bit of imaginary dust from his tattersall vest—that "squeaky brakes" were, in reality, The Rolls Royce Pedestrian Early Warning System. This system was developed during WWII to warn mechanics away from the propellers of the Spitfire airplane. It was later refined for use on the Rolls Royce automobile, to warn pedestrians of an approaching car.

I tried to tell him that I had had The Rolls Royce Pedestrian Early Warning System on my last Chevrolet and the fools charged me $500 to reline the brakes—but he had already turned his back on me.

At a later date, my Rolls Royce also exhibited what I naively described as an "oil leak" to the mechanic (same mechanic, different tattersall). Again, this time in what I can only describe as a haughty tone, he explained that this was The Rolls Royce Visual Lubrication Check. When those spots stop appearing on your garage floor, it is time to add oil.

If I had any doubts as to the perfection of the Rolls Royce, they were completely dispelled by my next adventure. I had smelled a gas leak for weeks. This was not too important until Annie got into the car and said, "I smell gas." *Now* we had a problem.

I took the car back and confronted the same mechanic (different tattersall). He was appalled. I really had him—even his British accent seemed a little Cockney to me. I left the car and swaggered arrogantly away.

Two weeks later, my motor car was returned to me by a beaming tattersalled mechanic with his accent restored to its old haughtiness. On the seat of my car, beautifully framed and placed in a position of honor, was a plaque attesting to the following:

THE ROLLS ROYCE MOTOR CAR COMPANY
IS PLEASED TO AWARD THE OWNER LISTED BELOW
THE HONOR OF DRIVING THE ONE OUT OF EVERY 100,000 ROLLS
ROYCE MOTOR CARS EQUIPPED AT THE FACTORY
WITH THE ROLLS ROYCE EAU DE GASOLINE.
THIS FRAGRANCE HAS BEEN INSTALLED WITH THE SAME
PERSONAL CARE AND OUTSTANDING CRAFTSMANSHIP
THAT IS EVIDENT THROUGHOUT ALL ROLLS ROYCE MOTOR CARS AND
WILL REMAIN A PART OF THE CAR FOREVER.

The Rolls Royce is truly a perfect motor car. I know that now.

The Prince and the Pea

Brutus the Doberman, lovable ball of fun that he was, was also a snob. He had delusions of grandeur. He would pogo around with that jaunty bounce of his, nose in the air and that smart-aleck look on his face. He thought he belonged on Rodeo Drive in Beverly Hills. Sometimes he could be absolutely embarrassing.

Take the low-fat cottage cheese that we mixed with his kibble. If the date on the box said, "do not use after April 10th," no matter how hungry he was, that dog wouldn't touch a bite on April 11th.

I'm not saying he read labels. What I am saying is that eating outdated cottage cheese was beneath his dignity. I don't know how, but he always knew when the fateful date came due.

Then there was the fit he threw about the car. When we had the Jaguar, he really loved it. Brutus would snuggle into those leather seats, lick away any stains or dirt that marred their pristine surfaces, and not allow anyone to approach closer than ten feet. The dog definitely had a car fetish.

When we got the Rolls Royce, I thought he was going to lose his mind. We couldn't get him to leave it. I couldn't even drive the car the first week we had it. He ensconced himself in the driver's seat and wouldn't let me in.

That Rolls was *his* car. He would stand by and stare menacingly while I washed it. Any unusual movements that seemed to threaten "his car" were met with a warning snarl and a throaty growl. The first time I tried to vacuum the inside of the Rolls, he attacked the vacuum cleaner with true Doberman ferocity. It was two or three hours before I could manage to pry the upholstery-cleaning tool from his jaws.

Brutus refused to ride in the Jaguar after we got the Rolls. When I would say, "Let's go for a ride," he would run hell-bent for the Rolls. If I would go to the Jag and open the door, he would look at me with disbelieving eyes and trot back into the house. This kind of snobbery really embarrassed Annie and me.

We took Brutus to obedience school, which was held at a local parking lot. Brutus wouldn't obey any command to lie down or sit.

We gave the command, "Sit," and Brutus looked at us with a blank and baleful expression. He just stood there as if he hadn't heard a word. The instructor came over. She yelled at Brutus, jerked on his lead, and finally offered him a bribe. But no bribe, no amount of threats or yelling, could make that dog sit.

Annie was starting to get really steamed at how the instructor was treating Brutus. Then the instructor finally got so aggravated, she hit Brutus. My wife went a little berserk and bit the trainer on the hand. That got all three of us thrown out of class.

We trekked home and decided to try our luck again. We went into the living room and Annie said, "Sit." Brutus sat down on the Persian rug as though someone had jerked a rope attached to his tail.

She said, "Stand." Brutus jumped to attention. I expected him to salute.

She said, "Down." You would think someone had cut that dog's legs off with a machete.

Then we went outside to the driveway, and that damn dog wouldn't obey a single command. I looked at Annie, and she went inside and got a small Oriental rug from the hallway. She laid it down on the driveway and put Brutus through his paces. He performed like a born champion show dog.

As long as he could sit or lie down on that rug, Brutus would obey any command he was given with lightning speed. Take away the rug, and damned if he was going to put his bottom down on the bare ground.

In all the years we had Brutus, he never did lie down or sit on anything but genuine Oriental rugs. And don't think for a minute that he didn't know the difference between machine-made and the real thing. I would never think of buying an Oriental rug without taking Brutus along to verify its authenticity.

Brutus carried a small Persian Saruk with him wherever he went. He selected it himself. It took him three days and twelve dealers before he found the rug he wanted. He just stood over it and kept growling and showing those enormous incisors of his until we bought the rug.

Brutus's rug became a sort of security blanket. He wouldn't move without it. He did anything we asked, as long as he could do it on his Saruk.

The Dominic Theory

You may remember that my daughter, Rotten Kid, was born with an amazing brain. Over the years she managed to surround it with an impenetrable shield of parental rebellion. It is unfathomable to me, as a parent, how she managed to function while avoiding the vast amount of parental advice we aimed at her.

RK was selling her graphic design business in Eugene, Oregon. She was fed up with the town's losing battle with economic depression throughout the '80s. RK was tired of fighting the good fight. She figured that the same amount of energy, invested in a different locale, would be more rewarding.

It only took her fourteen years to figure that out. We had it figured from the beginning, but that amazing brain surrounded by its impenetrable shield defeated us.

Unfortunately, there were a lot of people out there as smart as RK's parents. They didn't want her business, either.

You would think that some of the sound and oft-repeated economic brilliance of her prosperous father would have penetrated the cranium of the only child of such an astute parent.

The reason it didn't was revealed in a father/daughter telephone conversation. RK explained to me that her psychic advisor, Dominic, had been speaking to her for quite some time from Outer Cosmos. In her hour of need, he had come up with a formula for financial success.

Dominic had been reading the department store ads and noticed that Nordstrom was running a sale on furs. He explained to RK that she could recover any losses on the sale of her business by racking up some tremendous savings buying a new fur coat, on sale.

Dominic even gave her a hard arithmetic example. If, for instance, she lost $80,000 on the sale of her business, Nordstrom had a great lynx number marked down from $160,000 to $80,000. RK could make up her losses with only one purchase!

This was the first time I had heard of Dominic. Suddenly, a great number of inexplicable things became clear. Events that had bothered me throughout the entire fathering of RK took on a new interpretation.

Dominic was the one we had to reach—not RK.

To get in touch with Dominic, I would need to visit Outer Cosmos. This sort of thing was usually Annie's province, but she was out of town taming a pride of lions for an old friend. I decided to see if I could get there on my own.

I bought fifty candles and found an old cast iron cauldron. I set a fire of mulberry twigs and started cooking some chicken soup. Annie had never used chicken soup in her ceremonies, but this was my first time, and I needed all the help I could get. In any case, I make a pretty good soup, so I figured it wouldn't be a total loss.

After about an hour of chanting, Dominic showed up. We had a long talk about business and how to make and lose money.

The following Monday, I went down to Nordstrom to see if the lynx coat was still available.

That Dominic was one smart cookie.

The Mouthpiece

We always wanted a really sharp attorney. A tough and knowledgeable lawyer to protect us in case we got into trouble with the law or the IRS or the KGB or NBC or PBS. We figured he would also come in handy with our neighbor, Simon Hankle. Simon was always cutting branches off our favorite tree. The tree dropped leaves over the fence into his yard. Annie wanted to send him to prison and have him executed. She said he was killing the tree and deserved to die for it. We decided to call our attorney.

Every attorney we'd ever had forgot something important when he drew up our legal documents. There was the time we had one of our houses sold, and the buyer changed his mind after we had already committed to buy another house. Our attorney admitted he had forgotten to include a penalty clause in the agreement. "Guess I goofed on that one," he said, as he handed us the bankruptcy papers.

I do my own studying now. When we go into a deal, I read all the requirements and the legal rights we have and don't have. I have become a kind of legal expert. When we go into an attorney's office, I ask plenty of questions. Usually I get answers like, "You know, I never thought of that," or "Say now, you have a point there." We always leave our sessions thinking I should charge the attorney for the lessons I have given him.

After about a dozen attorneys and just as many years, Annie said she thought she might have finally found the perfect attorney. I figured we were in the right place when we were seated in the waiting room of his penthouse office. The office was furnished with lovely antique furniture, and we were served champagne and Russian caviar on a silver tray while we waited for our appointed time.

We were ushered down a book-lined hall to an inner office. The door closed noiselessly behind us. We sank into deep and comfortable leather chairs. Books lined the office walls. Eleven-foot windows looked out over the city. The carpet was thick and the air smelled like a courtroom. Behind an immense antique desk, piled high with obviously important papers and at a slightly higher elevation than our own chairs, sat Annie's old bookie: Carmine Costello.

During his last prison stay, Carmine had studied law—and discovered he could make much more money as an attorney and have just as much fun skirting the law, without the risk of jail time.

Annie, of course, had never met Carmine—and he'd changed his name when he started his new profession—but I recognized him immediately. On his left hand I saw he still wore "da muddah of all pinky rings."

I knew we had finally found our mouthpiece.

I told him about our neighbor, Simon Hankle, and he nodded wisely. "Your wife is right—we'll kill da SOB," he growled. Annie shot me a look of triumphant glee.

Carmine made out legal papers that even I couldn't question. He served Hankle with so much paper that poor Simon had his doorbell disconnected and wouldn't leave the house. Just before we were to appear in court, Hankle sold his house and moved away. Annie was deeply disappointed. She had wanted to "fry the bastard."

We got the attorney's bill the other day. Carmine Costello will be taking ownership of our house.

Not long after that, Annie said she wanted to sue Macy's Department Store for making her wait so long for sales help. She intended to have the entire chain wiped out. We visited our attorney. Carmine heard Annie's story and growled, "We'll kill da SOBs."

I put everything we had left in my kid's name.

Sport Makes a Deposit

It was early in the 1988 baseball season. Annie was having terrible pains in her shoulder. Despite the fact that Annie's visits represented about half the revenue of Dr. Fantastic's practice, we had left the good doctor behind when we decided to move permanently to Pebble Beach. After careful research, Annie decided to see the local doctor that all the professional athletes swore by. He was a shoulder/elbow/knee man. Every athlete in town had been to him for various muscle and bone ailments.

Remember, Annie was a pro when it came to doctors. She knew all the medical terms and what prescriptions contained what. She had made a kind of study of illness, and she spoke fluent Doctorese.

Annie was ushered into the doctor's examining room, and the nurse asked her what the problem was. She explained that she had edema and contusions in the left quadrant of the right sector of her shoulder joint. The nurse told her to take off all her clothes and that the doctor would be with her in a moment. Annie wondered why she had to take off all her clothes, but she knew that this doctor was a miracle man. For all she knew, he was going to examine her shoulder through her navel.

The doctor finally came in to examine Annie. He pressed here and he pressed there. He kneaded and probed with one hand and then with both hands. Annie fought to hold back tears of pain.

He finally looked up and said, "You have the biggest calcium deposit I have ever felt. We may just get to write this up in the Sportsmen's Almanac."

Annie told him she appreciated the fact that he had just crushed her "deposit," and asked if she could go home now. She also asked him if the Sportsmen's Almanac would give her an award dinner for having the biggest calcium deposit. Or, at the very least, an Oscar statuette. Preferably one with a bum right arm, since that was the one she couldn't raise. He didn't think she was funny. Most doctors didn't think Annie was funny.

He said, "We will have to operate first thing in the morning."

Annie said, "No, we won't."

"Then I'll give you a cortisone shot."

"I don't want a cortisone shot."

"Codeine tablets?"

"No."

"Aspirin?"

"How many grains?"

"You tell me."

"You're the doctor."

"I forgot that."

The doctor told her that without the operation, it was the end of her professional baseball career.

Annie hadn't had a baseball in her hands for about thirty years and thought the professional ball crack was really funny. It isn't often you find a funny doctor. She told the doctor he had made a very humorous crack. He told her she wouldn't think it was humorous when she was in the middle of a big game and the old flipper just froze up on her. And with a snort, he left the room.

A few months later, we ran into the doctor when we went to see the Giants play at Candlestick Park. He recognized Annie right away. He said, "Hey there. You're the calcium deposit. How's the old flipper holding up?"

Annie told him it didn't start bothering her until she had pitched about seven innings.

Let Me Count the Ways

It was in the middle or early 1990s that Annie died. The date escapes me. I think it escapes me because I don't like to think about her long and painful illness. I don't like to think about it, and I don't want to write about it. Annie died angry—the way she lived.

For a couple of years after Annie's death, my computer became my constant companion. Just the way Annie had been. The other day I came across my old computer and the memories flooded in. I started to draw a strange comparison.

Both the computer and Annie were not easy to make behave the way I would have liked. I started to think: how else were they alike or different?

My old computer was logically driven. When it was malfunctioning, there had to be a workable explanation for it.

Annie was emotionally driven. When she was malfunctioning, there was no way on God's green earth I could find a logical explanation.

I could erase the computer's memory.

Annie never forgot anything.

If I punched the right keys on the computer, I would generally get the expected results.

If I punched anything on Annie, there's no doubt I would have found myself flat on my back, nursing a bloody nose.

Then there was the cooking. Annie was a great cook. I don't know about the computer. The computer could probably have done well with a microwave oven, but those fancy dishes Annie cooked up would probably be pretty difficult for a computer.

There were a lot of things to think about.

I am sure the computer could have been programmed to tell me what color tie to wear with what suit, and when to wear black shoes instead of brown ones. Annie could even have written the program. She always knew things like that.

Annie would help me wash the dishes, too. I don't think I could have taken a chance on getting the computer to do that. I wouldn't have wanted it to get wet—and not only that, I am very particular about the dishes. Annie knew that.

The computer was rather square. Physically, I mean. I sort of liked the way Annie curved.

The computer did overheat sometimes. Annie used to do that a lot.

I do think I loved my computer, in a way. It never talked back. I could turn it off whenever I wanted. It never asked for anything we couldn't afford. It never complained. It never yelled at me. And with a bit of work, I could program my old computer to say "I love you" in amber and grey.

While it is true that I could have bought a color monitor and programmed the machine to say "I love you" in more colors than amber and grey, Annie could say "I love you" in so many colors and shades that a rainbow would blush in shame.

I don't think I could have gotten my computer to do that.

Majoring in a Minor Key

I resonate to a minor key. I think I was born with a "minor key" gene. I miss hearing a Jewish cantor, and sometimes I long for his plaintive song. I went to the local record store—one of the few still around. Mr. Gold, the owner, shuffled over and asked me what I was looking for. I replied, "I'm looking for a CD that features a Jewish cantor." He said, "Jewish cantors, I got. It's the *gentile* cantors I can't get." My first thought was that I had mistakenly stumbled into a New York deli.

There are few things funnier than the conversations you can overhear in a Jewish delicatessen. I am convinced that all Jewish standup comics begin their careers in delis, honing their comedic chops while they put in their time as butchers or waiters. The banter never stops, affronteries salt the air, and the insults have a rhythm that pulses back and forth like a metronome. The dialogue is always in a minor key.

I think if I got a really bad minor key attack and needed some music—and if I didn't have access to iTunes—I could go into a deli. I could have a bagel with a *bisselleh* cream cheese, throw in maybe a lox with a slice onion, and I could soak up my minor key fix.

At home, I can be involved in the most absorbing book or deep in conversation. The TV can be blasting, the dog can be barking, the gardener can be leaf-blowing, when suddenly…a violin plays a few notes in a minor key—a flute gives a lonely call—a sax sighs—a trumpet wails.

My world stops; my suffering begins.

203

An indescribable spark is ignited and begins to grow and fill me. The music soars with its stirring complaint, and I soar with it and absorb its soulful cry. The tears well up and the memories start. I turn up the sound, and I drown myself in my comfortable depression. I think all things are possible, and all things are right, and yet everything is wrong. All things are ugly and everything is beautiful. My mind is in a fantasy world, and I can travel to places I can only reach in my musical chariot.

I hear the melancholy wail of centuries of oppressed Jews. I feel the tug of kinship with the downtrodden and the poor. I am the lonely and disappointed lover. I am the sick and the hurt.

And the melody continues to shout and whisper and wail and lament, until I am spent from my travels and from the melody's plaintive beauty. Sometimes I feel better. Sometimes I feel worse.

But at least, I feel.

A Fantasy in Monterey

They collared me in the magazine section of the Monterey Bookstore. It wasn't the first time I'd been nabbed, so I knew how to fast-talk my way out. That's what kept me out of the slammer. But it could have gone either way.

It happened while I was knocking the magazines against the side of the rack. Iron fists grabbed me from behind. I turned and stared into the veiled fishy eyes of a couple of 205-pound female thugs. They muscled my arms to my sides and hustled me off to a barren storeroom on the top floor of the building and then slammed me down on an old wooden rocking chair.

The room was paint-peeled, cold, and dusty. The only furniture was my rocking chair and a stained and dilapidated desk. Behind the desk sat a chair the Goodwill would have thrown back. The two thugettes tied me to the rocking chair and left me there alone, sneezing from the dust. Each time I sneezed, I bounced back and forth in that squeaking chair, like a noisy, broken pendulum out of a Poe thriller.

The room was lit by a single naked bulb that hung from its cord like a displaced bug's eye, burning an incandescent tattoo in the top of my head. A bead of sweat ran down my back in a crazy corkscrew stream, like a downhill schusser with a busted ski.

My life began to pass before me in a kaleidoscope of vignettes. The time Coach Beldon told me at half-time I would never be able to play basketball unless I grew two feet taller by the end of the game. My spelling teacher hitting me in the back of the head when I argued that Filadelfia, in Pencilvania, was spelled with a capital F. Mary Webster turning her face at the last minute on New Year's Eve, causing me to kiss her passionately on her left nostril.

After what seemed like hours, the door opened and "She" walked in. She sat down behind that hideous desk. Her severely coiffed hair, tortoise-shell glasses and tailored suit failed to hide the fact that she was beautiful, with a body that a bikini would die to enwrap. I heard the muffled sexy swish of nylon on polyester as she crossed her legs and stared unblinking from behind her puce-colored lenses. She asked me why I had been mauling her magazines.

I sneezed again, and waited for my chair to stop bobbing. I told her I was tired of taking home magazines and having two dozen pieces of cardboard, seven or eight paper samples of perfume, and a six-pack of Miller Lite fall out from between the pages. From now on, I was going to shake out the junk before I bought the magazines.

I told her I had just read in Popular Science that the automobile manufacturers had made a technical breakthrough. They would soon be able to insert a full size automobile between the pages of a magazine. Damned if I was going to be the first person crushed to death when a Volvo fell out of the Christmas issue of my Playboy Magazine.

I told her that as long as I was talking to an expert on books and magazines, this seemed like a good time to find out a few things that had been bothering me lately. I asked her whether it was true that the Ku Klux Klan and the White Supremacists were getting together to force publishers to print their newspapers and magazines in white ink.

I also wanted to know if she thought the publishers would ever get around to numbering all the pages of their magazines, instead of just some of the pages.

I told her I was getting plenty steamed at having to find my page number by wetting my finger and counting. It seemed to me that if they were going to continue with the same system, the least they could do was to insert a scented finger moistener between the pages.

Right after that, I asked her out to Al's Diner for burgers and fries.

She pinned me to my rocking chair with her cornflower blue eyes and banged a book down on the desk. Dust flew around the room as though a small hurricane had struck. I went into spasms of sneezing. The rocking chair started skipping and weaving around the room like one of the Harlem Globetrotters looking for an open shot.

The book-slamming must have been a signal, because the two heavyweights instantly reappeared. They tackled the rocking chair, and light turned to black as they taped my eyes closed and crammed an old football helmet over my head.

I could smell the rotten wood of the stairwell as the two thugettes wrestled me down a narrow stairway and into the back seat of a stretch limo. I signaled illegal use of the hands, but they were having none of it. The ride felt like a roller coaster down a Big Sur cliff, and at the bottom I was pitched out the back door doing a headfirst slide into home plate. I heard the roar of the powerful motor as the car burned rubber. I wrenched off my helmet and peeled the tape from my eyes. I was in the parking lot of a deserted drug store. A grimy note, scribbled in crayon, was nailed to my shredded Armani jacket. It read, "From now on, buy your magazines at Walmart."

I guess that meant our date was off.

Shrinking

My Annie was gone, and I was back on the dating market at sixty. Less competent, and considerably less confident.

I was kissing a delightful and lovely woman on our first date. It was a blind date. Her name was Savannah. She was tall, blond and willowy, and very classy. She had grown up in an old Southern family in South Carolina. I usually didn't go for this sort of woman. I liked my ladies dark, small, and a little suggestive-looking, but I sure wasn't unhappy with my current date.

Savannah was a social worker moving her way "toward" a divorce from a crazy Texas doctor who carried a gun and made a habit of threatening to use it. She was a few months into psychotherapy, and I was more than a few years into my own shrinking. She was a mere babe in psycho-land and was awed that I spoke her new language with expertise. We hit it off at once.

And then the word "toward" rang a bell. Savannah was still married.

I thought about her gun-toting husband. I wondered at my courage—or stupidity. Who the hell in his right mind would voluntarily walk into a situation that involved a man who carried a gun? Of course, I hadn't known this until we were already on our date. The closest I had ever come to that sort of threat had happened long ago, when I was in the Army...

A girlfriend and I were in bed together when the window rattled. She said, "Oh my God, I think it's my husband."

It was a case of the incredible shrinking manhood. My penis

shot back into my body as though attached by elastic bands. I was sure I would never be able to function sexually again. It was going to take an operation by a skilled surgeon using a microscope to recover my willy.

I didn't know whether to move or play dead—or kill myself before her husband did the job for me. We lay very still together and listened to our hearts drum a rumba beat.

She finally said, "False alarm! It's not him. He would have torn the place up by now."

I said, "It really doesn't make any difference. I've become a eunuch. Why didn't you tell me you were married?"

"I forgot."

"You forgot to tell me, or you forgot you were married?"

"Both, I suppose."

Back then I was nineteen years old. It took me almost a month to coax my panic-stricken member back to life. A month is a long time when you are nineteen. It was a lesson I didn't ever want to repeat.

Yet, here I was again—decades later—with a married woman. I knew this blind date, great as it was, would be the last time I would see Savannah, my willowy blond beauty. I wasn't about to have some irate husband send me on another treasure hunt for my penis. This time I was quite a bit older and I might never find it.

But let's be realistic. You don't just cut these affairs off in the middle of passionate necking in front of the living room fire. It's just not fair to the woman. So, in the middle of the eighth or ninth or twentieth kiss, I figured I had nothing to lose. I did something I had never done before. I got crude. (If you can imagine such a thing.)

I said, "Let's quit this fooling around and go to bed."

I expected this classy lady to throw me out of her house. I didn't realize how the dating market had changed during my absence.

She said, "Great, give me ten minutes. You get undressed and I'll meet you in bed."

Instead of being happy about my success, I started to think. In cases like this, the dumbest thing you can do is start to think.

Hadn't I learned this by now? It was always the thinking that got me in trouble.

The first thing that occurred to me was that I had surely wasted a lot of time trying to get into bed with women. Why in God's name hadn't I used that line on first dates before?

I thought back on the girls I hadn't been able to lay throughout my life. I thought back on how long it had taken me to go to bed with the ones I *had* laid.

By the time Savannah came back, it was too late. The damage was done. Willy had disappeared as surely as if her husband had been rattling the window outside.

I swear, that's the last time you'll ever find me thinking.

Running

I always envy those marvelous running people who jog along the road in 95-degree weather with their tongues hanging out and their clothes stuck like wet sausage skins to their skinny bodies. They all look as if they are having such a good time.

I tried it once for almost ten minutes and decided it wasn't for me. My knees started hurting, my head began to ache, and my Walkman fell off and shattered on the pavement. I thought, let them have their good times. I would rather suffer and watch TV.

Then I met a runner. A lovely, slim, hard-muscled runner who went into a funk if she missed a day of blissful running. She kept insisting that I join her. I tried to explain that a running nose was as close as I ever wanted to come to running. She told me I would love it once I got into it. I told her, that's what Jim Fixx used to say.

We finally struck a compromise. She could run while I cooked breakfast. While she was out there having a good time, I would sweat over a hot stove cooking eggs Benedict or French toast, or a quiche to die for. (Quiches are always "to die for.") She didn't have to worry about her cholesterol. Cholesterol wouldn't dare breed in that perfect runner's body. For my part, I didn't worry about cholesterol either, because cholesterol is a part of life—like being overweight.

She would come back with her neon outfit stained in odd colors from righteous runner's sweat. Her breath would come in wrenching heaves as she told me about her wonderful and exhilarating run. I would look at her in envy.

I would listen, wishing that I, too, could enjoy a good run. Then, overwhelmed with shame, I would reach for another piece of French toast. She would sit gasping for breath, her lovely face contorted in pain as she extolled in panting syllables the glorious effect of endorphins.

I had heard about endorphins. Those extraordinary chemicals the body releases to affect pain and mood. They can be "turned on" by intense physical exertion such as running, or by chemical means, or by other methods not completely understood.

I was reminded of the famous Hershey Syndrome. It was based on an unbiased scientific article authored by the famous Doctor Frederick Hershey (unrelated to the famous Hershey chocolate family except by birth). Dr. Hershey conducted a series of impartial tests, funded by the Hershey Chocolate Company, to study chocolate's effects on the nervous system. The test concluded that chocolate, much the same as exercise, releases endorphins in the human body.

A thought began to form. Maybe my own beautiful runner and I could experience the same endorphin "kick" together. Maybe runners and people like me could have something in common!

I asked my sweet runner to explain more about the phenomenon of endorphins. She told me that after a long time of running, when the pain is almost unbearable and she feels as though she is about to die, the endorphins hit. She gets this wonderful feeling of euphoria. It takes over her whole body, erases her pain, and makes it all worth the effort.

She said it generally starts with a pleasant feeling in her mouth and spreads until she tingles all over and feels as if she could go on forever. She becomes completely satisfied and at peace with the world.

"Eureka!" I cried. "I knew it! It's the Hershey Syndrome. We can share. I get the same feeling eating chocolate! Instead of fixing breakfast, I'll just eat a candy bar while I watch you run."

I don't see my lovely runner much anymore. Oh, sometimes I pass her when I'm driving my car on the Seventeen Mile Drive. I see that perfect sweaty body, blond pony tail bouncing back and forth with each powerful stride, beautiful face distorted with effort and breath coming in fitful rasps. I start to wonder if I am missing something...and then I take a bite of my chocolate bar. The endorphins kick in and I am at peace.

Ode to a Jogger

He jogs his way
Through his private hell;
He sweats and strains
And starts to swell.

The hill is steep,
The path is new.
Don't stop him now—
Five miles to do.

His muscles burn;
His joints do, too.
Don't stop him now—
Four miles to do.

His breath comes hard,
His foot's askew.
Don't stop him now—
Three miles to do.

Pain wracks from head
Down to his shoe.
Don't stop him now—
Two miles to do.

His stride is weak;
His life's in review.
Don't stop him now—
One mile to do.

His sight is blurred,
His heart pounds, too.
So don't stop him now—
He's almost through!

He crossed the line!
He made the grade!
An old grave digger
Puts down his spade.

But his day will come,
When his race is done,
And his body's like lead,
And he drops stone dead.

To each his own, I always say.
Jogging's OK for those who must.
But I prefer my proven way:
Stay in shape from plain old lust.

Ridin' in the Rain

There were two of them—tall, lanky, each with lustrous long blond hair hanging down to her shoulders. They were dressed in tight, slim jeans that hugged their hips, big buckled belts, and slouchy cowboy hats tipped to the back of their heads. Their shirts were crisp, white, and tailored. They leaned easily on a wooden fence, one leg cocked up on a rail and one arm hanging over the top of the fence. They were both lookers—and I was looking.

After careful study, I decided I liked one better than the other. I don't know why. They looked a lot alike and I hadn't talked to either one, but one of them had some indefinable appeal. They looked as though they wanted to talk. I brushed through my hair with my fingers, sucked in my gut, and began the long walk to the fence.

That's when the dog barked for breakfast. I awoke from my dream, cursing that furry mongrel and vowing to force my daughter, RK, to give him away to the first person who would promise never to feed him again. I thought I had lost my dream ladies forever.

Thank God my visit with RK in Seattle was just about over. It had been raining in Seattle for the last 4,000 days. I usually knew it was time to head home when all my clothes were shrunken, wrinkled, and mildewed.

The next day, I journeyed home to Monterey. The airline didn't

214

let me carry my baggage on board. They said the luggage was too big and had to be checked. I didn't understand why. Another passenger managed to lug two seven-foot-wide duffel bags down the two-foot-wide aisle, hitting three unwary passengers in the head.

None of the stricken victims had moved during the entire flight. I asked the steward if he thought they had been knocked out or killed. He said they were obviously novices to flying or they never would have been sitting on the aisle. They deserved what they got. He said if they lived, they would know better the next time.

Even though it rains, or at least it drizzles, spits, showers, sprinkles, or mists continuously in Seattle, RK claims that the residents never actually get wet. I didn't seem to have their knack. I was looking forward to my return to the arid environs of Monterey, but the rain had followed me all the way home.

When my plane landed, I picked up my suitcases, the combined weight of which added up to somewhere between a piano and an automobile. I grunted and dragged my baggage to the taxi stand and waited to be picked up. Did I say I was glad to get back to Monterey, where it never rains *unless I am waiting at the airport for a taxi?*

All over the world, taxi drivers pray for rain. It gives them supreme authority over their customers. Everywhere but Monterey, that is. In Monterey, rain washes away our taxis. Like illusions in a watercolor, they just disappear.

I had been waiting a long time, drenched and bedraggled, when it happened. A car screeched past the empty taxi stand and came to a stop at the white curb. A slim, blue-jeaned, and booted leg popped out of the driver's seat, followed by a big buckle and a tilted hat, all wrapped around a tall blonde.

It was raining like someone upstairs had let a fire hose get out of control. She couldn't have cared less. She cocked one leg up on the curb and hung her arm over the opened door. A younger, mirror-image blonde got out of the passenger seat, put on her backpack, and headed into the terminal. Two blond beauties. It was my dream, come to life!

The driver took one look at my pathetic figure and said, "I came to drop off my daughter. You can't get a cab at the Monterey Airport when it's raining. You'll have to wait hours. Want a ride?"

I ran my fingers through my hair and sucked in my gut. I croaked, "Huh?" (I've always been pretty good with the repartee.)

"You poor wet person. Was that a gargle, or a yes?"

And with that, she tossed my baggage into her car's trunk, tipped her hat farther back on her blond head, and stared at me with blue-eyed laser intensity.

"Where to?"

(Silence.)

"I mean, where are you headed?"

"Huh?"

Come on people—give me a break. You've got to remember this was quite a shock. I had actually met my dream girl! I was tired. I had probably gotten a hernia from lugging suitcases that this slender woman had tossed into her car trunk as if they were gas-filled balloons. My stomach was beginning to hurt from holding it in and my brain was still waterlogged from being in Seattle for two months.

"I got a feeling," she said. "My name's Pamela. Let's just head toward Pebble Beach and when you get your breath, you can tell me where you want to go."

If I had been a movie director, there would have been a crash of cymbals and Judy Garland would have belted out "Somewhere Over the Rainbow"—because that's when it happened. The Monterey Peninsula put on its magnificent show. On that miserable wet day, the sun suddenly burst forth and sent glorious scarlet and golden colors arching along the horizon.

I settled back in Pamela's car and she took over. That was fifteen years ago. Pamela is still in the driver's seat and for me, the rainbow is still in the sky.

Fifty is Nifty

It is difficult to be sixty. As I write the number, I can't believe it refers to me. Why should it be more difficult to be sixty than fifty-five or -six or -seven? Because sixty is the beginning of old age. Everything thereafter is downhill. My memory certainly isn't what it was, and it takes me longer to assimilate things. I find myself searching for words that I *know* I know. Then when I find the word, I'm not sure it's the right one. Spelling has always been difficult for me; now even the simplest word looks odd.

I decided that I would refuse to be sixty, and got the brilliant idea to just say that I was fifty. And with the saying, it would be so. So far, it has not worked too well. As I write this, I feel myself slipping into fantasy. In fantasy, I could be any age—any weight—any height…

> *Handsome, with a gaunt and muscular build, his high cheek-bones suggesting some ancient Indian ancestor, he seemed to dominate the room. He towered a full head taller than his companions. His bearing was as alert as that of a jungle animal. Power radiated from his eyes as they ranged over the room, absorbing every detail with a single glance.*

That is the way I was at fifty. How come at sixty I got fat and short and have no muscles? What happened to that part-Indian guy with the high cheekbones? I think he slipped in some wild buffalo shit and got trampled to death. What happened to absorbing every detail at a glance with those powerful eyes? It's the damn bifocals—that's what. They just don't make bifocals the way they used to.

*Swinging his racquet back and forth while he awaited his op-
ponent's serve, his brown lithe body typified the professional
tennis player. He was fantastic. Since he'd learned the game
at age four, tennis had become as natural to him as walking.
He refused to turn pro because he loved the sport too much to
dominate it. It seemed unfair to the other professionals. It was
difficult enough to get someone to oppose him—even in a game
for pure fun. With practiced ease he smashed his opponent's
volley for the game point. The small gallery applauded in awe
as he strode from the court with that animal grace that served
him so well in all sports.*

That's the way I played the game at fifty. When the racquets
were lighter and easier to use. When they were also making the
shoes differently. They used to be springier. I'm glad I didn't turn
professional. Now that they make the courts bigger and the nets
higher, it just isn't the same game it used to be.

*As he wrote the last figure on the blackboard, the assembled
scientists from around the world stood in reverent awe. He had
solved, in a matter of minutes, the equation that had confounded
them all for decades. With a few strokes of chalk, the depth of his
genius was revealed. What a man! It was not enough that he had
been acclaimed as "Athlete of All Time." He was now assured of
receiving the Nobel Prize for "The Greatest Mental Achievement of
All Time—Including Even the Time Before That."*

How come honors like this are so easily won at fifty but seem
to elude us at sixty? As I think I said in the beginning, the mind
slippeth. It will probably take twice as long to solve the equation at
sixty as at fifty. The award will probably just be for "Greatest Mental
Achievement of All Time." They will leave off the "Time Before That"
bit. These are the facts we all must expect to face. Sad as they are.

Woe to sixty. Woe to me. Woe to us all—except those who will
not reach sixty. Double woe to them.

The Night I Fell in Love

In this world of billions, it seems silly that the number 100 is still an important milestone to me. I think we are all conditioned to think in even numbers and units—tens, twenties, one hundreds, five thousands. In my marble playing days, I had the goal of winning one hundred marbles. If someone had said, "Why not one hundred and seven marbles?" I would have thought they were being silly.

Once when I was giving an offer on a house, I bid $329,128.12 just to see the reaction. Under great protest, the broker submitted it. The owner thought I was a weirdo and refused to counter. I changed the offer to $320,000. The owner countered at $325,000 and we had a deal. No one stopped to figure out that the first offer was the better deal.

But back to the number 100. When I first started working for my father in the clothing store, we were selling a man's Arrow shirt, pure cotton, with the famous Arrow Collar, for seventy-nine cents. You could buy a pair of luxury brand shoes for less than five dollars. Ten dollars was a significant sale. Recovery from the depths of the Depression was slow in Bullneck. We didn't make many ten-dollar sales.

I was working as a salesclerk in my father's store after school and every Saturday. In the '30s, business was *all* business. There were no complacent retail clerks. You produced, or you were fired. Commissions were paid for results—not for gum chewing, or bathroom breaks, or telephone conversations with friends, or "I don't know," or "I'm busy right now." We were in a highly competitive atmosphere. Every sale counted. Every customer was all-important.

I was the youngest and therefore the last clerk to wait on a new customer. The older, more experienced salespeople had the first choice. I often waited a long time between turns. The system made sense, even to me, but it was sometimes hard for an ambitious twelve-year-old to take.

I was paid two dollars every Saturday. I didn't think it was enough. Everyone else was getting more money for the same job. So, I set my goal. If I could sell one hundred dollars worth in one Saturday, I would ask the boss (my father) for a raise.

I was a natural salesman. I knew the merchandise. I was pleasant. People would laugh with the "little person" who had the "sales pitch," and they would buy. I kept a detailed sales count in the sales book that every clerk kept in his back pocket to keep track of his total sales. The months passed. I came close to that elusive one hundred dollars, but I never quite made it.

And then, one Saturday just before Christmas, it happened: the one-hundred-dollar sales day. I had been busy and involved, and was surprised when I finally totaled my book. The total came to a magnificent One Hundred Twenty-Two Dollars and Thirty-Seven Cents. An amazing figure! I went to my father, showed him my book, and asked for a raise.

Payday was on Saturday. It was the custom, after the store had closed, for the sales people to gather around the cash register for their pay envelopes. I wondered if I would get my raise that Saturday.

My father's face had that tight-lipped look I had learned to dread. We were all gathered around the register, when he said he had an important announcement.

He said, "Burt had over one hundred dollars in sales last Saturday and has asked for a raise in pay. He has asked for a one-dollar raise. After thinking it over, I have decided to give him a fifteen-dollar raise."

I knew that big trouble was ahead. I said, "Never mind, I don't want a raise anymore."

My father said, "It's too late. Your money's already in your pay envelope. Open it."

I did as I was told. Three $5 bills and two $1 bills dropped out on the counter.

My father said, "Before you spend your new raise, I think we should settle a few accounts. I think five dollars a week rent on your room at home is fair. I'll take that out of the pile. Then there is a week's worth of meals. You're a big eater. Five dollars for a week's meals is a bargain. I'll just take that out. Then, there is that pair of shoes and the new pants you just got. That's another fiver.

"Look at that, you only have two dollars left. I thought about taking that out for your school notepaper and books, but I'm going to give that to you as a gift."

Not another word was said. I picked up my two dollars. Not one person around that cash register would look at anyone else. Not one person said a word. We all went home.

I never asked my father for anything again.

Sixty years later...Pamela and I were in bed and for some reason I felt sorry for myself. I told her that story. When I finished, she was crying. Not little tears that could seep out from those beautiful eyes and run quietly down those lovely cheeks. These were big, wrenching tears that came from the gut and spilled out like a river in a rush that washed down her chest and wet her breasts and the sheets and the bed, and didn't stop.

Until I cried with her.

And it was better.

And I fell in love.

The Wedding

Pamela and I were married in a tiny ceremony on the 6th green of the Cypress Point Golf Course, after the day's golfing had wound down and before they turned on the sprinklers.

My old buddy Frank and our immediate family were the only guests. RK had gotten herself ordained as a minister for just this occasion.

As I stood beside my beloved, swatting mosquitoes and waiting for RK to conclude her rambling nuptial blessing, I was reminded of a wedding I attended years ago—a far cry from our humble event...

It was 1954. The bride and groom were both spoiled from too much money and too many thrills. I didn't think anything could satisfy either one of them—but they were in love.

The wedding was the social event of the year. The Cohens and the Goldfarbs were finally tying the knot. Or, as the Los Angeles Times had put it, "The department store is marrying the dressmaker." There were receptions and showers and celebrations for weeks before the big event was to take place.

I had to buy a new suit to go to this affair. Buying new clothes is traumatic for me. I always take a size larger than I did the time before. The clothes are invariably so much more expensive than they were the last time I shopped that I go into "monetary shock syndrome." My eyes become glazed and I clutch my wallet with a death grip that can only be broken by the promise of wild sexual delights to be enjoyed when the spending has ceased.

The wedding was a glorious affair. The women all cried and the men were all busy trying to figure out how much everything cost. The groom (Cohen) was prettier than the bride (Goldfarb). The Goldfarbs kept trying to impress the Cohens with how lucky they were. The Cohens tried the same tactic with the Goldfarbs.

The bride's and groom's parents danced the Anniversary Waltz to an off-key orchestra. Uncle Albert (Cohen) made a pass at Aunt Ethel (Goldfarb). Uncle Rupert (Goldfarb) punched out Uncle Albert. Aunt Frannie (Goldfarb) passed out. Uncle Emil (Cohen) threw up. But things were peaceful enough, and everyone seemed to be having a good time, until the final hour. That's when the bride threw the bouquet.

I never saw such wild scrambling in my life. All the singles wanted that damn bouquet. The girls shrieked and clawed and jumped around like wild animals in a feeding frenzy. Wedding cake went flying in all directions. Thousands of dollars' worth of dresses were torn in a mad scramble, and fathers turned pale with the thought of what that spray of crummy flowers was costing them.

When the dust finally cleared and the commotion was over, Fred gave out his victory scream. He was clutching the flowers in his scratched and bleeding hands. His tuxedo was shredded and dirty, but his face was flushed with victory. He held the bouquet— the symbol of the next marriage—high in the air. He did a little dance around the room. With tears in his eyes, he embraced Tom. It was a beautiful and touching moment.

That's when the trouble started. The bride's family said it was a disgrace to allow Fred to catch the bride's bouquet. The groom's family said they didn't know how Fred had gotten into the wedding in the first place.

The Goldfarbs said the Cohens should take the bouquet away from Fred.

The Cohens said the bride must have been cross-eyed to throw the flowers in Fred's direction.

Things got so bad that the bride and groom started fighting. Somebody called the police, and the whole affair just kind of deteriorated. After it was all over, the bride and groom were so traumatized they decided to have the marriage annulled.

The whole thing aggravated the hell out of me. I had spent all that money for a new suit and there was a big glob of wedding cake on the right lapel, so I couldn't return the damn thing.

The Bunny Hop

After we were married, Pamela was ecstatic about taking up residence in Windrush. For months, she had been eager to establish her relationship with my resident population of rabbits. Those darling little animals sat out on my lawn and wriggled their noses and said to Pamela, "This is a happy bunny house and you must come live here."

So it was that Pamela came to inhabit the ugly, happy bunny house. She fed the little bunnies every day. They would sit up on their little bottoms and eat the carrots and lettuce that the kind lady had left for them. They would go into the bushes and do what bunnies do best besides eat. Sometimes, they didn't even bother to go into the bushes. The happy little bunnies prospered and multiplied.

Then we planted the flowers.

The little bunnies didn't want the carrots or the lettuce anymore. All they wanted were the flowers. And to do their thing in the bushes. No amount of noise or yelling could keep them away from either pastime.

It was a sad but common sight to see our gardener planting new flowers, while right around the corner of the house the rabbits were eating the ones he had just planted ten minutes earlier. Every week it was a race to see who would finish first.

It's not so easy to get rid of rabbits. Not when you are married to my darling Pamela. They are too cute and cuddly to poison. There are laws against shooting. They are too fast to hit with a baseball bat (which I know from experience). They are too smart to trap. Not only that, but what do you do with them after you trap them?

I had heard that if you take lion droppings and spread them all around the perimeter of the property, the rabbits would get scared and leave. You spread the lion droppings in proportion to the number of rabbits you have to get rid of. I decided it wouldn't work. There were too many rabbits. It would take three, maybe four truckloads to do the job. And at the rate they were going, I'd need double that in a couple of weeks.

That's when we decided to get an owl. Not a real owl, but one of those plastic ones the garden stores sell. According to the ads, one owl would clear an acre of four-legged pests. You merely staked it up in clear view of the gophers, rabbits, squirrels, or other un-wanted animals, and they would instantly make tracks for safer parts.

When I got a look at those owls, I could believe the ads. I never saw such ferocious-looking things. They had big yellow eyes, long claws, and a frightening expression of fury that made my blood run cold. I pitied the poor rabbit that encountered that horrible vision. But I was determined to be merciless. I bought the owl.

When I unpacked my prize, our magnificent Doberman, Bru-tus II, took one look at that owl and backed behind the couch. Brutus II was the second in a series of Bruteii who all seemed to defy the innate Doberman personality. I kept naming our Dober-man puppies Brutus with high hopes of getting a useful watch-dog, but each turned out to be, in one way or another, a disgrace to the Doberman reputation.

Brutus II just hunkered down behind the couch and refused to look at the owl, or at me. He seemed to be saying, "So, since there's nothing doing around here, I think I'll just relax behind the couch for a while. Hold my calls 'til later." I respect that. Some-times it's just too scary to be macho.

I couldn't wait to stake up that owl. If it could frighten Brutus, no doubt it could get rid of every critter on the place. I staked up the owl and, like magic, the rabbits instantly disappeared.

The owl had been scowling for three days. The setting sun

was casting long shadows across the lawn. The chewed-off stubs where the gardener had planted the latest flowering rabbit food poked up from the freshly turned earth. Pamela called me to the window.

There were big rabbits and little rabbits. Grey rabbits and brown ones. There were skinny rabbits and fat ones, tall and short, white tails and brown tails, standing and sitting, lying down and jumping. The ground was covered with sniffing, quivering fur for fifty feet. They were all gathered around that staked-up plastic owl.

It had taken three days for the rabbits to spread the word. All rabbitdom for miles around had assembled for a prayer meeting in our yard. The owl looked to be their preacher, and he must have been preaching a real fire-and-brimstone sermon. There was no other explanation.

I got rid of the owl the next day. The rabbits are still around. They are probably waiting for the second coming of the owl.

Farewell to Sport

About two months after Annie's death, I managed to back my car out of the garage without opening the garage door. I was taught that if you exit the garage the same way you entered, you will never hit anything. I had forgotten that first you have to open the garage door.

At the time of this collision, I was still driving the Rolls Royce. When the garage door ran into me, it caused extensive and costly damage. As if the initial cost of a Rolls Royce weren't enough, any replacement or repair is doubly stratospheric. When I got the repair bill, I felt as if I had been charged for the entire Rolls agency. I would have left the car for payment, but the agency said they couldn't get rid of the Rolls Royces they already had. So much for my "investment."

Except for the cost, I didn't think the accident was all that important. Since Annie's death I had been living in a dream world anyway. The sight of a garage door hanging as if in a Picasso painting seemed pretty normal to me. So I left it that way.

I still kept Sport's old T-Bird on the far side of the garage. I knew I had to put it up for sale, but I kept procrastinating. That white 1957 convertible had become as attached to Annie as a body part. I was convinced she and the car actually spoke to each other. No force short of death could have separated her from that car. Seeing it in the garage every day was my tie to the past.

A couple of years passed, and my life with Pamela was a joy. After we married, we began to make plans to remodel the ugliness out of Windrush. That was when the trouble started. It wasn't long before we determined that Annie's presence was still running around the place, and she was doing what she loved to do best: stirring up trouble.

Rightly or wrongly, we blamed her for broken glasses, misplaced items, forgotten appointments, and all sorts of minor accidents. We damn well knew she was still hanging around.

I seem to have a fondness for a certain type of woman. Ask me what I had for lunch today and I'll tell you I don't remember. Ask Pamela what we were doing August 11th, 1997, and she will ask, "Morning or afternoon?"

There lurked in Pamela's prodigious memory a ten-year old conversation with an old friend of hers, who had a friend, who fancied herself a type of seer. Pamela called her friend and learned the friend's friend might do us a favor and "cleanse the house" of Annie's lingering spirit.

Pamela and I talked it over and decided maybe a "good cleaning" would be best for Annie's sake as well as ours. Annie was a neat freak and probably would have agreed that a good cleaning never hurt, and besides, it was a chance for a good fight. The only thing Sport liked better than stirring up trouble was a good fight.

The seer arrived—dressed like a gypsy with a babushka on her head and a loud, flouncy flowered dress. She had on a broad belt with a huge silver buckle that looked like a wrestler's medal. Her eyes were black holes overarched by tufts of red hair. She sported a load of crazy jewelry that rattled when she breathed. She was like a character from a 1930s movie. Bela Lugosi had come back as a female.

The seer didn't waste much time. She asked us where we thought the spirit was hanging out. We told her we didn't know. But we knew Annie, and we predicted she would make herself plenty tough to find. She loved to play hardball.

"Bella" lit a long piece of woven dried sage salted with incense and assorted exotic materials, mumbled a couple of unintelligible words and said, "Start walkin'—feels to me like we should start in the bedroom."

We followed Bella into the bedroom and walked slowly through the rest of the house. The stink of sage and incense and the sound of Bella's incantations filled the rooms. The ritual was supposed to drive out the spirits, but Bella didn't seem too happy. As hard as she tried, she just couldn't find Annie.

Bella was so frustrated, her scowl crinkled her eyebrows into a single red brush across her forehead. She finally gave up, and we went outside. That's when Bella spied that crazy garage door hanging like a broken wing. It was swinging back and forth, though the air was as still as a sleeping dog.

"Gotcha!" Bella yelled.

We went into the garage and Bella went straight for the T-Bird. She held the smoking sage stick in the T-Bird's open window, and a sudden breeze blew the smoke away. Bella waved her hands and blew frantically into the smoke to guide it, but it just wouldn't enter the car. She leaned her ample body into the smoke and tried to push it as if it were a solid form. The smoke just fell away. Finally, she looked at us and said, "Rats! I need help."

We all surrounded the smoke and tried to blow it and push it into the car, but it wasn't working. Pamela ran into the house and came back with an electric fan. We used the fan to help us work the smoke toward the open window of the car. Slowly, with seeming reluctance, smoke began to enter the T-Bird in a narrow stream, and then it finally broadened until it filled the entire car. Bella sighed.

"We got her! What a tough cookie she must have been."

Pamela looked at me. I looked at Pamela. And that was that.

Until the next day. As I was walking to the bedroom, a book suddenly fell in front of me. It had dropped from the stacks that lined our hallway. I stooped to return the book to its place and noticed the title: Farewell to Sport.

You can believe what you want. I will believe what I want. We can compare or not. I believed one thing, but now I think I may believe another. I probably will change my mind many times. The only thing I really know is that I really don't know.

Life in the Construction Zone

*O*nce Windrush was spook-free, Pamela was hot to remodel. Too dark, too windy, too much, she said—and it was clear to me that my happy bride didn't need an ugly house to cure her depression. Strangely enough, neither did I.

We flew my old Laguna Beach architect, Eyeball Brown, up to Monterey to draw some remodeling plans. He came dressed like any self-respecting Southern Californian. He wore shorts, a lightweight short-sleeved shirt, and sandals.

July in Monterey is one of the coldest, windiest months of the year. When he got to the house, he was shivering like a leaf in a storm. He took one look at our Chinese-modern monstrosity, moved his eye patch over to cover his one good eye, and said, "Tear it down."

He vibrated his way back to the airport and returned to the comfort of the Southern California smog and Santa Ana breezes. It was a couple of months before we were able to convince him to draw us some remodeling plans, but he never set foot in Windrush again.

Puttering around

Meanwhile up in Seattle, RK had been promoting the talents of her chocolate-eating ex-partner in burglary, Adrian, and his dad, Arnie. They had set up business as A&A Construction, "the best builders this side of the Rockies." She suggested we lure them to Windrush with the promise of a few rounds of golf and try to talk them into taking on the remodel job.

We invited the pair down to the Peninsula to show them the plans. Pamela and I put them up in our guesthouse. We let them golf for about a week before we figured they were ripe for the reveal. We spread the plans out on the tenth green and waited while they looked them over. When they had digested what Eyeball Brown had in mind, they said, "Tear the place down."

Then they walked to the eleventh tee and hit two beauties straight down the middle of the fairway. I could see their game had improved quite a bit.

We said, "Think about it."

We left when they told us we were interrupting their game.

Home cooking

A few months later, RK called us up and said, "You're lucky! Adrian and his dad are having a dry spell in Seattle, and they're considering coming down to do your remodel!"

It seemed obvious that anyone who could have a "dry spell" in Seattle was indeed a miracle worker. We promised to house them in the guesthouse and encouraged them to bring their own cook and domestic slave (Adrian's mother, Florrie) for the duration of the remodel. We figured the job would take at least a year. So they loaded their tools, golf clubs, and kitchen equipment into a couple of pickups and headed south.

Windrush shook with a cacophony of hammers, power tools, and the crunch of wood being wrenched into rubble. We had to get out.

It was travel time! Annie had always been afraid to fly, and it hadn't seemed like much fun to go to exotic and exciting places alone. I had given up on my desire to ever see the places that Sarah and I had visited in fantasy so many years ago—but things were different now.

I was with a beautiful and loving partner who wanted to share the world with me. I was raring to go. Pamela was an ever-flowing source of energy, willing to go anywhere, do anything, and always find the joy in it.

Right after graduating from nursing school, Pamela had gotten a job that required her to travel around the world. Now she wanted to show the country boy, who had never been much of anywhere, what he had been missing.

During the first few weeks of the remodel, Pamela got out her maps and her travel books. We sat in what remained of the living room and planned our travels. After about a month of planning, my wonderful bride led her awestruck husband on the year-long journey of his life.

We started with the national parks of America and Canada. We soaked up centuries of history in the United Kingdom and India. We ate our way across Europe.

In the summer, we visited Scandinavia. In the winter we bungee-jumped in New Zealand, scuba-dived in Australia, and safaried in Africa. Pamela wanted to see over every hill and descend into every valley. She could never get enough. Her joy was boundless, and her exuberance carried me along.

Thirteen months after Adrian, Arnie, and Florrie had started the remodeling job, we returned to Windrush from our latest world adventure. We found our builders illegally playing the back nine of the golf course that surrounded the house.

They had made a deal with the golf stewards. Florrie would furnish the cake and coffee. The golf police wouldn't patrol the back nine after 3 p.m.

Between rounds, A&A had managed a remarkable transformation on our ramshackle dump. Our two wonderful craftsmen turned a 1950s Chinese modern monstrosity into a charming French country gem. I don't know how they did it.

Frankly, I think it was Florrie's cooking.

After the house was done, Adrian decided his golf game still needed some fine-tuning. He relocated to the Peninsula. We've done a lot of projects together since that first one, and have become dear friends. Each project has been better than the last.

Adrian hasn't had a dry spell since he moved to Monterey.

Perfection is only a dollop away

Richard, our ubiquitous painter, generally arrived on Monday at about noon. Depending on whether, or when, he got laid on Sunday.

He had almost become a member of the family, painting our house for a couple of years, on and off, when he got around to it. It was like having another dog, except we didn't have to walk him.

Richard was a great painter, but it could take three days for him to get comfortable with the color of one door. He didn't seem to care whether he got paid for one day or three. He did care *a lot* what the door looked like.

We kind of walked around him and tried not to get roped into a discussion of whether the door would look better with "a dollop more of burnt umber, or maybe two dollops?" If we got caught up and ventured an opinion, Pamela and I never seemed to agree. That made three opinions, each one involving at least two days of experimentation. The door-painting usually stretched on for more than a week before a decision could be made. When the final coat of paint was applied, one of the three of us was bound to be disappointed.

It was very safe for me to say, "When Richard finishes painting, I think I will start a new house."

I wished he wouldn't ask for any opinions. I was reminded of my dental hygienist, who informed me that I had a cavity. I said, "I don't remember asking you whether I had any cavities. All I wanted was to have my teeth cleaned."

There are some people you should never get smart with. A doctor who happens to be examining your testicles. A guy with a knife or a gun. Somebody with big muscles (male or female). Dental hygienists armed with sharp instruments but no sense of humor. And painters who like to mix colors.

Drunken Duncan and Gus

Gus was the unlikeliest vision of a wallpaper hanger, but he could wallpaper a telephone pole to a water hydrant, if that's what the job called for.

When Pamela and I first met him, he was already about seventy years old. He was allergic to wallpaper paste and would break out in huge welts within minutes of starting a job. He wore glasses that looked as though they had been fashioned from truck headlights. Anything more than six inches from his face was a hopeless blur to him.

Most fascinating of all, Gus had the worst case of palsy we had ever seen. It took him ten minutes just to unwrap a fresh razor blade to begin working.

He would haltingly cut a length of wallpaper, wobble toward the wall, and stagger up the ladder to place the paper. It was a study in precision timing to see that mottled arm and palsied hand aiming the seams of the paper toward each other.

Gus would lean toward the wall and hold the precious paper in his shaking hand. We could see his concentration make the tremors even greater. Suddenly he would make a lightning lunge, and the paper would be placed perfectly. He never missed.

After he plastered the paper in place, red-welted hand holding the trembling razor blade, Gus would creep toward the ragged end of the perfectly laid strip. We would watch the fluttering pause before the execution. But we both covered our eyes just before that snake-like strike of the blade as it sliced off the excess paper.

Stella, our interior designer, always used Gus to hang her wallpaper. She told us she quit watching him work several years ago. It was that last-minute spasm that finally got to her. Stella was always afraid his final strike would slice completely through the wall into a stranger's apartment next door.

She confessed that she was watching him one day just before he delivered one of his final strikes. Stella was completely enthralled. She said she felt as if her eyes and body were in perfect harmony with his palsied vibrations.

At the exact moment of truth, he struck, she screamed—and Gus fell off his ladder.

After that, he banned Stella from the job site.

Gus is almost eighty years old now and isn't quite as exact as he used to be. Last I heard, he partnered with a painter who drinks too much. Painters who drink too much are so common they should have their own heading in the yellow pages. This particular painter's name is Duncan. He could list himself as "Drunken Duncan" in the yellow pages.

Drunken doesn't care if Gus misses the top of the wall a bit. He just paints the ceiling lower. Gus doesn't care if Drunken paints the ceiling too low. He just papers over the paint. Between the two of them, they decorate a house pretty well.

Stella builds spec houses now and can't afford Gus and Drunken. She likes to have a drink or two with Drunken if she passes a job he's working on. But if Gus is there, he still won't allow her on the job.

Could it be your tool is too short?

During our remodel, wisely or not, we took quite a bit of advice from Frank. He was a pro—he had remodeled his own house seven times in the last ten years.

Frank had a little joke he liked to play on his jobsites. He made himself a thirty-foot tape measure with two feet added in. The tape was thirty-two feet long, although at its end it was labeled thirty feet. He figured that any contractor who was stupid enough to come for a bid without his own tape deserved to miscalculate the footage. For obvious reasons, Frank always managed to make sure that particular tape was unavailable after the job was bid.

Frank also kept a certain vigilance. He was constantly amazed at how his own tools always seemed to get "mixed up" with the workmen's tools. No matter how many trucks, tool kits, ladders, saws, nails and various other building paraphernalia were brought to the job, the one special tool that was needed always seemed to reside in Frank's bountiful tool chest and had to be "borrowed." Never to be seen again.

One day, Frank watched as an unfortunate cabinetmaker tried to cut a length of wood using the doctored tape he had evidently "borrowed" from Frank's tool chest. The woodworker, a diminutive young whippersnapper everybody called "Squirt," must have cut that board five times.

Squirt would measure the space using Frank's doctored tape. Then he'd put down the tape, walk to the saw, and measure the board for his cut with his own tape. Squirt would cut the board, walk back to place it, and it would be too short.

There was nothing Frank could do. Squirt had used the deceptive tape for his bidding estimate. So Frank just watched.

The cabinetmaker would measure. Walk to the saw. Measure. Saw the board. Walk back to fit the board. The board would be short. He would scratch his head. Repeat the process.

Squirt finally solved the problem. He said he was sick, and quit for the day.

Frank recovered his tape and destroyed it. The incident inspired him to write a best-selling How-To book. The meat of the book can be found on page 183, paragraph three:

If your efforts always turn up short,
it may be that your measuring device is faulty.

Repairs Through the Ages

*Y*ou have called five people the requisite four times each.

You have tried begging, cajoling, and crying. You have threatened and bribed. You have used the old "I've only a got few weeks to live" ploy. You've waited two months for the part that's "on order." Another two weeks for the repairperson to show up. Now, the day has finally arrived. Your repairman has made a *definite* appointment for some time between dawn on Monday and Thursday midnight.

Now, your service person has a real challenge. Not in fixing your problem—he knows he can't do that. At least, not on his first trip. His challenge is to put you off, hang you up, let you down, and *still* have you come back for more.

I must compliment the service and repair industry on how cleverly they have met this challenge over the years. The standard reason for not finishing a project or not showing up on a job used to be, "My horse threw a shoe." For my younger readers, a horseshoe is a thin oblong piece of iron, shaped about the same as a horse's hoof. It is nailed to the bottom of the horse's hoof so he has something handy to throw at other horses.

After the invention of the automobile, it was a relatively simple step from the "horses-throwing-shoes" excuse to that of "My truck broke down." It wasn't long until that phrase was included in all service manuals under the title, "The no-show excuse that preserves customer good will."

"My truck broke down" became the accepted standard in the service industry until late in 1970, when Clarence Smudlow, a New York appliance repairman, introduced an ingenious refinement.

Mr. Smudlow was the father of "The part's on order" schtick.

People were becoming more sophisticated. Mr. Smudlow knew that folks were starting to suspect the notion that 90% of the trucks used by painters, carpenters, and electricians were inoperable 90% of the time.

"The part's on order" was new and different. It had a high-tech ring of authority. It also shifted the blame to a third party. The repairman became your partner in raging against the "rotten service and miserable treatment of those damn fools up there who can't even ship out a lousy part."

As the father of "The part's on order," Clarence Smudlow has become a sort of folk hero to the service and repair industry. Songs have been dedicated to him, and a life-size statue is slated for installation in our nation's capital—as soon as they get the rest of the parts.

In the mid-1980s, the computer changed everything. The next logical step for the savvy repairperson was to morph "The part's on order" gambit into a computer scam. "The computer's down" soon became the state-of-the-art excuse. Computer downing can excuse any mistake or no-show in today's technologically advanced world. Since most of us can't work our own computers, we can easily accept any computer-related alibi.

Because of faulty computers, messages aren't delivered. Schedules evaporate. Part numbers are incorrectly entered. Instructions can't be printed. Trucks don't have to *break* down; they can't even be *tracked* down. Cell phones don't get reception. Work orders can't be processed. Two-plus-two becomes a problem requiring such long-neglected mental processes that the computer-dependent dispatchers quit in helpless frustration.

"The computer's down" gambit was the culmination of years of applied effort. These historical facts can't help but make you admire the thought processes that have gone into the creative excuses used during the last few generations. Your service people may not be able to fix things, but they have always managed to come up with timely and ingenious reasons for not doing the job.

They are truly a remarkable group.

Viva la France

Pamela and I had been vacationing in France for several months. As most tourists do, we had spent the majority of our time inside the dimly lit interiors of French restaurants. On this particular night, three impeccably attired waiters marched proudly into the darkened dining room, a gleaming silver food tray perched atop each upraised arm. Their faces set in serious concentration, they placed the stunning silver covered serving pieces precisely in front of six stern-faced diners.

Each waiter stood at ramrod attention equidistant behind his pair of expectant diners. There was a moment of expectant silence. Then, with uncanny precision, three pairs of hands grasped the six silver dish covers. As if controlled by one hidden wire, the six covers spun aloft, held high above each waiter's head like shields of triumphant gladiators. *Violà!* The main course.

In the center of a hand-decorated porcelain plate the size of a meat platter was a complicated and beautiful food design consisting of eleven green peas, three miniature ears of corn, one medium carrot sliced into forty-seven pieces, a roast bird the size of a sparrow, two slivers of mushroom, a parsley sprig, and one small snail.

The renowned French cuisine is one of France's most treasured traditions. It's wonderful unless you are a vegetarian, or an American with an American appetite. Pamela and I were in our short-lived but very committed vegan period. That's one step above (or below) a vegetarian: vegans eat no animal products at all, not even eggs or dairy. Vegans make up for the lack of animal products by increasing their consumption of everything else.

We were able to handle our veganism through most of our travels, except in France. The French found it to be *un problème*. When we told a French waiter we did not eat meat or dairy, we usually got an argument. We would keep trying until we found a French chef brave enough to chance expatriation and serve our food the way we wanted it.

At one restaurant, when we mentioned we didn't eat meat, fish, eggs, or dairy, I thought the Maitre d' was going to explode in a cloud of French perfume. He asked us to please leave. It was as if we were soiling his restaurant. It made no difference to him that he had held a table for us. He wanted us gone.

We tried to maintain a modicum of composure as we left in complete disgrace. I tried to tell him in my best sign language that I understood his traditions. I told him we deserved to be thrown out of his wonderful restaurant. I told him we should be reported to the French government, our passports should be shredded, and our effigies burned in front of his restaurant. I said we should be thrown into the Bastille and left to rot. He agreed with it all, and further pronounced that it was not enough. I should be made to learn French—so we would better comprehend his contempt. We left the restaurant, our heads hanging in vegan shame.

Pamela and I spent nine weeks traveling in France and Italy. We don't speak a word of French or Italian, so you know we gained a deep understanding of both countries.

We learned that what they say about the French is not true. Well, at least some things are not true. The French, for example, love Americans. In fact, they love Americans more than they love their own people. Ask a French innkeeper whom he prefers as guests and he will tell you without pause: "Americans." He will then begin a long monologue about what's wrong with every country in the world, including France.

We also learned something about French traditions. A Frenchman will put himself into the poorhouse to maintain his family *chateau*. These stately homes have been owned by the same families for hundreds of years. Generations of dedicated *chateau*-own-ing dynasties have struggled with crumbling walls, leaking roofs, deteriorating foundations, deplorable smells, and countless inconveniences. Tearing them down, letting them sink into a pile of rubble, or changing their basic structure are simply not options.

For upkeep and expenses, some French families turn their *chateaux* and manor houses into bed-and-breakfast inns. They welcome visitors to share the smells, the deterioration, the inconveniences, the crumbling. They charge astronomical prices for the privilege of staying in one of their lovely, dilapidated old places.

After staying in bed-and-breakfast inns run by charming French innkeepers for several weeks, we developed a great fondness for this country's historic and wonderful traditions. I think the trouble between France and the United States started during that period when we got angry with the French and tried to rename French fries.

It just doesn't pay to fool around with French cooking.

We traveled directly from France to Italy. Since we didn't speak French or Italian, to us both languages were the same. The biggest difference we noticed between the two countries was this: when we ordered our vegan meal—unlike the Frenchman's "*un problème*," our Italian waiter would say, "*No problema!*"

Our waiter would then bring us the same meal he served to all the diners. If we complained, he would swear—with a broad smile and a big shrug—that it was exactly the way we ordered it.

242

Brutus and the Snake

Walk a Doberman, and you have plenty of room on the sidewalk. Women look faint and strong men cross the street. Brutus II would prance up and down with the Dobie's characteristic haughty gait, ears at point, eyes alert, body poised to attack. He was a magnificent animal. People would ask me whether he would bite. I did my best to uphold the breed's intimidating image. I would say he hadn't bitten anyone for almost a week.

But the sad truth was: let one person come within touching distance, and all poise would melt from this splendid beast. He would become a limp furry rag, panting for a kind word or touch. He would nuzzle anyone who came within his reach and put his long snout where it definitely did not belong.

Brutus II was the antithesis of the classic Doberman. The local Doberman Club refused our membership. They claimed Brutus was a sissy and would ruin the reputation of the entire breed. They said we should paint spots on him and call him a Dalmatian.

One day, Pamela opened the door to let Brutus outside. He jumped back and collided with her. There was a snake on the doormat. No way was that dog going to step over a snake to get outside. Our magnificent Doberman was fairly good at frightening rabbits and birds—if they ran in the opposite direction. But a snake? Forget it.

Pamela turned to me and said, "You will have to do something with that snake. Your dog won't go outside."

I said, "Snakes are not my thing. Let Brutus do something with it."

Pamela and the dog stood at the door expectantly—Brutus II well behind Pamela, with his ears straight up and his eyes glued to the snake. If he could talk, I am sure he would have said to me, "Well? *Do* something."

So I picked up the snake on the end of a broomstick and threw it over the fence. The dog watched the whole procedure from behind Pamela. When the snake slithered away into the bushes, Brutus went outside and attacked the doormat where the snake had been. He started tearing that doormat all to hell, barking and snarling. Those ferocious teeth of his were an awesome sight.

I grabbed the phone and called the Doberman Club. If they could get there in time, maybe they would reconsider our application.

"Does This Hurt?"

The last time I had a pain of any consequence was when I had my last physical. Dr. Costly gave me the usual "turn your head and cough" routine, and managed to drive his hand inside me far enough to *cause* the hernia he was so diligently searching for. I walked around with my insides aching for a month.

My previous physical had involved a "stress test." That's when you run on a treadmill with all kinds of wires hanging from your body. The wires are connected to a machine called an EKG to monitor your heart. Today the doctors are not satisfied if you merely pass the tests. They like to see how far they can go before you collapse...

> *The doctor entered the waiting room, sat down, paused dramatically, and said to the gathered relatives in his most sympathetic voice, "I'm so sorry. He looked perfectly healthy to me. Who knew he had a heart condition? He might have lived another twenty or fifty years, except for that stress test. It's something we'll just never know."*

During my last stress test, the nurse asked me to tell her if I had any chest pains. After about three minutes of running on that silly treadmill, I told her. She ran into the doctor's office and said, "The EKG Patient says his chest hurts." The doctor said, "They always say that. Tell him to keep running."

I used to like it much more when the doctor reminded me of

a kindly grandfather. We only called him when we were sick. He always came to the house. We never made him wait in some room with outdated magazines to read.

Old Doc Kindly would exude the aroma of medicines and cigars, and he'd smile and laugh. He would thump my back, and I would cough a couple times. Next would come the worn stethoscope. Listen and smile—listen and smile. Doc Kindly would open his case full of many colored pills. He would hum a happy tune as he put a few pills into a little container with instructions to take three each day for a week. I always got better.

I figure the mistake we make with doctors is that we tell them too much. With all their machines and tests, they should be able to figure out what's wrong without our help.

We ought to be able to go into a doctor's office and say, "I'm sick." When the doctor says, "What seems to be the trouble?" we'd say, "That's what I'm here to find out." If the doctor says, "Where do you hurt?" we could tell him, "In the same place where you pressed too hard the last time I was here."

Heaven Can Wait

There was a sharp crack—no other sound—and he was dead. My kindhearted wife came running into the living room, looked at the floor with a horrified glance, and said in a low, accusatory voice, "You killed him."

"You're damn right I killed him. He's guilty of breaking and entering, and he should have known better. He got what he deserved."

With those heroic words still echoing throughout the house, I flushed what was left of the cricket carcass down the toilet.

Pamela saves any insect that walks, runs, flies, crawls, creeps, slides, or slithers. She carefully captures them in a glass or has them crawl onto a piece of paper and then tenderly hands them to me, to toss outside to join their brethren.

Pamela also believes in her own version of heaven and hell. I'm not sure about heaven or hell or insects, so I stomp, splat, or spray and send them off to whatever section of Pamela's heaven or hell she thinks they belong in. It makes no difference to me. Let a higher power decide.

Pamela started raising such a ruckus over that dead insect, you would have thought I was the one in the wrong. I tried to explain it to her, using her logic: I did a favor for a criminal! I personally sent that insect to cricket heaven.

She said, "Don't be ridiculous."

Then she thought for a while and said, "Do you think insects go to heaven?"

That started me thinking. Take the black widow spider, for

instance. That winsome little lady sees a muscular eight-legged guy hanging out in the woodpile and invites him up to her apartment for a good time. Then in the morning—after she's had her fun—she eats him for breakfast. That doesn't seem like behavior that qualifies you for heaven. But in a way, it's not her fault. She's programmed for it.

Should the black widow go to heaven? According to my attorney, Carmine, absolutely yes. Not only that—she should be able to recover damages from the owner of the woodpile and child support from the estate of the deceased male spider.

I asked Pamela if she thought there would be fleas and ticks in a heavenly world. We hoped not in our dog's heavenly world. Yet don't fleas and ticks deserve to go to heaven? To their way of thinking, they're just trying to keep food on the table. I think they lead pretty righteous lives. At least they don't eat their mates.

You start not allowing things into heaven just because they bite or sting, and you're treading on dangerous territory. That's like interfering with the food chain. First thing you know, there won't *be* any heaven. We're already doing a pretty fair job of ruining things down here on earth—I think we should leave heaven alone.

Pamela and I kept knocking it around all day. We didn't come up with any answers, but we sure came up with a lot of questions. That's what happens when you're retired— you do a lot of thinking about heaven and hell. You begin to realize one or the other is not that far away.

The thought occurred to us that there just might be a separate insect heaven and a separate people heaven, and lots of separate heavens. I'm sure it's all figured out.

Personally, I kind of like the heaven I'm in, right here on Earth. Of course, it would help if the Republicans would listen a little less to God and a little more to the people. And it wouldn't hurt if the Democrats listened a little more to the Republicans and a little less to the media.

The Agony of the Ecstasy

As Pamela will confirm, I have (and have always had) a problem controlling my hormonal drives.

At the tender age of fifteen, I sold ladies' shoes in my father's store. One day we were visited by Jenny Bresthaven, past runner-up of the Miss Illinois beauty pageant. Jenny lost the Miss Illinois contest when she answered a question put to her by the judging committee. She was asked, "What do you love best about living in these great and wonderful United States of America?"

Jenny answered, "What I like best, about this great and wonderful country, that I live in, is that I am allowed to live with my boyfriend Philip, and no one cares that we aren't married."

This was during Reverend Elijah "Spud" Hall's tenth year as president of the judging committee. When he heard Jenny's answer, the good Reverend fell out of his chair and off the judge's platform. When he fell, Reverend Spud hit his head on the edge of the judge's stand. His face was bathed in blood from his slight but flowing wound. The Reverend rose from the ground like a bloody avenging angel. He surveyed the crowd, shook the blood from around his glazed eyes, and began to speak in tongues. The entire committee flew into pandemonium. All judging was halted while two doctors attended to the Reverend.

It was the end of the contest for poor Jenny Bresthaven. Of course, this was many years ago. That would never happen in today's open-minded society.

Even though she had lost the beauty contest, Jenny still needed shoes. And of all the lucky fifteen-year-olds in this unlucky world, it happened that I was to be tapped as Jenny's shoe salesman. Jenny was a stunning woman of statuesque proportions given to wearing tight sweaters and even tighter skirts. When she entered the store, I was "up." In retail parlance that meant it was my turn for the next customer. I was certainly "up" for this one. Jenny picked out a pair of shoes from our display, and I hurried to the back room to search for her correct size.

When I returned with her shoes, Jenny adjusted her exquisite bottom and arranged her tight skirt. She aligned her lithe limbs to insert her delicate feet into the shoes I offered. In performing these gyrations, the lady exhibited a significant expanse of perfectly formed inner thigh. By divine coincidence, at that precise moment my fifteen-year-old hormones locked onto the target they had been created to find.

As I sat on my shoe stool and assisted this fascinating lady into her shoes, her exhibitions had made it difficult for me to rise to a standing position without exposing myself to considerable embarrassment. My only consolation was that she had not tried on boots. I would never have lived through the experience.

Immobilized, I talked to the lady. I talked and talked some more. I talked about the rain. I talked about the snow. I talked about the mileage per gallon one could expect from a Ford as opposed to a Chevrolet. I talked about the Pythagorean Theory of Geometrically Opposed Angles. I was willing to talk about anything but curves.

I finally talked my hormones back to where they were a lot more comfortable and considerably less visible.

After this first encounter, Jenny thought I was the most intelligent and interesting person she had ever met. Subsequently, when she needed shoes, she always requested that I be the one to wait on her. She displayed the most varied and provocative wardrobe I had ever seen. She knew the discomfort she caused me. She had fun trying to talk me into standing when I preferred to remain sitting. She made my service in the shoe department the greatest combination of delight and agony I had experienced in my fifteen years.

I told Pamela this story of my youth, and she didn't find it amusing at all. I had no sooner finished my narrative than she insisted we go shopping together. She further insisted that I accompany her to the dressing room while she undressed and tried on various costumes.

After a few try-ons, the old hormones started acting up. At this stage in my life, while they are not as active as they once were, they can still get out of control. Especially where Pamela is concerned. When Pamela was sure she had accomplished her purpose, she got dressed and left the dressing room. Immobilized, I could not follow. She explained to the saleslady that I would probably be there for some time, and that I would be glad to explain the Pythagorean Theory of Geometrically Opposed Angles to anyone who wanted to listen.

Real Men, Chocks,
and the Taper Effect

When is the last time you saw a real man punch another on the shoulder and say, "Coach, I love the way you're doing your hair"?

Real men don't compliment other men.

Women compliment other women all the time. They compliment each other on their clothes, their makeup, their anything that strikes them as attractive or unusual. It's natural to them.

Pamela and I had spent the entire day trying to buy some shirts for me. For some unknown reason, men's shapes have changed in the past few years. All men are tapered now, and shirts are tapered to match the new figures.

I am tapered too, but in the wrong direction. Between the shirt's taper and my taper lies a vast expanse of stretched material and protesting buttons.

Pamela says she loves my figure and she wouldn't trade one of me for a hundred Arnold Schwartzeneggers. I admire my wife's taste in all things, and damned if I will start to doubt her expertise about bodies.

I was recuperating from the trauma of shirt-shopping with an overflowing platter of fettuccine. I have found that is one of the few things that will restore my natural good humor.

I can now eat pasta with a complete lack of guilt. I read, somewhere that escapes me, that if you eat pasta before the year 2015, you can do it without gaining any weight.

A detailed scientific study has proven that pasta contains

complex carbohydrates that are not only non-fattening, but in the jargon of the scientist are "chock full of energy." These chocks were not discovered until 1986. Some of you may remember that prior to 1986, we were told to avoid pasta like the plague if we ever wanted to lose any weight.

The reason I terminate the pasta-eating period in 2015 is because my inside medical sources inform me that a new study is investigating other types of chocks in pasta. It is feared these new chocks may be full of calories. The results of this study will not be released until early 2015.

My advice to those of you who love pasta is to load up fast, before it becomes fattening again.

Sitting across the room in the Spaghetti House was a man tapered about the same way I am. His shirt fit perfectly. Pamela suggested I go to Perfect Shirt's table and tell him I liked his shirt and ask him where he got it. I told her real men don't do that. You'd never see John Wayne do that to another man.

She said, "Don't be ridiculous. John Wayne never had the kind of trouble you do finding shirts."

Sometimes there's no arguing with Pamela.

I swaggered over to Perfect Shirt and drawled, "Pilgrim, that's a great-looking shirt you got on. Where'dja get it?"

He very slowly wiped the spaghetti sauce from his scarred and swarthy face. He looked up and snarled, "You lookin' to eat your tie, buddy?"

I slunk back to the table and joined Pamela. She asked me whether the man had told me where he got his shirt. I told her he didn't remember, but he did say that he just adored my tie.

"I Say, Buffie..."

Montecito, an exclusive upscale suburb of Santa Barbara, California, has some of the most expensive real estate in the country. Elegant estates valued in the millions of dollars stretch their acreage around the base of the Santa Ynez Mountains, and the sun glistens on the sea as if the wealthy had tossed a few of their jewels on its surface. The scattered oil derricks poking skyward out of the ocean seem to be giving "the finger" to the rest of the world.

I was working on an article about this picturesque coastal village. Pamela and I checked into the Santa Barbara Biltmore for a weekend while I gathered my information.

The Biltmore is a world-class hotel on twenty-two beautiful manicured acres in the heart of Old Montecito. This Mediterranean style resort was lovingly constructed in the '20s, and has since been visited by royalty and heads of state from all over the world.

It is a writer's nirvana. With a little encouragement, I could compose a few thousand words in an environment like this. With more money and even less encouragement, I could write a novel. I felt like Ernest Hemingway, in Spain, between wars.

There are events we all remember. The first date. The first kiss. The night we ended up in the slammer. Our first night in the Biltmore was one of those memorable events.

Pamela and I had retired early. Around midnight, the room started to shake and the windows began to rattle. Even in the dark

I could see Pamela's eyes, opened wide. "My God," she whispered. Pamela always whispers in hotel rooms. "It's an earthquake!"

Then the Amtrak engineer announced his train's passage with a blast from his horn that Gabriel would have envied. We started to laugh in relief and spent the rest of the night betting who would be the first to feel the earthshaking vibrations before the next train passed by.

Incredibly, a railroad runs through this beautiful and luxurious community. The railroad easement runs about fifty feet from the boundary of the Biltmore property. A couple of times each night, Amtrak invades this playground of the rich and famous like a ghetto blaster at a harp recital. The train music starts with a faint humming in the tracks and grows increasingly louder with each passing second, until it becomes a roar. Then the ground shudders in resonance with the "Amtrak Heavy Metal Concert."

The concert always ends with a blast from an overzealous engineer who must have graduated *summa cum laude* from Train Horn Blowing School.

As we lay in bed that first night in our hotel room, Pamela and I speculated: was it possible that this was some anti-elitist plot? Was the same noisy blast designed to trumpet bison from train tracks in earlier days now being used to explode the wealthy from their beds in the pre-dawn hours?

Or could this be the perfect combination of the Peter Principle and an engineer "around the bend?" Long past his level of competence, he approaches the outskirts of this quiet and refined community. He compensates for his lack of skill with an endless series of deafening horn bursts, which echo long after he has thundered past the town.

Pamela whispered, "Methinks there's more here than meets the eye." Pamela often says "methinks" in hotel rooms.

We turned over and tried to nab as much sleep as possible between train visits.

The next morning, we complained to the distinguished-looking manager of the hotel about Amtrak's earth-shaking clamor. He stared at me, and then at Pamela.

He said, "Train? What train?"

It was like being thrown into an old episode of the Twilight Zone.

I began conducting research for my article. I wanted it to include the entire spectrum of Montecito life. With Pamela at my side, I interviewed scores of Montecito residents. I conferred with heads of state and captains of industry. I spoke to movie stars and to the moguls who hire and fire them.

I talked to people in their $1.9 million teardown shacks. I harangued them in their multi-million dollar mansions. I spoke to people in Mercedes automobiles as well as those who drove Rolls Royce motor cars. I painstakingly surveyed the wide variety of Montecito citizenry, from the less fortunate upper class wealthy to the filthy rich.

There is not a single resident of Montecito who is even aware that a train runs through their village. No one hears it. No one sees it. It is very difficult to find anyone who even knows what a train looks like. Trains run in Los Angeles. Trains run in Denver, New York, Chicago, and maybe even in Paris.

But any of Montecito's residents will tell you: *no* train runs through *their* town.

I Haven't Even Started
and I'm Almost Done

When I was a kid, I used to thumb through a new book until I found a key word like "breast" or "silken bodice," or if I was very lucky, "throbbing member." I knew then that it was time to quit thumbing and start reading. Scenery was irrelevant, dialogue a waste of time. When does she rip off his clothes and slam him down on the bed? That's all I wanted to know. Even then, my attention span was not that great.

In the cinema, they know all about attention spans. A movie can't even wait for a scene to change.

SCENE: *The main characters are stranded in a rowboat in the middle of the Pacific Ocean.*

SOUND: *A telephone rings.*

As there are no cell phone relay stations in the middle of the ocean (yet), I know there are only two alternatives: either the rowboat is hooked in to a telephone cable running on the bottom of the Pacific, or the director has jumped the sound to the next scene. That technique speeds up the action by as much as one to three seconds.

I once watched a movie for over an hour. It portrayed a man's struggle to cross the Sahara Desert—not a drop to drink, his lips parched and cracked. The camera kept moving from his pain-wracked face to the burning sun in the cloudless sky.

"Water—water," he croaked. Then he fell, exhausted, to the sand.

Just as he fell, a toilet flushed. I thought, "Thank God, water." Wrong. The director had overlaid the sound from the next scene. Not only had they saved three seconds, they had really added some class to the drama.

Speaking of class, today's movies move things so fast there isn't even time for the actors to take bathroom breaks. They just put a toilet in the scene and film the actors as they use it. It's the writer's job to work this action into the script.

The producers of TV commercials are also experts at timesaving. They squeeze thirty-eight seconds into a thirty-second spot. That's a savings of eight seconds. It's done by speeding up the video track. The sound generally goes with it. If it's just a little out of sync, what the hell, nobody listens to commercials anyway—they're too damn loud.

TV can promote an entire who-done-it (including who done it) in a fifteen-second flash of tonight's coming attractions. Fifteen seconds—that's all you have to watch. That can save as much as an hour and a half.

It can't be long until some sharp film producer figures out how to run all those car chases backwards. That way we would be through with them before they started—another saving of at least forty minutes out of most action movies. And why can't the bad guy be killed in the first scene? The next logical step would be not to make the movie at all. Just think of all the time that would save.

There is one timesaving device that displays true genius. It is TV's fifteen-second political sound bite. In this short span, we are privileged to see a condensed presentation of the lifetime of sacrifice, infallibility, and sacred inspirational service of our favorite political candidate. His love of God and country and his thriving crop of perfectly coiffed hair is brilliantly displayed in front of the flags of his beloved state and country.

Can you imagine, when God made the world, how much time He could have saved with these techniques? He probably could have done the whole shebang in ten or twelve hours instead of six days.

This discourse was originally going to be a lot longer, but my computer just started barking. Either I've been typing on a dog, or the scene has changed.

Holiday on the Tarmac

Pamela and I were in the Seattle airport on Christmas Eve, awaiting our connecting flight to Vancouver. I looked outside and saw a full-blown blizzard raging.

"How wonderful," someone exclaimed. "A white Christmas!"

She was too far away to strangle.

The scene outside was surreal. I could see the stacked planes from the airport's windows. They looked like shivering ghost-machines reflected in the blurry evening light. Half-tracks with their chemical tanks and attached hoses were frantically spraying some chemical (probably lethal) all over the planes. I was convinced they were de-icing the wings so the planes could load up, take off, and then immediately crash into Puget Sound. It was a diabolical plan to free up the tarmac.

From time to time, a uniformed captain (or lieutenant or unfortunate steward who had drawn the short stick) would appear outside for a brief inspection of a frozen plane. A mechanic would also skate his way to the plane. There would be a huddle. They would look very official, flap their arms to keep warm, and peer at the frozen equipment. Their breath fogging in the cold, they would shake their heads in agreement: no takeoff yet. Having performed their ritual, they would scurry back to the airport's warmth. That would end the official ceremony for another hour or so.

While I was watching this scene and suffering my usual holiday blues, Pamela, cut from another cloth, was in heaven. The flakes were falling, the holiday music was playing, and she was going to a foreign land for a new adventure. She was humming Jingle Bells. All was right in her world.

Finally, we got the long-awaited call. Flight 225 to Vancouver was ready to take off. We would board at gate 13—not an auspicious number.

We were told to board the plane by walking down exposed and icy stairs leading to the tarmac. From the tarmac, we were to ascend another flight of frozen stairs to our assigned seats in the aircraft.

Anyone slipping and/or falling would be left on the tarmac to die.

The world is a scary place. Foolishly and recklessly, we place a lot of trust in our fellow human beings. When I speed along at sixty miles an hour, I trust that the corkscrew road of the Big Sur highway will not lead me over a cliff at the next blind curve. When I turn on my bedroom lamp, I trust I will not be electrocuted. When the waiter dips his thumb in my mashed potatoes, I trust that Swine Flu is not the special of the day.

I thought of trust as I fastened my seat belt and looked out the frozen window. Who okayed this flight—the captain, or the steward who drew the short stick?

Our plane sat on the tarmac for about an hour. We watched the worsening weather. The passengers made stale jokes to show how brave they were. Finally, the intercom crackled with the announcement that we were to deplane. The flight had been canceled. Oddly, there seemed to be more smiles than frowns. We were all going to live to crash some other day.

We all gingerly descended the icy stairway to the tarmac and placed our boarding passes (folded into the shape of Christmas ornaments) on the frozen bodies of the two passengers who had slipped and fallen when we had boarded the plane.

Pamela was still humming Jingle Bells. I think her brain was frozen.

Deciphering

I have a friend who says he wants a divorce and then sets about buying a whole houseful of new furniture.

I have another friend who says he hates the automobile business and then adds another agency to his chain.

My daughter says she wants to move out of town and then starts arranging financing to buy a house just down the block from the one she already owns.

The neighbor says he hates kids, and two weeks later, his wife is pregnant.

What's going on?

If you just listen to what people say, life will be a constant mystery. People usually don't mean what they say, or they don't listen to themselves talk. The first friend doesn't want a divorce. He thinks his wife does. He is protecting his ego. When she said she wanted new furniture, he jumped to please her.

My other friend goes to work at 7 a.m. every morning and works until 9 p.m. every night. He doesn't need the money. He is a millionaire five times over. He loves the business. He just likes to complain.

The neighbor had been trying to get his wife pregnant for five years and finally gave up. He then went about trying to convince himself and everybody else that he had hated kids all along. When he quit concentrating on making babies, both he and his wife started having a good time. Not only did she get pregnant, but her acne cleared up.

The trick is not to listen, but to decipher. When Pamela says, "I think the plants are dying in the greenhouse," what she means is that it's time for me to water.

When she asks, "When are we going on another trip together?" she means I'm not paying her enough attention.

But when she says, "I don't care what it costs," she means exactly that.

An Old Fiddle
Can Still Play a Good Tune

I believe you are all entitled to a report concerning my life as a younger man. You may remember that when I turned sixty, I decided to become ten years younger. It didn't work too well at sixty, but it sure works at seventy.

It took me a while to realize that there is a difference between *claiming* you are ten years younger and actually *losing* ten years. At seventy I don't tell people I am ten years younger. In fact, I never mention my age. It's nobody's business how old I am. I just decided to *become* ten years younger.

I was born very close to the witching hour of midnight on Friday, October 31st. Pamela claims my mother was a witch. Was that aimed at my real mother? Or did she mean I was born of a witch and raised by a woman who *called* herself my mother? I don't know. I prefer not to pursue the subject.

Being born on Halloween has always been a bonus. Halloween heralds the beginning of the festive fall season. Every year, people welcome the holiday season and celebrate my birthday at the same time.

This last birthday was the best one I ever had. All in all, losing ten years was a pretty smart move. Why not? Age never got me anywhere except to the doctor's office. Rodney Dangerfield was right: you don't get no respect. You would think the nurse could call me Mr. Harris. No way. It's "Burt, hang this out." Or, "Burt, cover that up." What's the advantage of being older if nobody ever calls you "Mister"?

Ten years was a good choice. It's easy to remember. Even at this younger age, my memory is not as good as it used to be. Ten was also a good number because less than ten is rather meaningless. Physically, two years or four years wouldn't have made much difference. With ten years, you can really tell something is different.

Since I became younger, I notice I can walk a lot farther and my hair seems thicker. Younger girls smile at me. Of course, I am not as smart as I was, because nothing educates like experience. Ten years is a lot of experience to lose.

All in all, things have worked out pretty well. It feels great to be young again. I may be ready to ease into the next decade when the time comes—or I may not. I will look around in ten years and if I don't like it, I'll just lop off another ten or twenty years.

Pamela is aggravated that I'm now younger than she is. She can hardly wait for her next birthday. My ten years impressed her so much, she figures she will drop fifteen. I told her to be careful. I am having enough trouble keeping up with her now. If she gets too young, it could kill me.

Pills

I've got a pill for every ill,
And a color for every pill.

It's red for my heart—
But red makes me fart.
Green cures the gas,
But gives me a rash.

My cholesterol is down
Because I take brown.
But brown makes me sad,
So a pink makes me glad.

It's blue for a screw!
(No one knows it but you.)
But blue makes me see
How great it used to be.

When my back aches a lot,
It's a purple pill I pop.
But purple causes vertigo;
I take a white to make it go.

White stops vertigo for sure,
But added weight comes with the cure.
I can't ever seem to win,
No matter what the pillmakers spin.

The winners are the makers of pills;
They sell us out for dollar bills.
There is no color without its cost.
Color me colorless before I'm lost!

Contact Me

The whole adventure in optometry started because I was having difficulty reading. The proof of my failing vision was when Pamela congratulated me on finally coming to maturity. She had passed naked in front of me, and I hadn't ogled. I wondered: what other visions had I missed?

The examination had gone well. The doctor's assistant had been impressive with her capable and efficient manipulation of the machinery. The colored lights were fascinating, and she had let me play with some of the dials.

Now was the time to ask her the hard questions about the contact lenses. Do they hurt? Is there any pain? Do they sting? Are you positive they don't hurt? You are telling me that I will never feel any pain at all?

I decided to contract for the contacts.

The assistant displayed another eye chart on the wall and asked me to read the smallest line I could see. I said I would appreciate it if she could make the room brighter, because I was having difficulty finding the display. Right after that, she put the drops in my eyes and gave me cookies and milk.

This wasn't so bad. I was getting more heroic by the minute.

After all the tests were over and while I was still vulnerable and virtually blind, the door to the examining room swung open and in came a tall, sober-faced man with military bearing. Dr. Seymour had found time to visit me for a few moments. The doctor told me my contact lenses would be ready in about two weeks. He warned me to drive carefully and handed me a white cane.

During the next few weeks, Pamela thought nothing about going around the house nude, apparently enjoying a false sense of security. She didn't know what I had discovered. While seeming to read and squinting very hard, if I looked out the left side of my right eye at an exact angle of fifteen degrees over the cover of a book, I could see pretty well.

I kept it to myself.

The third week after my exam, the doctor's receptionist called to tell me my contacts had arrived. As I drove to Dr. Seymour's office, I found myself wondering if I had asked his assistant if the contact lenses would hurt.

I always ask the doctor's assistant my doctor questions. Doctors don't like it when you ask them questions. That's why they teach them in doctor school to charge extra for those unwelcome queries. $100 extra for questions about what they are going to do to you. $150 and up for questions about what their diagnosis really means. There is a surcharge if they have to use more than twelve doctor words.

As I drove into the parking structure, a twelve-year-old attendant with the name "Spike" emblazoned on his Polo shirt took my car and twenty bucks. I listened to him burn rubber for three stories before he finally crashed into a parking space somewhere in the bowels of the building.

I had almost read my way through the 1948 Argosy magazine in the waiting room when my name was called. I was ushered into a smaller room where I resumed reading the Argosy. I waited for the doctor as he finished his two-hour lunch and performed his subsequent 2 p.m. inspection to "count the house" in the waiting room.

Dr. Seymour finally entered the room, pried open my eyelids and rammed the contact lenses home. The nurse gave him a high-five and said, "Good job, Doc."

It's been six weeks since I got my contacts and they hurt like hell. The doc's assistant keeps telling me I will regain my vision any day now. Meanwhile, both my cars are in the body shop.

I can't even see to find my white cane.

The Flying Dog

He arrived in a cage, his black eyes staring out, unafraid. He was only three months old, and this was his first time away from home. It had been minus 10 degrees when they put him on the plane in northern Minnesota. They had bumped, scraped, and dropped his cage. He had traveled almost two thousand miles in a dark hold with no company but a pile of smelly luggage. The ride had been full of strange tilts, turns, and noises. His dismal prison had vibrated constantly from the roar of powerful jet engines.

Now he was finally on the ground—or at least on something that wasn't moving. The noise and vibrations had stopped, and things were quiet except for some idiot who kept smiling and saying, "Hello, Brutus. Hello, Brutus. Come on out."

Brutus III, descendant of a fierce Doberman ancestry, was the third in our ever-hopeful attempts to snag ourselves a watchdog. He had arrived in Monterey. Did you know that until twenty years ago, Dobermans were considered untrainable except by professionals? I didn't know that. What miracle happened twenty years ago? I am still waiting for it to happen to me. I spend $1,000 to purchase each dog and $3,000 each time for obedience lessons. The only thing I keep learning is that my Dobermans are smarter than I am.

For his long trip, our little puppy had been placed in a cage sized for a full-grown dog. I couldn't reach back far enough to get him out. No matter how persuasively I coaxed, he wouldn't budge. We had been waiting twelve weeks for this little shrimp, and now I couldn't get him out of his cage.

268

Looking at it from the dog's perspective, he had a point. About five hours ago, he had been sold a bill of goods from a sweet-talking somebody who looked suspiciously similar to this idiot who was now trying to coax him out of his cage. The other somebody had told him everything would be okay. Then more somebodies had hauled his cage out and put him beside a roaring dragon that had devoured him. Now that the dragon had spit him out, he had no inclination to be talked into anything.

Brutus III had to be asking himself, "What are they trying to sweet-talk me into this time—the slaughterhouse? No thanks."

Once burned, twice careful, and he had backed to the rear of the cage where he sat and stared stonily at his latest tormentor. I felt the blanket on the floor of his cage. Everything was dry and clean, but he had been confined for five hours, and I knew things weren't going to be dry and clean much longer. I had tried everything short of dumping over his cage, but nothing seemed to work. I looked at Pamela and shrugged in frustration.

"Maybe you can do something."

Pamela took over. She began to explain to our little Dobie how lucky he was. He was in California now, the best state in the union. Not only was he in California, he was on the Monterey Peninsula—the best place in the world!

She told him we were going to love him and baby him. She said the temperature here never got below perfect or above ideal, it rained only ten days out of the year, and the skies were always filled with rainbows. She told him about the ocean that foams and rolls and the surf that tickles a puppy's feet.

She explained to Brutus III that there were sand dunes to run in and rabbits to chase and deer to watch. There was a beach full of wonderful smells where dogs could roam free. She suggested that any self-respecting dog would give all his buried bones just to visit this place, and he—lucky dog—was going to live here all year 'round.

I don't know whether nature won out, or whether my wife's persuasive words finally got to him, but he finally emerged from his cage. The gutsy little guy walked out, looked around, stretched, shook himself, adjusted his six-gun and sauntered over to the nearest grass patch, where he spent a long time doing what a guy's gotta do.

He didn't utter a sound. He just looked both of us in the eye and sneezed with what seemed to be contempt. We watched in respectful silence as he ambled quietly back to re-enter his cage. He lay down on his blanket and fixed us with a black steely stare, as if to say, "Okay punks, I'm ready for you now."

Blockhead

I once read an article about a sculptor. He said he could look at a piece of marble and see a figure trapped inside. He said that he didn't really sculpt—all he did was chip away the marble and allow the figure to escape. That may be an old story to sculptors, but to me it was a revelation.

I had always wanted to be a sculptor. I thought, after I learned the secret, that the rest would be easy. I started looking in stone quarries and marble places for pieces of marble that had somebody hidden inside, beckoning me to turn them loose. I went to every marble workplace within 100 miles. I never found anyone trapped in the stones.

I would go up to a piece of marble in the back lot and ask the quarry worker to turn it this way and that way. I would look at the ends and at the back and the front and the top and the bottom. I could never find anybody in there. Then I would knock on the marble. I figured if the figure were asleep, I'd wake it up and then it would call to me.

The quarry worker would usually assume I was a bereaved person who had a strange way of picking out a gravestone. Sooner or later, even the most understanding of them would give up in disgust.

Moving marble by yourself can get heavy, and I was becoming impatient to find my imprisoned friends. The quarry workers were beginning to look upon me as slightly odd, and I was not welcomed the way I had been at first.

After a while it occurred to me that maybe marble was not my thing. Maybe marble figures didn't like me and preferred to be liberated by a different type of fellow, or maybe even a woman. I wondered if what I'd read about marble could be true for brass or iron. Who knew what delightful people and things could be silently waiting within an iron prison—waiting for my powers to deliver them to a grateful world?

The junkyard became my next target. Junk dealers are much more tolerant than marble quarry workers. They don't care what you do—just don't try to feed their dogs. I spent days knocking on iron and turning brass pieces over and over, trying to find a little man or woman clamoring for liberty. Nothing. I was becoming very depressed.

One day I came home from a particularly trying and frustrating hunt. I was considering giving up iron and brass, and trying wood sculpting instead. My next venture would be to the lumberyard, or maybe a trip to the live Christmas tree farm in the valley. I had been studying tree stumps as a kind of side venture for a few days, and I thought I saw the figure of a squirrel in one of them. I became very excited until the little fellow ran away.

When I got home, my wife was sitting at the kitchen table sculpting the figure of a beautiful young girl. I asked her what the hell she was doing. I told her that I was the sculptor in the family, and she had a lot of nerve infringing on my territory.

Pamela told me she was sorry, but she was cleaning out the garage and had come across this lump of clay. She saw the figure of a girl inside, and she was just setting her free.

I really got mad. I had been knocking myself out looking in marble places and junk yards and lumber yards and forests, had combed the area for miles around—and my wife, in her innocent way, had just stumbled upon a lousy piece of clay, in our own garage, with a figure trapped inside.

The Twelve Hour Workday

My day begins at 6 a.m. when Brutus III starts howling for bathroom privileges. There is no way you can ignore a Doberman. If he doesn't get what he wants, he gives you a shove. These dogs are very muscular. A Doberman shove can lift you right out of bed. If that doesn't work, they have a little trick with a yawn. They open wide, show you their choppers, and make clicking sounds. You figure, what the hell, it's late, it's past 5 a.m.—I think I'll take the dog for a walk.

Brutus and I have an understanding. He gets up at six o'clock and we start the day. He works a full twelve hours. He patrols and barks. He frightens squirrels until they retreat up trees. He snarls at snails and chases objects only he can see. He does this until 6 p.m. He doesn't like to be disturbed after that.

We have a home fire alert bell about ten feet from our bedroom. We all sleep in the same room. Brutus III, Pamela, and Burt—in that order. The dog has the big queen bed; my wife and I share the single.

The guys who installed the fire alert bell used to work as firemen. They installed a commercial alarm that clangs like oversize cymbals. It shakes the windows and rattles your brains. It also signals a monitoring service. The service calls the Pebble Beach security guards and the fire department.

Last month, in the middle of a horrendous coastal storm, the fire alarm went off at 2:30 a.m. I thought it had to be a false alarm. No self-respecting fire would even attempt to get started during a hurricane.

The bell was clanging. The rain was coming down in torrents. The wind was howling. I was running around half dressed trying to figure out how to turn off the damned racket.

I finally located the reset button and turned off the alarm. I was just beginning to breathe normally when I saw red lights coming up the road. It was the security police and, close on their heels, the hook-and-ladder from the fire department. They were headed hell-bent to put out the big fire.

The whole menagerie pulled into the driveway, complete with flashing lights, sirens, and hissing air brakes. Firemen lined up with axes at the ready, helmets dripping with rain, ladders rattling. The security police were armed and prepared for battle.

They could see there was no fire. They could also see a frustrated man standing outside, half dressed and dripping wet, looking very embarrassed, telling them it was all a terrible mistake.

With expressions of disgust on their dripping faces, they started to leave. One of the security policemen took out a notebook and thumbed through a couple of wet pages. He said, "We got you down for having a dog. A vicious attack Doberman. Where is he? If you don't have him anymore, I should take it out of my notes."

I told them. "He doesn't get up until six. You might want to put his schedule in your notebook. He works from 6 a.m. to 6 p.m."

Outlaw Cameras, Not Guns

I don't like having my picture taken. The only thing I hate worse than someone taking my picture is when people want to show me *their* pictures. I have to hear how bad she looks. How fat or skinny he seems. She has to explain that the zit on her nose is the first pimple she's had since high school. I know better: I've known her since high school. I realize this picture memorializes the only time she ever had just *one* zit.

This whole picture-taking business is very aggravating. It makes it impossible to lie to your children. Show your kids an old picture of you as a skinny, vacant-eyed teenager, staring with slack jaw into a camera lens. Then try to convince them that all your teachers thought you were going to become President of the United States.

Perhaps my favorite person is the one who looks at a photo of me and says, "My God, is that thin person really you and *what happened to all your hair?*" After I have shot that person, I would like to take aim at grandparents. Those lovable people who, with or without your expression of interest, will let fall from their wallets that plastic photo album that unfolds from their navel to the ground.

Photographers are the only people I ever wanted to shoot. Does that make cameras more dangerous than guns? It makes me realize that cameras—not guns—can kill people. Maybe the National Rifle Association is right. Let's keep our assault weapons and outlaw cameras.

When we were back in Bullneck, my friend Frank won a $1,000 first prize in an amateur photo contest. His picture of a dripping icicle, dimly lit by the winter sun and displaying the colors of the rainbow, was a work of art.

I had a camera back then, too. It was just about the most expensive thing I owned, but it never took very good pictures. The photos were always out of focus or missing heads or feet. I finally got tired of my camera's off-center and blurry images and gave it away.

It was the same camera Frank used to shoot his first-prize-winning $1,000 photo.

"It's Only a Flesh Wound"

I never knew what a hammertoe was until I got one. I was minding my own business when my toe decided to hammer the entrance to my house about one inch wider than it is. In the battle of doorframe vs. toe, the doorframe clearly won. My toe hurt like the devil for about a day, and then seemed to be all right. I was willing to let it end there.

Evidently, the toe thought differently. It began to think it really *was* a hammer. It decided to specialize in widening door entries. "HammerToe" decided the bathroom doorframe also needed enlarging. This time the frame not only won, but decided to teach HammerToe a lesson. It broke the bugger. My toe was bent into a ninety-degree angle and getting bigger and meaner looking by the minute.

Why is it that whenever I have the slightest accident, I end up in the emergency ward of Community Hospital? Why can't I be more like the guys in the movies or on TV?

A dozen men fight with bare fists, and the blows sound like cannon shots. Fists are flying and bodies are falling. The hero is pummeled, kicked and knifed. He is shot, speared, broken and dragged. He falls down cliffs and turns over in automobiles. He jumps out of windows and falls out of trees. They drag him behind horses and hit him with cars. He is handcuffed, tied, twisted, bent, strangled, burned, hacked, sawed, frozen, drowned, cut, suffocated, and drugged.

The hero smiles. He wipes away the trace of blood that trickles engagingly from the corner of his mouth. He turns to the sexy lady at his side and mutters, "It's only a flesh wound."

Why can't I be like that? Why can't I reach down and straighten that toe with a heroic yank, look my adoring wife in the eye and say, "Hell, it was nothing but a flesh wound. Pass me another steak."

I'll tell you why—because I protect my heart now. I don't eat steaks.

As my visits to Community Hospital are fairly regular events, the nurses treat me like a long-lost friend.

My last trip had something to do with a trash masher and a finger. After they gave me a tranquilizer, one nurse held my right hand while the doctor sewed up my left. A second nurse stroked my head and told me what a brave person I was.

It is always important that Pamela accompany me on a trip to the emergency room. It's a revelation to compare notes with Pamela afterward. She knows all about doctoring. She used to be a registered nurse, until she started fainting at the sight of blood. I never hear a doctor say anything bad. Pamela hears nothing but bad news.

Pamela is clued into the secret signals all doctors send. A smile is merely a cover-up for the grave news of a deadly disease. A sigh is a sign that an exotic and debilitating South American fever has been diagnosed. Coughing is a sympathetic comment on an incurable lung problem.

If the doctor talks about the rain or the cold, I assume he is discussing the weather. Pamela is sure he is telling his patient how to dress on the way to the hospital.

I didn't want to take HammerToe to Emergency. I knew that after the visit, Pamela would reveal all the ominous signals I had missed. Visions of amputations and permanently crooked digits crossed my mind.

We went together anyway. The doctor on duty touched the toe and I screamed. The doctor said, "Wow, that's one of the worst-looking broken toes I've ever seen. That's got to be about a ninety-degree angle. It must hurt like hell." And then he laughed.

I don't know what secret message Pamela got from that, but she started laughing, too. I didn't see anything funny about a busted toe. If either one of those laughing smart-asses had a bet on the Forty-Niners and I was the kicker, they sure as hell wouldn't be laughing.

Pamela and the doc had barely wrapped up their little private moment when Dr. Laughalot saw my eye twitch and said, "I think your toe must have affected your eye, because it's twitching." That sent them both off again.

Pamela said, "Does this mean Burt and I can never have sex again? Or do we just have to stop using his toe?" Then both of those damn fools really broke up.

I was getting madder by the second, and my swollen toe was shooting pains all the way to my hair. I thought about the TV hero and wondered what he would have done. But there was no way of knowing. All he had ever suffered was a lousy flesh wound.

Then a horrible thought struck. What if they weren't kidding? Was it possible that Dr. Laughalot was sending one of those secret messages Pamela was always picking up? What if my toe really *could* affect my sex life?

I made a mental note to ask Pamela, when we got home, what the doctor really meant.

Anyone for Lunch?

We boarded a single-engine Cessna that looked as if it had been used to carry mail when Lindbergh was doing the deliveries. The pilot looked about fourteen years old and had a case of acne that threatened to explode all over the plane's control panel. It wouldn't have made much difference. Most of the glass covering the instrument dials was broken or missing, and the needles were smothered with spider webs and insect carcasses. There were patches of fabric glued to the fuselage. We wondered what they covered. We were afraid to ask.

Pamela and I had been traveling in Africa for several months. We thought we had gotten used to the condition of the short-hop airplanes. However, we weren't quite prepared for this day's journey. We settled into the dilapidated seats, strewn like piles of firewood on each side of the fuselage. We assumed the forced smiles you might reserve for attending your own funeral. The passengers behind us said something in Spanish and genuflected. Pamela muttered some half-remembered fragments of The Lord's Prayer.

We took our last close-up look at Africa's dry earth spotted with the dung of animals who wisely transported themselves as nature intended. We wondered who had been foolish enough to invent flying.

The plane's engine shuddered, sputtered and spit, and then stopped. The pilot said something unintelligible. The engine shuddered and spit again. The plane bumped and jerked its way onto the dirt runway. It gathered speed like a three-legged turtle until the only readable dial wavered its needle to an unbelievable twenty-five miles per hour.

The Spanish couple started yelling and pointed out the broken glass window. The child pilot finally looked out to notice a half-naked man frantically waving a soiled cloth and screaming at the plane. The engine choked to a stop.

The half-naked man climbed onto the wing, reached into the innards of the exposed engine compartment, and grasped an oil can—its snout still poking into the oil intake pipe. He jerked it out. With a satisfied smile, the "mechanic" carefully placed a cap on the intake pipe and threw the empty oil can to the ground. He jumped from the plane, stood at rigid attention, and then waved his soiled flag wildly in a frenetic signal for the pilot to take off. Our pilot grunted, adjusted his goggles, and off we took.

We were officially on our way to Phunga Camp in South Africa.

The balance of the flight was reasonably uneventful. The unfolding sight of African veldt was spellbinding. We flew at low level along the savanna. Our plane cast a shadow on the ground that resembled a giant speeding animal. The sound of the engine frightened the herds of grazing animals. We looked out from the cracked windows of our plane and watched them run for safety.

About the time we started congratulating ourselves on having survived our two-hour trip without incident, our pilot went into a series of frightening vertical maneuvers. It made us think he had either lost control of his plane or his mind. He finally pointed our trembling plane into a shallow dive that took us so low over the grass, he should have had a mower attached.

We collected our breath and saw a worse-for-wear windsock, disinterestedly drooping from a crooked pole. Our pilot buzzed the grassy spot a couple of times to scatter the grazing animals that were in his appointed path. He waved a red flag from his window, evidently signaling to someone that he was going to land (or parachute from!) the plane. We were approaching a typical African landing field. The more "sophisticated" airports had field attendants to scatter the wild animals before the planes landed.

As soon as we touched down, a Land Rover roared its dusty way to our landing spot and two immaculately dressed attendants greeted us with grins and handshakes. "Welcome to Phunga Camp," they intoned in unison, as they extended documents for us to sign.

Our escorts explained, with smiles, that the documents must be signed before they could transport us to Phunga Camp. It was a new regulation. Apparently the last group of tourists had been rather careless. There had been a bit of an "incident" with lions.

The episode in question had happened the previous week. On advice of their attorneys, the Phunga management was now insisting that new arrivals waive their rights to sue should there be another "incident." The details were not specified. We didn't have much choice. It was sign away our rights or return with our pilot—who suddenly looked eleven years old instead of fourteen. We all opted to sign.

Our Phunga Camp chauffeurs congratulated our pilot on completing his first solo flight. The child pilot grunted, adjusted his goggles, revved his sputtering engine into its bone-jarring rhythm, and flew off into the wild blue yonder.

Pamela and I thought we were seasoned African travelers. We had gone on safari in other camps so many times we lost count. We had seen elephants, lions, gazelles, crocodiles, cape buffaloes, and monkeys. Our guides always assured us that to the wild animals, our Land Rover appeared to be a single, frightening animal; the humans inside were just texture on its hide. In one camp, our vehicle had gotten so close to a feeding pride of lions we could smell their dreadful breath. We had watched the lions and their cubs feed and play. They seemed like a bunch of cavorting giant housecats.

There was always an armed guide or two who accompanied us on safari. We smiled knowingly. We were sophisticated; we knew the guns were for show, and probably were not even loaded. Our African guides were splendid actors! One camp had let us choose: guard with a gun, or guard with a spear. We figured signing away our rights at the "airport" was a stroke of pure theatrical genius.

When we got to camp, we learned the whole story.

A group of seven tourists on a photography safari had been staying at Phunga. They opted to travel in a Land Rover without guides. On their safari, they had come upon a pride of lions who had just consumed a fresh kill. The lions were satiated. Half the pride was asleep. The others were grooming each other and playing with their cubs. The scene seemed so lazy and benign that two of the photographers decided it was a wonderful chance to get some close-ups. The two climbed boldly out of their Land Rover to get some once-in-a-lifetime shots.

Things are not always as they seem. The once-in-a-lifetime shots turned out to be the *last* in a lifetime of shots. Lions being lions, they knew a tasty people-meal when they saw it. They promptly ate the two photographers.

Post Scripts

Among his many other talents, my friend Frank is a poet. He is the kind of a guy who falls in love with fence posts. He can write about them with such wit and beauty that I could almost join him and fall in love with his adorable wooden sticks. There would be hell to pay if we both desired the same post. Fortunately, Frank goes for the heavyweights and I prefer the skinny ones.

There is a chorus line of very desirable and shapely fence posts just north of the entrance to Point Lobos State Preserve, just south of Carmel. According to Frank, these fence posts sing, they dance, and anyone can see they are completely bark-less. A fence post with her bark removed leaves nothing to the imagination and is particularly sexy.

These posts are true eye candy, and they lie in wait for adoring post lovers. A post lover doesn't even have to dig them out of their earthen holes. They stand in their naked beauty with abandon and joy. They are yours forever—impassive and immobile, awaiting your arrival. Such are the enchantments of a fence post to a post lover. And Frank is a champion post lover.

Frank threatens to hide a few fence posts in his oversize pants. Who knows what delights await? I tell him to calm himself. The Point Lobos Preserve people wouldn't like him taking their fence posts. Frank says he only wants to borrow them for a little while. He might get away with it. His pants are all a little baggy anyway.

As if loving fence posts were not weird enough, Frank also writes poems about a tree in his front yard. Today he was complaining that she (the tree) was throwing her leaves all over his front yard and sidewalk. I tried to explain to him that she was probably jealous of the fence posts and trying to get him to pay more attention to her. I know this from Peter Youthburner's book on the feminine mindset—it's kind of my bible when it comes to understanding women.

I told Frank to just go on loving that tree. She is shedding her leaves before she dons her beautiful new spring dress especially for him. It seemed to satisfy Frank. He hasn't been to Point Lobos for a couple of weeks.

Frank and I went out to lunch last week, and he shared another poem he'd written about his fence posts and the tree in his front yard. I had to admit I felt a pang of jealousy. Why couldn't I write poems as clever as Frank's? And then it hit me. The posts and the trees were Frank's muses! All I needed was a post muse or a tree muse and I could write poems, too.

I began to take road trips looking for fence posts or trees that I could fall in love with. I traveled for hours down country roads and canyons looking for just the right muse. Pamela became disgusted and stopped speaking to me. The price of gas was eating a hole in our budget. I didn't even care. I was going to find my muse.

Suddenly, there it was. In a cow pasture in Carmel Valley at the top of a small knoll, I spied the most beautiful oak tree I had ever seen. It stood in lonely grandeur overlooking its bovine domain, its spreading limbs waiting to embrace me in loving splendor. I stopped the car and looked with open-mouthed awe at its magnificence—MY MUSE.

I had come prepared:

> My blanket I did unload,
> To later on the ground unfold.
> My sandwich of cheese and baloney
> Would keep me from being lonely.
> Next came my jug of wine,
> To spend a day sublime.

I was rhyming already! I was filled with unbounded joy. I picked my way through the cow droppings and proceeded to unfold my blanket under the spreading oak. I started to consume a delicious baloney and cheese sandwich that had been expertly prepared by Chef Barfalonius at our local deli earlier that day.

I won't bore you with an account of the hours I spent under my tree that day, notebook in hand, with no results. Except for that first magnificent burst, not a single new rhyme came to mind. Finally, the cows and the flies got to me. I downed the rest of the wine and started across the field to the car. On the way, I had a rather unfortunate accident. I took my eye off the path while brushing away the flies and I stepped into a fresh and very moist cow pie.

When I got to my car, I bagged my aromatic shoe and sock and drove home. Defenseless, with one foot shoeless, I faced the silent treatment from Pamela. Those shoes had cost us $200.

I couldn't wait to talk to Frank about my failed muse-hunt. On the phone, he was very sympathetic and suggested we visit my marvelous tree to find out why it had failed me.

I told Frank that since Pamela wasn't speaking to me anyway, we could go right away. I told him to bring an extra pair of shoes, just in case. I picked him up and we headed for Carmel Valley to see what was going on with my oak tree.

When we got there, Frank took a look at my tree. Waving away the flies, he carefully walked all around the oak's magnificent base. He gazed at its powerful limbs and muscular trunk.

He looked into my worried eyes and said, "I didn't know you were gay."

I said, "I'm not gay."

Frank reflected for a moment and said, "Well then, no wonder it's not working. This is a male oak. You got to find yourself a female."

It's a good thing Frank brought an extra pair of shoes.

Don't Offer Me Advice,
Just Give Me Money

I have been struggling with trying to cheat the phone company out of six dollars and fifty cents a month. The effort has occupied untold hours of my time and approximately $800 in equipment costs. My system still isn't working. However, my phone conversations have impaired my hearing. Pamela has had to massage my swollen ear for the past week instead of massaging other preferred body parts that have become incapable of swelling until I solve this earth-shaking problem.

My last conversation was with an AT&T tech. After I'd waited an hour to get to him, I explained what I wanted to set up.

His first response was, "We don't have what you want."

I have not been in the problem-solving business for all these years without recognizing a typical response. "We don't have it" or "It can't be done" are the standard answers when service people don't understand something and prefer to dismiss the problem instead of trying to solve it. In other words: when they are too lazy to do their jobs.

I told the tech he *did* have what I wanted, because another tech on another day had told me he had it, and even quoted me the price. LazyTech decided to look further. He came back after about half an hour. He said he didn't have the part. I told him to talk to his supervisor. He came back and said the supervisor said they didn't have it.

By this time, *I* had had it.

I decided to pull out the big guns. I told him I didn't think he had talked to anyone at all, and that I had been dealing with AT&T for forty years, and because of him, I was going to change to Cingular.

He said, "We *own* Cingular."

This was very deflating.

He then added that what I was trying to do was illegal and in breach of contract, and that if I got caught, the punishment would be death.

Now that some time has passed, I must admit he might not have actually said "death." That might have been a mental juxtaposition of my thoughts for him.

I am now trying another avenue (also illegal). I have spent some time in the local telephone store and at Radio Hutch. I have bought and returned three items to the AT&T store and another three items to Radio Hutch. In the process, I have made many friends at these two establishments and they have decided to help me.

It eventually dawned on them that it was easier to help me than to enter sales and re-enter refunds for every electronic component in their vast inventory. More importantly, they also decided that I might discover a little work-around that they could use to cheat the phone company themselves.

It's just a question of finding people on your own criminal level.

I am adding the expenditures from this current project to my losses in the stock market. The project costs seem minuscule in comparison, and it soothes my psyche. There is nothing like looking on the bright side.

Local Pair Mugged in Pebble Beach

We were mugged. It happened in broad daylight at about 8 a.m. on a Tuesday morning. The odious crime occurred on a footpath bordering the Seventeen Mile Drive, in the gated and protected community of Pebble Beach. If I hadn't been there, I never would have believed it.

Brutus III and I were prancing alongside the ocean and admiring the rolling waves and the glorious weather. At least Brutus was prancing; my prancing days stopped the last time I pranced myself into a pile of dog poop. Now I walk slower and have a tendency to look down instead of ahead. Every time I start to feel good and catch myself beginning to prance, I know something stinky isn't far away.

As we walked, my proud Doberman carried his prize stick in his mouth. He had found and rescued the stick a few weeks earlier. Brutus III had seen it bobbing back and forth in the surf like a yo-yo. The ocean would drop it on the beach, and the next wave would suck it back out to sea.

At first, Brutus thought the stick was alive. He would watch as the ocean deposited the stick onto the sand, and he would warily approach it. After a cautious sniff, he would begin to bark furiously and then attack. At the same time, the ocean would roll in and the stick would retreat into the sea as if frightened and defeated. This gave Brutus a great sense of power. He thought his vicious attack had worked! He had scared the dreaded stick away.

Brutus soon learned that the frightened stick would reappear on the sand, and he could bravely attack it and play the game again. He was as happy as only a dog can be.

Dogs and dog owners with any experience know that there are ordinary throwing sticks, and there are super deluxe Primo Sticks. A Primo Stick is a piece of wood of a special size and weight. Add some horrible smell and it becomes a true five-star Primo.

This particular piece of driftwood was a most wonderful stick. It had soaked in the ocean and acquired the characteristic stink of rotten seaweed. It had traveled from some exotic far-off shore, cavorting with the fishes along the way, soaking up delicious tastes and smells and acquiring a seasoning of sea salt. This was a Primo Stick worth keeping. So, when Brutus III got enough nerve to pick it up in his mouth, he rescued it from the ocean's grasp.

My dog had brought this prize on his walks for three weeks straight, and this extraordinary stick was the one he was carrying when we saw the mugger.

Even from a distance, I could tell the name of the approaching low-slung and powerful German shepherd was Big Trouble. Brutus III, however, was oblivious to the danger ahead. He was doing his prancing number. He seemed to be smiling broadly, and his Primo Stick was balanced perfectly in his mouth as the menace came closer and closer.

Big Trouble was drawing near, slinking toward us with an alert and shuffling gait, his brown eyes searching, his enormous fangs drooling, and his head weaving menacingly from side to side. He knew a five-star Primo when he saw one. His leash was stretched to its limit as his owner struggled to keep the muscled beast on the narrow trail. Soon they were going to pass very close beside us. And as they passed us, it happened.

In a move so lightning fast it was only a blur, Big Trouble snatched my dog's priceless Primo Stick right out of his mouth! Brutus didn't even know it was gone until Big Trouble had passed and was ten feet down the trail. He gave an anguished howl, but it was all over. His stick was gone—brazenly stolen in broad daylight by a ruthless and unprincipled German shepherd.

That was a month ago. Brutus and I go down to the beach quite often. My dog is constantly searching for his old Primo stick.

I'm just hoping we can find one to replace it. It's pretty hard to find a replacement for a five-star Primo.

Brutus III and I have talked about reporting the theft to the sheriff or the security people at Pebble Beach, but we haven't done it. We probably couldn't get the stick back anyway. That long-fanged monster has undoubtedly chewed it into a thousand little pieces. It's matchsticks by now.

Why is the sheriff never there when you need him? It's pretty sad when you can't take a walk in broad daylight in your own neighborhood without being mugged.

A Study in Evolution

Two things of great import have happened. One is that I picked up a dozen eggs at the supermarket, and one of the twelve had a sharply pointed end. (More on this later.) The other thing happened five minutes ago, and I can't recall it.

I am hoping the memory will return before I finish this. If it does not, five minutes will have set a new record for my retentive abilities. This new record could very well be as important as the thing of great import that I have forgotten.

There is a third thing I just remembered, and I will substitute it for the second thing that I have forgotten.

In addition to my shopping trip to the supermarket, I stopped to pick up an extra suitcase for my houseguests. The suitcase is to hold the various household items our guests have appropriated during their visit. Items that used to belong to us. It seems natural enough that since I supplied the merchandise, I should also supply the container in which to carry it all home. I am happy to do this as long as the guests will leave as promised.

But I'd be damned if I was going to purchase a new suitcase—I do have a few limits. Pamela suggested I go to the Goodwill. It was there that I lucked into just the right container.

It was a handsome devil, black with fine zippers and exceptionally attractive roller wheels. It was love at first sight. I was so delighted, I offered to pay five dollars more than the marked price. This caused quite a commotion and a brief encounter with a security guard.

Apparently, no one had ever paid above the marked price. I waited as the security guard struggled with the decision of whether to throw me out of the store or accept my offer. We finally compromised at two dollars above the original price.

But that's not the point of this amazing story.

When I got the case home, I realized that it was the same case we had donated to the Salvation Army ten years ago. It looked the same as it had then, and was complete with our old identification tags. Fortunately, someone had removed the dead mouse.

Isn't it amazing that after ten years, my tastes have not changed?

Now, back to the pointed egg. It is rare that we are able to see evolution in action as plainly as it was demonstrated by that pointed egg I had just purchased at the supermarket. This may be the first pointed egg that has ever been laid. Can you picture the admiration of the other chickens when they set eyes on that egg? Can you imagine their conversation?

"Clementine, did you see that egg?"

"You mean the one with the point?"

"Yeah, just think—no more torn vaginas! Let's ask Bernice how she did it."

And right there starts the modern-day evolution of the egg. In ten years, there won't be a rounded egg available in any store in the world. Rounded eggs will become a delicacy.

Sell all your stocks and buy rounded eggs! It's a sure thing.

If I remember the thing I forgot, I'll come back to it—it has to be very important, or I wouldn't have forgotten it.

Preparing for Armageddon

The U.S. doesn't issue $5,000 currency bills any longer. However, they do honor those still in circulation. Pamela had been bugging me for months to have some cash hanging around, so we can at least eat when the really big economic crash happens. According to Pamela, the really Big One is only one Ponzi scheme away, and that could happen anytime in the next twenty-four hours.

Fortuitously, I came across a listing on e-Bay to sell a rare 1965 $5,000 U.S. currency bill. The sellers wanted $6,000 for this antique, and it seemed like a bargain to me. I love rare items, and at the same time I could satisfy my wife's wishes for emergency cash. I had the bill checked for authenticity, negotiated a price of $5,500 and bought the thing.

Telling myself it was really for Pamela, I enclosed it in the traditional plain white envelope, put a ribbon around it, and gave it to her as a prize for being the foremost nervous hysteric of Carmel. She propped that $5,000 bill up on the breakfast table and spent the next few days mooning over her new insurance policy against economic disaster.

After three days, Brutus III, feeling he had been deserted for a green piece of paper, jumped on the breakfast table and ate Pamela's $5,000 insurance policy.

Pamela, as is her habit, left the scene by fainting. I grabbed Brutus's head and forced his mouth open, but it was too late. The bill had gone to that place where currency bills go when swallowed by disobedient animals that I don't want anyway and who are always having to go to vets whose charges total more money than I would pay to correct my own physical ailments.

I called the vet. When he stopped laughing the maniacal laugh that doctors and veterinarians are usually trained to suppress, he said there were two choices:

1) He could operate and maybe retrieve the bill. However, it would cost between $4,000 and $5,000, and there would be no guarantee that the bill would be salvageable.

2) We could rigorously examine Brutus III's solid eliminations for the next week, and maybe we would get lucky.

I thought about running a classified ad: "Valuable dog for sale. Contains a $5,000 U.S. currency bill." But I decided the explanation would be too complicated. I told Pamela I would be happy to perform the operation myself. She wrested the knife from my hand, and the choices became narrower.

That's how we became experts in the aromatic field of dog poop. We could tell the time of day by the color of Brutus's deposits. We both knew exactly when our valuable dog needed to dump just by looking at the way his tail was working. Brutus started to growl at us for following him around with tongs.

One morning, as the sun rose majestically over the forested beauty of Pebble Beach, Pamela screamed, "I think I see something green!" I threw a rock at Brutus III before he could ingest our prize again and instructed Pamela in the preferred method of bill extraction. We finally got it.

Our errant bill had suffered a bit on its trip through the dog, and had lost its magic for Pamela. She wanted it cashed. We cleaned the bill, and I proceeded to my local bank.

I presented the $5,000 currency bill to the teller for deposit. The manager was summoned to inspect the bill. He said it looked okay, though it smelled a little odd. He figured the smell was probably because it was so old. I agreed with him as he ruminated, "You just never know where a bill has been in the years since 1965."

He approved the deposit, but said I had to wait a week before I could get the cash. I asked him whether he thought the bank would survive until next week. He said he didn't know. He further whispered that Upper Management had misplaced the TARP money they got last week. They couldn't seem to find it, but they would be getting more soon.

When I got home, Pamela was beside herself again. The stock market had dropped another three hundred points, and Armageddon was surely coming within the next twenty-four hours. She said, "If we only had a few thousand dollars in cash, at least we could eat."

I told her I would see what I could do, and went online.

Breinigsville, PA USA
08 November 2010
248944BV00001B/2/P